"Pretty much all the important questions are in this book. Randall Smith has looked at death from every angle, and he has given us an extraordinary testimony to Christian faith in the face of it. In this eminently reasonable and readable guide, Smith shows himself to be a profound master of the most sacred and important things. This is a book that everyone needs."

MATTHEW LEVERING

James N. Perry Jr. and Mary D. Perry Chair of Theology,
Mundelein Seminary

"Randall Smith's new book *From Here to Eternity* is both delightful and wise. The author marshals stoic sages, insightful poets, contemporary psychologists, Christian saints, and most of all Jesus Christ to help us reflect on what death and the Resurrection are really about. In prose both clear and profound, Smith raises the ultimate questions that arise from the human reality of death and offers consoling answers. This book is so good, I may teach a course on the topic of death just so I can have my students read it."

CHRISTOPHER KACZOR

Professor of Philosophy, Loyola Marymount University and
Author of The Seven Big Myths about the Catholic Church

"Catholic teaching on the four last things has faded from the collective consciousness of the Western world. Yet, as recent events have reminded us, the reality of our mortality is something every person must face. Our culture, no matter how confused, has never stopped hoping for a newer and better life beyond death. In *From Here to Eternity*, Randall Smith illuminates these perennial questions of the human heart with penetrating insight that is at once accessible and profound. He reminds us of the wisdom of the greatest teachers of our tradition, stirring us to hope and eternal healing in Christ. I highly recommend it."

SAM GUZMAN

Founder and Editor of CatholicGentleman.com

"Discovering the meaning of death unlocks the purpose of life. Over and against the limits of ancient myth and the distortions of modern utopian visions, Christ's resurrection has made death into a source of hope. Randall Smith helps us to face the reality of death, seeing in it a choice either to rebel against the limits of life or accept them as a sacrificial means of entering into the greater gift of life in Christ."

JARED STAUDT

Associate Superintendent for Mission and Formation, Archdiocese of Denver and Author of The Priority of God

"If Catholics are going to re-evangelize a decadent West, we will have to speak prophetically about the reality of death and the hope of Resurrection. Randall Smith shows us the way with this engaging meditation on humanity's standing before God in light of eternity. Characterized by impressive theological depth, Smith weaves together the wisdom of the Catholic tradition with illuminating references to literature and film. The final product is a moving spiritual reflection on what it means to be a finite creature subject to death yet destined for eternal communion with the Triune God."

BUD MARR

Professor, Author, and Co-Host of "The Uncommon Good"

FROM HERE TO
ETERNITY

FROM HERE TO
ETERNITY

*Reflections on Death, Immortality,
and the Resurrection of the Body*

RANDALL B. SMITH

EMMAUS
ROAD
PUBLISHING

Steubenville, Ohio
www.emmausroad.org

Emmaus Road Publishing
1468 Parkview Circle
Steubenville, Ohio 43952

Library of Congress Control Number: 2022936692
ISBN 978-1-64585-218-6 (Hardcover) | 978-1-64585-219-3 (Paperback) |
978-1-64585-220-9 (Ebook)

Cover design by Patty Borgman.
Layout by Cori McCulloch.
Cover image: *The Icon of the Feast of All Saints*, Greek Orthodox.

To my wife

TABLE OF CONTENTS

ACKNOWLEDGMENTS

"A book on death? Are you alright?"

"Trying to work through some issues?"

"It's kind of morbid, isn't it?"

These were the reactions I kept getting from people when I told them about the book I was working on. "But the point is to talk about the resurrection," I assured them.

"Well, okay then. *That's* good."

Such, I suppose, sums up our culture's attitude toward death. For the most part, we would prefer to ignore it. We have for decades tended to insulate ourselves from death by stashing away people who are dying in hospital rooms where there are stringent rules for "visitation." It's probably safe to say that the topic makes many of us more than a little uncomfortable. We prefer to focus on heaven the way we prefer to focus on cute little babies in swaddling clothes in their mother's arms and then largely put out of our minds all that painful part a woman goes through giving birth. The problem is, in the real world, you don't get the nice, sweet, pleasant thing without the more troubling precursor to it.

Now to be clear, I am very much a product of this culture, having grown up nominally Protestant, not having become a Catholic until I was an adult, and I share this discomfort about death—in spades. Indeed, I am probably the last person in the world whom you would expect to write a book about death. I have friends who love walking through cemeteries to look at all the headstones. I don't. Cemeteries creep me out. I don't like funerals (but I go). I don't even like vampire movies with all the coffins and other paraphernalia surrounding death. So make no mistake, the author of this book did not write it from a disposition of blessed peace about the prospect of death. If the reader picked up this book, wondering: "Do I really want to read a book that talks about death?" that would be this author's general attitude.

I would love to report that writing this book has made me more comfortable around cemeteries. But it hasn't. The only thing that has made me more comfortable around cemeteries has been (a) the Catholic doctrine of the communion of saints, (b) the agreement I made when I was in graduate school and was forced to routinely walk by a cemetery in the dead of night that I would pray for the souls of the dead if the souls there would agree not to creep me out (I prayed, and they didn't haunt me), and (c) the fact that several of my dearest friends and mentors are now buried in that same cemetery, so now I go out of my way to walk by there to pray for them and ask for their prayers.

I wrote this book in the spring of 2020. COVID had hit hard; we were in the midst of the pandemic, and I thought the subject of "death" might be on people's minds. These reflections had been swirling around in my head for over a decade, but I thought the COVID crisis might be a good time to write them down and see whether I could interest a publisher.

So I wrote the entire book in about six weeks and sent it off for consideration. Looking back after months of revision, I can honestly say, with no small amount of embarrassment, that the draft was pretty terrible. I cannot fathom the faith the editors at Emmaus Press showed in me (or adequately express my gratitude for it) when they accepted the draft, adding only that the manuscript needed to be "tightened up" a bit. Saying it needed to be "tightened up" a bit was like saying the Titanic needed a bit of a patch job after hitting the iceberg. Well, yes, but that hardly expresses the breadth and depth of the problem.

Also to their credit, Emmaus Press allowed me to enlist as an editor the talents of the inimitable Susan Needham. Years ago, an article of mine was accepted at the journal *Nova et Vetera*, founded and managed by that redoubtable and unstoppable machine of scholarly production, Matthew Levering. At the time, Susan Needham was the subject editor of the journal.

Up to that point, I had always been a bit allergic to editors. But when I got my article back from Susan Needham, the comments were so interesting, so illuminating, and so obviously *right* that I said to my friends, "From now on, I want this woman to read everything I write." Little did I know that just about everyone I respected writing books in theology was also sending their work to Susan Needham. So when I said to myself, "I want this woman to read everything I write," this was like a second-string high school quarterback saying, "I want Peyton Manning and Tom Brady to watch me practice throwing the ball."

Since that first article, I have burdened Susan Needham with more of my turgid prose than should in all decency have been allowed, and she will certainly have earned substantial time off in purgatory for agreeing to read as much of my work as she has. This book would have been much worse if it weren't for the tireless efforts of Susan Needham to help me "tighten it up," which in some cases meant re-organizing and re-writing entire chapters. When my students look downcast at the editorial notes and comments I place on their college papers, I am tempted to show them a page from that first draft with Susan's mark-ups on which scarcely a word has been left untouched. I'm not sure whether this would reassure them or depress them, but at some point they need to realize that re-writing is simply part of the process. At least it is for me. So thank you Susan Needham.

I should also thank again the editorial board at Emmaus Press, and in particular Chris Erickson, for having faith in me, allowing me to employ Susan Needham, and then having patience as

I made the extensive edits that were needed. I also owe a debt of gratitude to Caroline Rock, who did the final copyediting on the manuscript.

Finally, I wish to thank the director and staff of the University of Notre Dame de Nicola Center for Ethics and Culture for their friendship and support as I was finishing this project: Carter Snead, Laura Gonsiorek, Margaret Cabaniss, Ken Hallenius, Petra Farrell, Pete Hlabse, and Tracy Westlake. Thanks also go to John and Alicia Nagy, Phil Bess, and Dr. Catherine Peters for their friendship, help, and support. But most especially, I must thank my good friend Professor John O'Callaghan, Director of the Notre Dame Jacques Maritain Center, for hosting me all these years. Most of the work revising the manuscript of this book was done there. The Jacques Maritain Center continues to be, as it was under the directorship of the late, great Ralph McInerny, one of the premier centers for important scholarship in service to the Church, and that is due in large part to the tireless efforts of its present director.

This book, as with every book or article I write, is dedicated to my wife, the amazing Tamara Nicholl-Smith: poet, Muse, better half.

Randall B. Smith
Christmas, 2021

It is in the face of death that the riddle of human existence grows most acute. Not only is man tormented by pain and by the advancing deterioration of his body, but even more so by a dread of perpetual extinction.

Gaudium et Spes, §18

INTRODUCTION

THE QUESTION OF DEATH AND THE MEANING OF LIFE

Pope John Paul II began his encyclical *Fides et Ratio* with the admonition "Know yourself." He spoke of how "in different parts of the world, with their different cultures, there arise at the same time the fundamental questions which pervade human life: *Who am I? Where have I come from and where am I going? Why is there evil? What is there after this life?*"—questions, he declared, "which have their common source in the quest for meaning which has always compelled the human heart. In fact, the answer given to these questions decides the direction which people seek to give to their lives."[1]

In the Second Vatican Council's Pastoral Constitution on the Church in the Modern World, we find this admonition: "It is in the face of death that the riddle of human existence grows most acute. Man is tormented not only by pain and by the advancing deterioration of his body, but even more so by a dread of perpetual

---

[1] John Paul II, Encyclical Letter on the Relationship between Faith and Reason *Fides et Ratio* (Sept. 14, 1998) §1, http://www.vatican.va/content/john-paul-ii/en/encyclicals/documents/hf_jp-ii_enc_14091998_fides-et-ratio.html.

extinction."[2] And so it is. Few things challenge our tranquility and provoke a sense of existential dread more profoundly than the thought of death. The great eighteenth-century writer Samuel Johnson is reported to have quipped, "Depend upon it, sir, when a man knows he is to be hanged in a fortnight, it concentrates his mind wonderfully."[3]

Of all the fundamental questions we face, perhaps the most difficult to confront fully and honestly are those concerning our own mortality. Certainly Pope St. John Paul II is right to point out that if we are to know ourselves rightly and truly, we cannot avoid the question of our own death. Indeed, few things force us to face the question of the meaning of things and of our very existence more powerfully and more insistently than having to consider the end of our existence.[4] If all we have striven for—all we have learned and experienced, everyone we have loved—simply comes

---

[2] Second Vatican Council, Pastoral Constitution on the Church in the Modern World *Gaudium et Spes* (Dec. 7, 1965), §18.

[3] James Boswell, *The Life of Samuel Johnson*, ed. David Womersly (London: Penguin Classics, 2008), 612.

[4] The Spanish poet and novelist Miguel de Unamuno (1846–1936) writes: "And if I die, then, nothing has any meaning for me." See *The Tragic Sense of Life*, trans. J. E. C. Flitch (London: Macmillan & Co., 1921), 37. The central theme of many of Unamuno's novels is the question of the immortality of the person. William James called death "the worm at the core" of man's existence and pretensions to happiness. "Back of everything is the great spectre of universal death, the all-encompassing blackness." See *The Varieties of Religious Experience* (New York: Longmans, Green, and Co., 1901), 139–40. Psychologists Sheldon Solomon, Jeff Greenberg, and Tom Pyszczynski write, "There is now compelling evidence that, as William James suggested a century ago, death is indeed the worm at the core of the human condition. The awareness that we humans will die has a profound and pervasive effect on our thoughts, feelings, and behaviors in almost every domain of human life—whether we are conscious of it or not." See *Worm at the Core: On the Role of Death in Life* (New York: Random House, 2015), x. References of this sort to the existential challenge of death could be multiplied across time and cultures.

to nothing in the end, is there any point to life? Does life have any meaning?

In a scene near the end of the 1982 movie *Blade Runner*, the android "replicant," Roy, moments from his own death, saves the life of Deckard, the man who has been hunting him to terminate him. Rather than letting Deckard fall to his death, Roy pulls him to safety and says: "Quite an experience to live in fear, isn't it? That's what it is to be a slave." We know that the fear he is referring to here is the fear of death that Deckard had been facing just moments before. Now that Roy has finally come face-to-face with his own death, his built-in, four-year replicant "expiration date," he no longer lives enslaved to that fear. But he tells Deckard ruefully as he dies: "I've . . . seen things you people wouldn't believe. Attack ships on fire off the shoulder of Orion. I watched C-beams glitter in the dark near the Tannhauser Gate." We the audience have no idea what these things might be, nor are we meant to. The point isn't the details. The point is to ask what will become of all these marvelous experiences, of all that Roy has seen and done and learned. "All those . . . moments," whispers Roy, "will be lost . . . in time . . . like tears . . . in rain." "Time to die," he says finally, and does.[5]

A dove he has been holding is released at that moment and flies upward, implying that perhaps, in the end, Roy, too, though an android "replicant," had a soul—something that survived his physical death. We don't know for certain. But we, like Deckard, are left with the same question about ourselves: All that we have seen and learned, all our experiences, the life, the loves, the sorrows, the joys: what comes of them? Are these things just lost when we die . . . like tears in rain?

---

[5] *Bladerunner*, directed by Ridley Scott (1982; Hollywood: The Ladd Company, 1992), DVD, 117 minutes.

It is not only the prospect of our own deaths that causes fear and anxiety, however; there is also the distress we incur watching others suffer through the process of aging and dying. We wonder, *Is that what is in store for me?* Indeed, the experience of the agony of others can be more terrifying than our own. For our own life, as the poet T. S. Eliot has written,

> is covered by the currents of action,
> But the torment of others remains an experience
> Unqualified, unworn by subsequent attrition.
> People change, and smile: but the agony abides.[6]

Experiencing the death and dying of others will often expose more clearly our own mortality, our own vulnerability, a clear sense of which can be missing when we are younger. Facing the reality of death is difficult; it is much easier to live in the illusion of immortality, of never having to face death. How do we tolerate it? How do we live with it? Should we even try? Do we gain wisdom by simply ignoring death as long as possible and focusing on the present, or is wisdom found by facing up to the reality of this inevitable fate? But if we do allow ourselves to live with an awareness of death, how might this be done so as not to make life seem merely dark, empty, and desolate?

So Roy's challenge to Deckard about enslavement to fear is also a challenge to us. What would it be like to be free of the fear of death even in the face of the inevitability of death? Would life be more vibrant and more meaningful if we were no longer anxious about extending this life endlessly, if we were assured that death is

---

6 T. S. Eliot, "The Dry Salvages." See also Nicolas Berdyaev, *The Destiny of Man*, trans. Natalie Duddington (London: Geoffrey Bles, 1937), 251: "We die not only in our own death but in the death of those we love."

not the final word on a meaningful human life? If one were liberated from the fear of death and the slavery that can accompany endless efforts to merely perpetuate life, would we be able to eat, play, read, contemplate, spend time with friends, or risk one's life for one's country with a new and expansive sense of freedom? It's a nice thought. But is it possible? Or is it another false promise distracting us from the grim reality we must face?

Does Hope of Heaven Diminish One's Concern for This World?

If we say that for there to be meaning in this life there must be life after death, we must also be careful what view of "life after death" we hold. If heaven is so wonderful, why not get there as quickly as possible? Why loiter in this life? If God has made man for heaven, why does he make us waste our time here on earth? Just to give us a chance to fail? And we continue to be faced with the same question as before. What about all we have struggled for—all our relationships, our loves, our dedication to others? Do we simply leave all that behind? For many, even those who believe in an afterlife, their greatest fear is losing contact with their loved ones. Although some sort of life after death seems necessary for this life to be meaningful, some views of life after death can make this life seem meaningless.

It has seemed to many people throughout history and across many cultures that there is something within the human person that would transcend the limitations of our current earthly life, whether we call whatever survives beyond this earthly life a "spirit," a "soul," or a "ghost," and whether we envision that afterlife as entailing a cycle of reincarnations culminating in nirvana, everlasting happiness in the Elysian Fields, or union with God in heaven.[7]

There have been exceptions, of course: those who were convinced (and felt it important to convince everyone else) that belief in life after death was not only irrational and wrongheaded but detrimental to living well in this life. Some theorists, especially in the modern world, have been convinced that an individual's hope for heaven decreases his or her concern for the rest of mankind and diminishes his or her desire to fight this-worldly injustice. Karl Marx (1818–1883), for one, held that *those who suffer injustice patiently now in the belief that they will receive their reward later are having their senses deadened by what he called "the opiate of the masses."*[8] A contemporary socialist author, echoing Marx's view, writes that "organized religion . . . with few exceptions, is used to maintain the positions of those who rule in our class society. For the most part, organized religion teaches that we should accept hardship and inequality because it is 'God's will.' We are encouraged not to resist our exploiters because we are all the 'children of God.' We are also told, especially in the Christian faith, that we should 'love your enemy.' Carrying out such dictates carries with it the promise of a place 'with God' or a new and better rebirth after death. . . . As it stands," continues this author, "religion, for the most part, does not provide motivation to discover more about matters about which we are ignorant, instead, it provides

---

[7] For an overview, see Catherine Wolff, *Beyond: How Humankind Thinks about Heaven* (New York: Riverhead, 2021).

[8] Originally written in the "Introduction" to *A Contribution to the Critique of Hegel's Philosophy of Right,* but first published in *Deutsch-Französische Jahrbücher,* February 7 and 10, 1844 in Paris. For this "Introduction," see *Marx's Critique of Hegel's Philosophy of Right,* trans. Joseph O'Malley (Oxford: Oxford University Press, 1970) or the online version, accessed March 3, 2021, https://www.marxists.org/archive/marx/works/1843/critique-hpr/intro.htm.

convenient answers which calm fears, but which encourage ignorance. Such ignorance, linked with the acceptance of inequality, usually diluted by gestures of patronage and charity to the less fortunate, helps maintain a system of extreme wealth and crushing poverty in a world of plenty."[9] Another prominent critic, the Frenchman Auguste Comte (1798–1857), who has often been called the "father of sociology," believed that hope for the afterlife produces only "slaves of God" and of the Church. In order to develop what is needed, namely "servants of Humanity," men had to turn away from the fictitious notion of a life after death and concentrate on helping others in this life.[10]

Do we live as "slaves" to the fear of death, seeking for an opiate to relieve our fear (as Marx thought)? And are we kept in slavery to the Church by our hope for the afterlife (as Comte believed)? Much depends upon what notion of life after death we hold.

If Christianity caused people to devalue this life, and if it caused people to have less concern for justice and for the welfare of others, then Christianity would have a problem not only because of these external critiques but also because it would be holding a view of the afterlife that was inconsistent with its own stated principles. It is not as though Marxism is concerned with the poor and Christianity isn't. Quite the contrary. It was the influence of Christian teaching on the cultural ideals of the classical Greeks and Romans—cultures that placed little or no value on the poor, the lower classes, and manual labor—that transformed those cultural

---

[9] Terry Bell, "Religion, Opium and Karl Marx," Terry Bell Writes (blog), Dec. 29, 2010, https://terrybellwrites.com/2010/12/29/religion-opium-and-karl-marx/.

[10] See Henri de Lubac, *The Drama of Atheist Humanism*, trans. Edith Riley, Anne E. Nash, and Mark Sebanc (San Francisco, CA: Ignatius Press, 1995), 172–73, esp. nn101–3.

norms so that the poor, the weak and the vulnerable, women, and laborers were now believed to have a unique value as especially loved and cared for by God (see 1 Sam 2:8; Pss 12:5, 14:6, 34:6, 35:10, 70:5, 86:1; Isa 41:17, 61:1; Jer 22:16; Ezek 22:12; Luke 4:18). Thus if, having preached as a central principle that the Lord has special concern for the poor and that Christians have a special responsibility to exhibit a "preferential option for the poor," Christians held a view of the afterlife that resulted in diminishment of that care and concern, then, quite independent of any claims or arguments of Marxists or other secularists, Christian doctrine would be in conflict with itself.

But does belief in life after death really result in a lack of concern for the injustices in this world? The long history of Christian charitable organizations dedicated to caring for the poor, the sick, the widow, and the orphan, and the Church's centuries-long struggle against social injustice at times and in places when others did nothing, should put to rest those claims. Even the Roman philosopher Cicero wrote, "No one would ever have exposed himself to death for his country without good hope of immortality."[11] Does the hope of life after death make us more complacent in the face of human suffering? Or might it not make at least some of us more willing to risk life in the fight for justice?[12]

---

[11] Cicero, *Tusculan Disputations*, trans. J. E. King (Cambridge, MA: Harvard University Press, 1927), 1.15.

[12] Russian orthodox writer Nicolas Berdyaev more likely has the accurate view when he writes: "It would be more correct to say that the unbelievers rather than the believers make life easy for themselves. Unbelief in immortality is suspicious just because it is so easy and comforting; the unbelievers comfort themselves with the thought that in eternity there will be no judgment of meaning over their meaningless lives." See Berdyaev, *Destiny of Man*, 264.

The Challenge: Finding a View of the Afterlife That Does Not Make This Life Meaningless

In the pages that follow, I will argue that popular criticisms of the Christian teaching about the afterlife are based on fundamental misconceptions—misconceptions that, unfortunately, are sometimes spread by Christians themselves. Christians need to make clear that their notion of the afterlife does not result in less concern for justice and the care of the needy but supports a greater freedom to act justly, that it does not bring about less concern for the things that are truly important in this life but undergirds a greater devotion to them. Just as the Church has long held that grace does not violate nature but perfects it, so, too, Christians should enunciate a notion of the afterlife that does not negate the value of this life but is perfective of it.

In accord with Pope St. John Paul II's claim that the answers people give to the fundamental questions "will decide the direction which people seek to give to their lives," I propose that a person's notion of the afterlife reveals a great deal about what they think makes life meaningful. A person who thinks intellect is the most essential element of our humanity will likely believe that intellect is what survives death. Further, if a person believes it is intellect that survives death, this is likely because he believes that intellect is the most essential element of our humanity. Whatever it is that a person believes survives death—whether the guilt of their sins, the nobility of their heroic deeds, or the union of love they established with their beloved spouse—this will likely reveal what they think is the most important and defining element in human life.[13]

---

[13] "There is a strong connection," writes psychologist Robert Kastenbaum, "between ways of life and ways of death in every culture in every epoch." See R. Kastenbaum, *Death, Society and Human Experience*, 11th ed. (New York: Routledge, 2012), 95. For useful historical examples, see Philippe Aries, *The*

Christians should understand, therefore, that their notion of the afterlife should accord with the Church's teaching about human nature and human flourishing. If, for example, a Christian were to claim that death entails the liberation of the soul from the body, as Socrates seems to have thought, their view would be at odds not only with St. Paul's teaching about the resurrection of the body but also with the Christian understanding of the intrinsic unity of body and soul that we find throughout the Scriptures, from the Genesis account of the creation of mankind to the Gospel accounts of the Incarnation of Christ.

Thus we have a twofold challenge. In addition to proclaiming the "good news" that there is life after death, Christians ought also to enunciate an understanding of life after death that does not make this life meaningless and does not undermine the Christian teaching about the human person.

Justice in This Life, Justice in the Next

Every notion of the afterlife has real-life consequences. If I believe that acts I do now stay with me and affect my future after death, then my actions will likely tend to accord with those things I believe will bring me to a good afterlife. If, on the other hand, I believe that death is the ultimate end beyond which there is nothing, then preserving my life and living well in this life will likely become my preeminent goals. So, too, if I believe that victims and victimizers both end up just the same—either both in heaven or both simply obliterated in death—then why resist the temptation to be victimizer rather than victim? And yet, don't most of us feel that, if the

---

Hour of Our Death (New York: Knopf, 1981); Edelgard DuBruck and Barbara Gusick, *Death and Dying in the Middle Ages* (New York: Peter Lang, 1999); Colin Murray Parkes, Pittu Laungani, and Bill Young, *Death and Bereavement across Cultures* (New York: Routledge, 1997).

Jews murdered by the Nazis and the Nazis who murdered them end up just the same in the end, then there is something wrong in the universe, some ultimately unfinished business?[14]

In Book 2 of Plato's *Republic*, Socrates's young friends Glaucon and Adeimantus pose to him this very question. If men acted justly only in order to get a reward, even if it would be a reward in the afterlife, and then, if it became widely believed that in the afterlife the differences between the just and unjust were erased and both attained the same reward, would anyone still choose to undergo the trials and torments often visited upon the just? Further, what if there is no afterlife at all and in this life, the just man gets treated like an unjust man and the unjust man is lavished with all the rewards of the just man? Given this possibility, could Socrates still make a case for being just?[15]

This was not a merely theoretical question when Plato wrote his *Republic*, since Socrates, the most just man in Athens, had already been put to death by the Athenians for being unjust while various groups of tyrants and criminals seem to have prospered. The pressing question Plato had to ask himself and his fellow students was this: What reason would they have to be just if it might result in them being executed for crimes against the city as Socrates had been?

Death as a Liberation? As an Escape from This Life?

One answer to that question might be the one Socrates himself proposed shortly before his execution. In the *Phaedo*, Socrates

---

[14] See Berdyaev, *Destiny of Man*, 253: "It is base to forget the death of a single living being and to be reconciled to it. The death of the least and most miserable creature is unendurable, and it is irremediable, the world cannot be accepted and justified. All and everything must be raised to eternal life."

[15] The challenge is found in *Republic* 2.358b–2.367e.

famously argues that the philosopher should always be preparing for death and should actually welcome it because death would mean the final liberation of the soul from its "imprisonment" in the body.[16]

Socrates's friends had come to him with an offer of escape—a bodily escape from prison in this life. They tell him that they have bribed the prison authorities so he can escape to another city to live out his days. Socrates refuses this offer, asking how he could turn his back on his city when he owed it his life, his education, and his well-being. He had accepted the benefits of the city; how could he now deny it his service? He had always encouraged others to be willing to sacrifice for the good of the city; how could he refuse to sacrifice himself now that the city required it of him? He owed the city his life; how could he refuse the city even if *not* refusing should cost him his life?

And yet, Socrates's students ask him, might it not be better for his friends and fellow Athenians for him to remain alive, continuing his efforts to teach from abroad? Socrates refuses this proposal and asks how he could have any credibility among his fellow Athenians if he refused to abide by the lawful decisions of the city. This challenge has been posed to martyrs throughout history. Wouldn't it make more sense to stay alive and continue the fight? What can one do after death? Doesn't death signal the end of any meaningful activity on behalf of one's friends, family, and community? Aren't those who allow themselves to be persecuted in this way simply fleeing their responsibilities? Isn't an "escape" from this

---

[16] See, for example, *Phaedo* 66c3–5, 66d5–e2. For a more positive interpretation of Plato's account, see Joseph Ratzinger, *Eschatology: Death and Eternal Life,* trans. Michael Waldstein, ed. Aidan Nichols, OP (Washington, DC: The Catholic University of America Press, 1988), 78–79 and 141–143.

life tantamount to an abandonment of one's obligations to one's fellow human beings?

Ready to Give Reason for the Hope That Is in Us: The Promise of Eternal Life

Christians are admonished in 1 Peter 3:15: "Always be prepared to make a defense to anyone who calls you to account for the hope that is in you." The source of that hope, as St. Paul repeatedly makes clear, is our faith in the death and Resurrection of Jesus Christ. "For I delivered to you as of first importance," Paul tells the Corinthians, "what I also received, that Christ died for our sins in accordance with the Scriptures, that he was buried, that he was raised on the third day in accordance with the Scriptures, and that he appeared to Cephas, then to the Twelve. . . . Last of all, as to one untimely born, he appeared also to me" (1 Cor 15:3–8). For St. Paul, the Gospel message included the "good news" not only about Christ's Resurrection from the dead but also about ours. He is the "first fruits" of what we, too, will enjoy.

Indeed, so fundamental is this message about Christ's Resurrection and the general resurrection of the faithful that Paul tells the Corinthians: "If for this life only we have hoped in Christ, we are of all men most to be pitied" (v. 19). But, he goes on to insist, Christ *has* been raised from the dead, "*the first fruits of those who have fallen asleep*" (v. 20) The message is clear: the victory Christ won, he won for us all. The Resurrection with which he overcame death is a resurrection in which we all will participate in union with him.

Elsewhere in the Scriptures we find the promise of "eternal life" as a central theme. Among the many examples are these:

Matthew 19:29 (also Mark 10:30 and Luke 18:30): "And everyone who has left houses or brothers or sisters or father or mother or wife or children or fields for my sake will receive a hundredfold and inherit *eternal life*."

Matthew 25:46: "And they will go away to eternal punishment, but the righteous into *eternal life*."

John 3:14–16: "And as Moses lifted up the serpent in the wilderness, so must the Son of man be lifted up, that whoever believes in him may have *eternal life*. For God so loved the world that he gave his only-begotten Son, that whoever believes in him should not perish but have *eternal life*."

John 3:36: "He who believes in the Son has *eternal life*."

John 4:13–14: "Jesus said to her, 'Every one who drinks of this water will thirst again, but whoever drinks of the water that I shall give him will never thirst; the water that I shall give him will become in him a spring of water welling up to eternal life.'"

John 5:24: "Truly, truly, I say to you, he who hears my word and believes him who sent me, has *eternal life*; he does not come into judgment, but has passed from death to life."

John 6:40: "For this is the will of my Father, that every one who sees the Son and believes in him should have *eternal life*; and I will raise him up at the last day."

John 6:47: "Truly, truly, I say to you, he who believes has *eternal life*."

John 6:54: "He who eats my flesh and drinks my blood has *eternal life*, and I will raise him up at the last day."

John 10:27–28: "My sheep hear my voice, and I know them, and they follow me; and I give them *eternal life*, and they shall never perish, and no one shall snatch them out of my hand.

John 17:3: "And this is *eternal life*: that they know you, the only true God, and Jesus Christ, whom you have sent."

Romans 2:6–7: "For he will render to every man according to his works: to those who by patience in well-doing seek for glory and honor and immortality, he will give *eternal life*."

Romans 6:22–23: "But now that you have been set free from sin and have become slaves of God, the return you get is sanctification and its end, *eternal life*. For the wages of sin is death, but the free gift of God is *eternal life* in Christ Jesus our Lord."

Galatians 6:8: "For he who sows to his own flesh will from the flesh reap corruption; but he who sows to the Spirit will from the Spirit reap *eternal life*."

1 Timothy 1:15–16: "The saying is sure and worthy of full acceptance, that Christ Jesus came into the world to save sinners. And I am the foremost of sinners; but I received mercy for this reason, that in me, as the foremost, Jesus Christ might display his perfect patience for an example to those who were to believe in him for *eternal life*.

Titus 1:1–2: "Paul, a servant of God and an apostle of Jesus Christ, to further the faith of God's elect and their knowledge of the truth which accords with godliness, in hope of *eternal life* which God, who never lies, promised ages ago . . ."

Titus 3:7: ". . . so that we might be justified by his grace and become heirs in hope of *eternal life*."

1 John 1:1–2: "That which was from the beginning, which we have heard, which we have seen with our eyes, which we have looked upon and touched with our hands, concerning the word of life—the life was made manifest, and we saw it, and testify to it, and proclaim to you the *eternal life* which was with the Father and was made manifest to us

1 John 2:25: "And this is what he promised us, *eternal life*."

1 John 5:11: "And this is the testimony, that God gave us *eternal life*, and this life is in his Son."

1 John 5:13: "I write this to you who believe in the name of the Son of God, that you may know that you have *eternal life*."

Jude 1:21: "Keep yourselves in the love of God; wait for the mercy of our Lord Jesus Christ unto *eternal life*."

This long but by no means exhaustive collection of quotations manifests a clear and consistent message proclaimed throughout all the books of the New Testament. Christians have been promised eternal life (in Greek *zōē aiōnios*, sometimes translated "everlasting life"). Taking these texts out of context in this way, we lose much of their depth and richness, but we gain a relatively undiluted witness to how ubiquitous is the promise of eternal life and how central to the Gospel message throughout the New Testament.

Looking back carefully over the list, we will notice the essential connection between eternal life and Christ but also the importance of grace, faith, mercy, life in the Son, the Eucharist, doing good, and love. We see that the promise of eternal life gives us hope, that it requires faith, that it was promised from the beginning of time, that the Scriptures were written so that we may believe in Christ and have eternal life, and that eternal life is contrasted with the classic pair: sin and death.

There are other key texts we would need to consider if we were making a fuller examination of the biblical concept of eternal life: texts about heaven, the kingdom of heaven, or kingdom of God, especially the ways in which this kingdom becomes present with Christ but is not yet complete and will be fulfilled only with Christ's Second Coming. And we would need to consider the meaning and significance of other important texts, such as that marvelous passage in which St. Paul says, "For now we see in a mirror dimly, but then face to face. Now I know in part; then I shall understand fully, even as I have been fully understood" (1 Cor 13:12–13)—a text that suggests we will need to take seriously the possibility that eternal life depends, first and foremost, not on our knowing and loving God but on our being known and loved by God. But since we are not making a textual analysis of a biblical concept but are, rather, reflecting more broadly on the Christian teaching of the significance of the resurrection of the body, I ask the reader to keep these ideas somewhere in the back of his or her mind as we examine other questions.

What Should Be Obvious: Eternal Life Does Not Mean We Never Die

That Christians are promised eternal life should be clear enough. What that promise entails, however, is not always so evident. We can dispense with one obvious and yet stubbornly persistent mistake right off the bat. Clearly Christ's promise about eternal life is not the promise that we will never physically die.[17] This would have been an odd promise in a community that had as its chief symbol a dead man on a cross. The early Christian evangelists

---

[17] I am putting aside for the moment any consideration of whether, early on, St. Paul held that Christ would return imminently, whether during Paul's own lifetime or shortly thereafter. At the very least, Paul understood that many Christians would die before Christ returned, including himself. How many would die and how long it would be before Christ's return is something about which he seems to have been unsure, perhaps unsurprisingly, given that Christ himself had said, "But of that day and hour no one knows, not even the angels of heaven, nor the Son, but the Father only" (Matt 24:36).

did not include Christ's promise of eternal life unaware of the fact that Christ himself had suffered death on the Cross. Quite the contrary: Christ's death was for Paul and for the Gospel writers after him the central event of Christ's earthly ministry. They did not repeat Christ's promise of eternal life in spite of his death on the Cross, as though it were an embarrassment at odds with the promise of the resurrection of the dead. No, they preached Christ's death and Resurrection precisely as that which brings about our victory over sin and death.

Moreover, it was well known in the early Church that nearly all the original Apostles had been martyred, many in decidedly gruesome ways. This fact was also not thought to be a scandal at odds with the Gospel promise of eternal life. Rather, the willingness of these martyrs to suffer death was a source of great pride. So whatever early Christians believed Christ had promised when he promised "eternal life," it could not have been that the faithful would not die physically.

An Understanding of Faith, Not a Rational Demonstration to Convince Everyone

If the promise of eternal life does not mean that we will never die, what does it mean? What is being promised? At the heart of the Christian teaching about our resurrected life after death is the promise that we will be united with God, that we will, as it is said, see God "face to face" in the beatific vision.[18] Since the knowledge of God in his essence is infinitely beyond our grasp in this life, a

---

[18] The Catechism of the Catholic Church, (hereafter CCC), §1023: "Those who die in God's grace and friendship and are perfectly purified live for ever with Christ. They are like God for ever, for they 'see him as he is,' face to face [1 Jn 3:2; cf. 1 Cor 13:12; Rev 22:4]." CCC, §1028: "The Church calls this contemplation of God in his heavenly glory 'the beatific vision.'"

full comprehension of what eternal life is will remain beyond our intellectual grasp. Hence what we can know about our union with God has to come primarily through divine Revelation, and, as with many aspects of divine Revelation, it remains enigmatic. We should no more expect God to lay out for us in clear and distinct categories, subject to deductive verification, what it means to live eternally in union with him than we should expect a person to be able to demonstrate in clear and distinct categories what love is. Just as lovers often have recourse to creative imagery, poetry, and music to give us a glimpse of true love's character, so, too, God has often revealed himself to us in ways that give us an invaluable glimpse of him without ever capturing his essence completely.

Although there are things we can know about God by our unaided reason alone, life after death is not likely to be one of them since death is not an experience we can have and then reflect on or write about. What we know, we have received from Christ, and so we will need to pay special attention to what he reveals.

Resurrection of the Body

One of the things we find in divine Revelation, confirmed most fully in the Resurrection appearances of Christ, is that Christ's promise of eternal life includes the resurrection of the body. Sadly, many Christians seem unaware of this central tenet of their faith. And yet, it is so central to the Gospel that we find St. Paul saying, "But if there is no resurrection of the dead, then Christ has not been raised; if Christ has not been raised, then our preaching is in vain and your faith is in vain" (1 Cor 15:13–14). And again, "If for this life only we have hoped in Christ, we are of all men most to be pitied" (v. 18).

The resurrection of the body, from St. Paul and the time of the Apostles until the present, has been at the center of the Christian proclamation of the faith. Indeed, the Church proclaims her belief in the resurrection of the body in all her major creeds: the Apostle's Creed, the Nicene Creed, and the Athanasian Creed. The Fourth Lateran Council (1215) infallibly defined that, at the Second Coming, Jesus "will judge the living and the dead, to render to every person according to his works, both to the reprobate and to the elect. All of them will rise with their own bodies, which they now wear, so as to receive according to their deserts, whether these be good or bad."[19] And more recently, the Catechism of the Catholic Church reiterated this long-defined teaching, stating, "Belief in the resurrection of the dead has been an essential element of the Christian faith from its beginnings. 'The confidence of Christians is the resurrection of the dead; believing this we live' [Tertullian, *De res.* 1, 1]" (CCC, §991). And again (CCC, §1017): "We believe in the true resurrection of this flesh that we now possess" (Council of Lyons II: DS 854). We sow a corruptible body in the tomb, but he raises up an incorruptible body, a 'spiritual body'" (see 1 Cor 15:42–44).

Despite the fact that we proclaim our faith in "the resurrection of the body" every time we repeat the creed, I have found, over many years teaching theology, that awareness of the Christian teaching about the resurrection of the body is in short supply. The overwhelming majority of Christian students believe that Christianity teaches that, after death, we cast off our bodies so that our souls are free to go to heaven. A mentor of mine, the late, great Ralph McInerny, was once reported to the dean at the University of Notre Dame by one of his Catholic students for teaching what the student thought was heresy. McInerny had suggested to his

---

[19] The Fourth Lateran Council, Constitution 1 "Confession of Faith," 1215, https://www.papalencyclicals.net/councils/ecum12-2.htm#1.

students that Aristotle's notion that the soul was the "substantial form of the body" helped Christians like Thomas Aquinas make better sense of the "resurrection of the body" than the older Platonic view that the soul left the body behind after death. This student believed that the Catholic view was that *Christ* was raised bodily from the dead, and Mary after him, but no one else. Fortunately, the then-dean of the university was able to set him right on this point, undoubtedly to the benefit of the young man's adult Christian faith.

Even Christians who are aware that their faith includes belief in the resurrection of the body will often ask, "What does that mean?" So, too, with the promise of "eternal life." If it does not mean never dying, what does it mean? Since Christians have been admonished to be prepared to give an answer for the hope that is in them, our task in the following pages is to provide an account (albeit one that is necessarily inchoate and incomplete) of why the teaching about the Resurrection of Christ and the general resurrection of the faithful gives us hope. But it must also be an account of what kind of hope it gives us: why, for example, it is a hope *for* this life and not merely the hope of an escape *from* this life. To provide context for that discussion and in order to give a sense of the distinctiveness and significance of the Christian promise of eternal life, let us begin with some of the things *not* promised by the Gospel and some of the misinterpretations to which the Christian view has been subject.

These are some of the questions that will occupy us in the chapters that follow. But I think it is important to signal right at the beginning that the goal of all these reflections is to gain a clearer understanding of what it means to believe in the Christian promise of eternal life, how our faith in that promise can contribute to our living more meaningfully now, and how the hope founded on that faith can help us face death more meaningfully whenever the time comes.

Not an Argument against Other Traditions

Our discussion of things not promised by the Gospel and of possible misinterpretations of the Christian teaching will require an examination of other approaches and other possible answers to the fundamental questions we are posing about death and the afterlife. Recall that Pope St. John Paul II noted in *Fides et Ratio* that these are "fundamental questions" that have "always compelled the human heart" and that have arisen repeatedly throughout history "in different parts of the world, with their different cultures."[20] And yet, even though all human persons throughout history and across different cultures have faced the same fundamental questions, the answers they have provided have been far from identical. To clarify Christian teaching, it will be necessary to distinguish it clearly from other possible answers to the fundamental questions. Readers should not mistake this effort—an attempt to clarify Christian teaching by comparing it with other possible answers—for an argument against the views held by other religious or philosophical traditions. In some cases, we will be examining positions that resemble teachings held by other religions. But the hypothetical possibilities I propose here should not be mistaken for the teaching of any other religious tradition in its fullness, understood in its original context. Christians are under orders to treat others as we would wish to be treated, and since we would not wish for our views to be made into a caricature of what they really are, we should be careful not to do that injustice to the views of others.

---

[20] John Paul II, *Fides et Ratio*, §1.

The discussion of the afterlife we are about to undertake is based in large part on the Christian view of the human person as revealed in the Scriptures and the person of Jesus Christ and as passed down over the centuries through tradition and the teachings of the Church. It would be possible to have a very different view of the human person, and many people have. Christians think it reasonable to believe in a human reality that survives the death of the body. Christians are not the only ones in history who have accepted that notion, but there are others who would not. If a person held rigorously materialist presuppositions and believed that human beings were nothing other than their bodies, then it would only seem reasonable, based on those presuppositions, to conclude that nothing survives the death of the body. For a Christian to convince such a person to, at the very least, *consider* the Christian view of the afterlife, the Christian would first have to convince the materialist that his or her materialist beliefs and convictions were misplaced or in error. This book is not an argument against materialism, and a devoted materialist would likely find the discussion contained herein to be either "question-begging" (presuming a conclusion that the arguments should be proving) or utterly divorced from reality. So it is important to note that I am not formulating arguments against the materialist or the Hindu or the Buddhist; rather, I am attempting to clarify what the Christian promise of eternal life entails or does not entail by comparing it with a series of logically possible alternative views in order to point out difficulties that Christians should be careful to avoid.

As I have already mentioned, we want to avoid views of the afterlife that would make this life meaningless. If, for example, we believe that the "best life for man" is the life of virtue, then we cannot, without being guilty of a serious inconsistency, claim that the life of the blessed in heaven is filled with dissolute sex. So, too, if a Christian believes that heaven is a realm of selfless love of God and others but lives a life devoted to the pursuit of wealth, power, and status, that person has failed to grasp the essential relatedness between this life and the next. One's view of the good life for man in this life should not contradict the life of the blessed in heaven, and vice versa. To claim that the dead will enjoy in heaven a life that we (and they) would find reprehensible on earth is to introduce an unacceptable contradiction into the heart of the Church's proclamation of the Gospel message. Any adequate response to the challenge of the shadow of death must, therefore, show the essential continuity between one's view of the best life now and one's view of life after death—between one's view of human nature and human flourishing in this life and one's view of the ultimate end for mankind after death.

It will become apparent, especially in later chapters, that I take it as axiomatic that the Christian view of the afterlife is revealed most fully in the person of the risen Christ. There are other scriptural images of "heaven," and they are not unimportant. But they are still just images. The most central and important revelation about the afterlife is given by Christ himself in his own resurrected body. The Christian promise is that when we live our lives in continuity with Christ crucified and risen, we are living even now a foretaste of the life enjoyed by the blessed in heaven.

Indeed, I believe it is in the light of Christ's sacrificial death and Resurrection that we must view Christian teaching about purgatory. I do not say much about purgatory in the following chapters, not because it is a subject of controversy among Christians but primarily because I am more concerned in this work with illuminating the goal of the journey rather than the means to it. But there is something more. It is clear that purgatory cannot be considered a method of purification from sin that is somehow independent of

Christ's sacrificial death and Resurrection. However we envision purgatory and whatever we think happens there, as Christians, we must believe that this final purgation of our sinfulness and preparation for our union and loving communion with the Triune God is made possible by Christ as our Head, the "first fruits" of what we, too, will enjoy. So however the transformation is effected, its goal is to rid us of whatever is false in ourselves, whatever is the product of selfishness, death, and the privation of being, so that we may be at long last fully united with the risen Body of Christ, because it is only in the union with Christ, the incarnate Son, that our union with the Triune God is possible.

The Christian promise is that, when we live our lives in continuity with Christ crucified and risen, we are living even now a foretaste of the life enjoyed by the blessed in heaven. "We were buried therefore with him by baptism into death," St. Paul tells us, "so that as Christ was raised from the dead by the glory of the Father, we too might walk in newness of life."

> For if we have been united with him in a death like his, we shall certainly be united with him in a resurrection like his. We know that our former man was crucified with him so that the sinful body might be destroyed, and we might no longer be enslaved to sin. For he who has died is freed from sin. But if we have died with Christ, we believe that we shall also live with him. For we know that Christ being raised from the dead will never die again; death no longer has dominion over him. The death he died he died to sin, once for all, but the life he lives he lives to God. So you also must consider yourselves dead to sin and alive to God in Christ Jesus. (Rom 6:4–11)

The Christian message, then, is this: Begin the life of heaven now—which is the life of Christ crucified and risen, a life purged of our false self and its selfishness—to make way for an "eternal life," a life devoted to the selfless love of God and neighbor. The "good news" is that no power on earth, no matter how great, not even death, can separate us from God's love and from the grace that inspires his divine love in us.

Distinguishing Approaches to the Question of Death

We begin our survey of possible views about death and the afterlife with the most basic distinction: between those who believe in life after death and those who do not.

Under the general heading of those who have been convinced we need not or should not live with any expectation of life after death, we can make a twofold division between (a) those who believe death is inevitable and who try to find some way of dealing with that fact and (b) those who believe death is not inevitable and try to find a way of achieving immortality. In chapter 1, we examine some of the claims of the first group—those who believe that the way to deal with death is simply to accept that there is no afterlife. Among these, there have traditionally been two diametrically opposed approaches. One group claims that the wise thing to do is to realize that death is not something we can control or do anything about—it merely upsets us unnecessarily—so we should not let it affect our lives now, while another group holds that wisdom is found by spending one's life in preparation for death and always being aware of the imminent possibility of death. We consider both views in chapter 1.

In chapter 2, we examine the claims of those who believe that death is not inevitable and who have dedicated themselves to achieving immortality in this life. Although the dream of immortality has been harbored by many individuals throughout history—perhaps we all harbor this dream to a certain extent—the scientific advances of the modern world may seem to have put immortality finally within our grasp. In this chapter, we examine the claims of the modern "trans-humanists" and consider whether the extension of human life they envision is reasonable and whether it would ever be desirable.

In chapter 3, we take up our examination of those who believe in life after death. We begin, however, with an examination of various pre-Christian pagan views of the afterlife held by certain classical Greek and Roman authors. Many of these authors held, as the Platonists did, that death brings about the soul's liberation from the body. Others believed that the soul, once liberated, would return and be reincarnated in another body. The mind-body dualism underlying such views has been something orthodox Christianity has always opposed and nowhere more controversially than in its insistence on the resurrection of the body.

In chapter 4, we begin our examination of the Christian teaching about the resurrection of the body and the eternal life we hope to enjoy in union with the Triune God after our death. In chapter 5, we discuss how, in the light of this teaching, Christians might transform their communities to better deal with the challenges of death and dying. And finally in chapter 6, we consider some issues related to the Christian belief in "the end times" and the Second Coming of Christ. Christ told us that "no one knows the day or the hour," but that does not make the promise of the Second Coming irrelevant to our lives now.

Outline of the Chapters

I. Those who do not believe in life after death

    A. Those who believe death is inevitable and try to deal with this fact (Chapter 1)

        1. Those who believe that death is nothing we can control or do anything about, and since it upsets us unnecessarily, it need not affect the way we live, nor should we really even think about it much

        2. Those who believe that we should daily be aware of death and live in its presence

    B. Those who do not believe death is inevitable and try to achieve immortality (Chapter 2)

II. Those who believe in life after death

    A. Non-Christian approaches to life after death (Chapter 3)

    B. The Christian teaching

        1. Christ and the resurrection of the body (Chapter 4)

        2. Facing death in light of the Christian teaching (Chapter 5)

        3. The "end times" and the "Second Coming" (Chapter 6)

A Final Note: Why This Book Is Not Enough

Will reading this book help people when they face death? Perhaps in some ways, yes. One can always hope that would be a result. But the author's own view is that the answer is ultimately no. Instead, the argument of the book should make clear why, in the author's view, an intellectual approach to the challenge of death is not enough and why Christians will need to develop certain habits and engage in various practices if they wish to prepare themselves to face death, whether their own deaths or the death of a loved one. Hence the ideas put forth in this book need to be embodied in communal practices if they are to be helpful and provide the needed consolation and peace. We need the right theology, that is, the right understanding of death and the afterlife, but we need as well a community in which those ideas and theology are embodied. In short, we need the Church. And we need the Church to do what it was created to do: namely, to incorporate the faithful ever more fully into the risen Body of Christ.

Death is nothing to us.

Epicurus, "Letter to Menoeceus"

Authentic Being-towards-death can not evade its ownmost non-relational possibility, or cover up this possibility by thus fleeing from it.

Heidegger, *Being and Time*

A free man thinks of nothing less than of death, and his wisdom is a meditation, not on death, but on life.

Benedict de Spinoza, *Ethics*

When Spinoza wrote that the free man thinks of nothing less than of death, and that his wisdom consists in meditating not on death but on life . . . he did in fact think about death, and he wrote it in a vain endeavour to free himself from this thought.

Miguel de Unamuno, *The Tragic Sense of Life*

Chapter 1

DEATH: IGNORE IT OR LIVE TOWARD IT?

The questions about how we should face death and what we might expect in the afterlife are obviously not unique to our age; they are two of the most "pressing" of the "fundamental questions that pervade human life" about which, as we mentioned in the introduction, St. John Paul II speaks in the opening paragraph of his encyclical *Fides et Ratio*. These are questions, declares the saint, that "have their common source in the quest for meaning which has always compelled the human heart"—throughout history and across cultures. Indeed, few things cause "the question of the meaning of things and of their very existence" to become "ever more pressing" than the challenge of having to face death, whether one's own or of those we love. So should we spend our whole lives, as Plato and Socrates advise, preparing for death?[1]

---

[1] See Plato, *Phaedo*, esp. 64A–68C.

Or would it make more sense to forget about it and focus on the pleasant things available to us now?[2]

The latter view was one that was held, for example, by Epicurus and his followers. As Epicurus says in a famous letter to his disciple Menoeceus: "Death is nothing for us."[3] By this, Epicurus meant not only that death was something they ignored but also that they ignored it precisely because they thought that after death there was nothing. Why be frightened, they wondered, if there is nothing after death? You won't suffer. You won't be conscious. You won't even exist. So there is nothing to fear. Simply focus on those things that are pleasant now and put aside any concern about death.

But does our fear of death come solely from belief in an afterlife in which there might be punishments, as Epicurus assumed? Or is the reality somewhat more complicated? In a scene from near the end of Henrik Ibsen's wonderful play *Peer Gynt*, Peer is confronted by a character identified only as "the Button Molder," who tells Peer that because he has "never yet been himself," he is to be melted down and recast as a "new button," a new person.[4]

"No, I say, no!" protests Peer. "I'd rather, far, put up with anything than that!"

---

[2] See Diogenes Laertius, "Epicurus's Letter to Menoeceus," in *Lives of the Eminent Philosophers*, trans. Robert Drew Hicks (Cambridge: Harvard University Press, 1926), esp. secs. 3–4. Online at http://classics.mit.edu/Epicurus/menoec.html

[3] Ibid., 3. To be fair, it is not merely thoughts of death that Epicurus wanted his followers to put aside. It is any hope of immortality. When you lose any hope of immortality, Epicurus believed, then you no longer fear death.

[4] I am quoting throughout from the English translation of *Peer Gynt* by William and Charles Archer (New York: Charles Scribner's Sons, 1929). Ibsen's play is written in a poetic form, and Archer attempted in his English translation to be faithful to that intention. In my quotations, I have altered Archer's punctuation and poetic lines to make the lines easier to read.

"But what do you mean by 'anything'?" asks the Button-Molder. "You're not the sort that goes to Heaven."

"I'm humble," says Peer; "I don't aim so high as that; but I'm not going to lose a single jot of what's myself." He would rather be sent to "him with the Cloven Hoof" (the devil), sentenced "for a certain time, say a hundred years, if the sentence must be a very severe one," which Peer can't understand because he has never done anything quite so bad.

But this is the problem, replies the Button-Molder; Peer has done nothing bad enough for him to be relegated to hell or good enough for admission to heaven. He has never chosen anything sufficient to *become himself*. He has always chosen only things that allowed him to get by. Instead of "to thine own self be true," his motto was "to thine own self be—sufficient." This sort of life, explains the Button-Molder, has earned him neither heaven nor hell; rather, he is to be melted with other defective buttons so that the Maker can start again and make new ones. Since "you have never yet been yourself," says the Button-Molder, "what difference can it make to you if, when you die, you disappear?" Since he has never become himself during his life but has chosen, rather, to "disappear" behind appearances, to be nothing, an empty cypher, a nonperson, why would it bother him now to become literally nothing, to cease to exist altogether, since this has been the reality of his life?

But Peer is not comforted at this thought; he is horrified. "To be swallowed up, like a speck in a mass of strange material," he cries—"this ladle business—losing all the attributes that make a Gynt: that fills my inmost soul with horror!"

The prospect of nothingness rather than hell does not quiet Peer Gynt's fears; quite the opposite. Better hell than nothingness.

But only nothing can come from nothing, and Peer has chosen to be a nothing.

Ibsen was likely not much interested in life after death, merely that people choose to live a real life *now*, but he has hit upon an important insight. Christians who think that it is best to "play it safe" so that they don't risk getting condemned to hell are making a very grave mistake about what Christ means when he says that he came "that they may have life, and have it to the full" (John 10:10).[5] Whatever else "living to the full" means, it cannot mean simply avoiding doing sinful things. It must involve the kind of passionate, loving fidelity to God and to others that Peer Gynt lacked.

What Can We Control?

The Epicureans argued that people should focus only on things that they could control, not those they couldn't. The key to happiness, thought Epicurus, was to be content with what was available and not to desire things beyond one's limits. Since death was not something subject to one's rational will and immortality was something beyond human limits, worrying about death and/or wishing to attain immortality would simply bring pain and frustration, and so the concern about death or immortality should be avoided. Why worry about something you cannot control or let yourself be troubled by what you cannot have? Better to seek wisdom by reflecting on how to live well *now*, in *this* life, because this is the only life we have.

There is something to recommend in this approach. Recognizing that we cannot control death—that it can come at any time and unexpectedly—and so we should make as much as we

---

[5] This is also the message of the Parable of the Talents in Matt 25:14–30.

can of life each day makes a great deal of sense. And yet, the sort of life the Epicureans thought made sense with this view of death suffered from its own difficulties. For one thing, since the Epicureans were convinced that there was no afterlife filled with rewards and punishments, nor was there any reincarnation to a new life, they concluded that people should simply live their one and only life satisfying their desires for moderate pleasures so that, upon their death bed, they would have no fear and no regrets. In *Peer Gynt*, Ibsen aptly describes the motto of such a life: "To thine own self be—sufficient."[6]

With further reflection, we come to realize that it is not only our own death we cannot control but also the deaths of our friends and loved ones. And if "wisdom" means minimizing pain and not worrying about things I cannot control, then the natural conclusion for an Epicurean would be that one should not get too involved with or dedicate oneself to a friend or loved one, for to do so would be to court heartache and disaster. Passionate attachments to others would be things to be avoided, not embraced.

We might also wonder about the consequences of the Epicurean emphasis on control and self-sufficiency. Loss of control is taken to be a loss of freedom, which is thought to represent a diminishment of the subject's dignity. In a similar spirit, increasing numbers of people in the modern world are interpreting their loss of self-sufficiency as just such a diminishment of their dignity, so much so, in fact, that when they (or a loved one) lose that self-sufficiency, they consider life no longer worth living and wish to end it. It is worth noting that Epicurus himself committed suicide rather than face the pain and the diminishment of his powers brought on by aging.

---

6 Ibsen, *Peer Gynt*, act 2, scene 6.

5

Stoics made similar judgments about the diminishment that accompanied any loss of self-sufficiency and control. The Stoic philosopher Epictetus distinguishes between things in our power and those not in our power. When we concern ourselves with things in our power, says Epictetus, we remain "by nature free, unhindered, untrammeled." When we worry about things not in our power, however, we become "weak, servile, subject to hindrance, dependent on others."[7] "Exercise yourself then," says Epictetus, "in what lies in your power. Each man's master is the man who has authority over what he wishes or does not wish, to secure the one or to take away the other. Let him then who wishes to be free not wish for anything or avoid anything that depends on others; or else he is bound to be a slave."[8] Clearly death is one of those things that is not under our control, so it would be foolish, on this view, to worry about it, which would mean becoming a "slave" to it. In contrast to the Epicurean wisdom, which advised that one should simply avoid thinking about death, the Stoic sage wanted men to keep it before their eyes from day to day, along with "exile and all things that seem terrible, but death most of all," because then "you will never set your thoughts on what is low and will never desire anything beyond measure."[9] Besides, "death is nothing dreadful," says Epictetus, "or else Socrates would have thought it so. No, the only dreadful thing about it is men's judgement that it is dreadful."[10]

But if death means the death of the soul, the total obliteration of the person, then merely thinking it not a bad thing will

---

[7] Epictetus. *Handbook*, trans. W. A. Oldfather, Loeb Classical Library, vol. 1. (New York: Putnam, 1926), sec. 1. References below will be given to section numbers.

[8] Ibid., 14.

[9] Ibid., 21,

[10] Ibid., 5.

not make it any less horrible. Socrates did not fear death because he believed that the soul, the seat of our thinking and remembering, survives death. But Epictetus misunderstood Socrates. How could a being defined by rational, conscious activity entertain the possibility of a complete loss of conscious, rational activity with anything other than dread and as anything other than a complete contradiction of his or her very being? Nor is it clear that merely reflecting on death would cause a person to act nobly. One might, like the Epicureans or the modern followers of the nineteenth-century philosopher Friedrich Nietzsche (1844–1900), decide that, since life is short and there is no afterlife in which we will be judged for our actions, why not maximize my pleasure and my own will-to-power as far as possible? Since Epicureans and modern-day Nietzscheans do not believe in life after death, neither concludes that it is worth being "shackled" to society's standards of "morality" or other people's notions of "duty."

Does Lack of Control Diminish One's Human Dignity?

But should we accept the basic premise underlying the view: namely, that the lack of control over one's life diminishes one's dignity? Would such a life really not be worth living? Are we ready to conclude with Nietzsche that caring for the poor and disabled displays a kind of "servile" morality we need to get beyond? Because if we conclude that the lives of those who are in any way dependent are "diminished," what are we going to say to the disabled in our society? Will we not be disposed to look down upon them as less dignified, as suffering through lives not worth living? Many people in our society believe just that although most might not be willing to say so out loud.

And yet, actions speak louder than words. Undoubtedly the

best witness one could give to the intrinsic value and dignity of the lives of the elderly or disabled is to confess our own dependencies and embrace our own weaknesses. If human beings are not only rational animals but, as philosopher Alasdair MacIntyre has argued, "dependent rational animals," then the emphasis the Epicureans and Stoics (and many of us in modernity) put on individual self-sufficiency is excessive and potentially deleterious to human flourishing.[11] To wish to actualize one's capacities fully and do one's part is natural and healthy; it is the root of virtue. To imagine, as many Stoics and Epicureans seem to have done, that allowing oneself to become dependent on others is a grave fault is to indulge a foolish and harmful illusion. For when in our lives are we *not* dependent? From infancy to old age, we depend on others, and the people on whom we depend in turn depend on yet others in ever-expanding circles. Epicureans depended on the efficient functioning of the city and its civic life, just like everyone else. They did not grow their own food, make their own clothes, or gather the resources needed to build their houses. So they had to depend on others within the context of a well-functioning *polis* to provide these things for them. That is to say, they had to depend on a civic order that they themselves did little or nothing to nurture or protect. An Epicurean life is most often parasitical on a civic order established and protected by others who are more aware that human flourishing relies on communities of virtue on which the members can depend.

And what about refusing to think about something simply because it cannot be controlled? I cannot control whether other people love me or whether they will react positively to my

---

[11] See Alasdair MacIntyre, *Dependent Rational Animals: Why Human Beings Need the Virtues* (Chicago: Open Court, 2001).

altruistic acts on their behalf, but is this a good reason to refuse to think about them or about the vast complexities of love? I cannot control the seasons or destiny or nature or the order of the cosmos. Many things—and largely those most worth reflecting on—are beyond my control. Should I refuse to think about them and focus solely on my next meal? Would that be a meaningful life? Isn't one of the most sublime accomplishments of the human species precisely that we can contemplate the whole of reality and not just the parts that we can control directly?

Avoiding Death's Sadness by Forgoing the Joys and Responsibilities of Life

Both Epicureans and Stoics seem intent on denying the sadness of death, the sadness that accompanies death. But perhaps we should consider whether this denial can keep us from facing fully some realities we must face if we are to be not only psychologically healthy but fully human. The American psychologist William James in *The Varieties of Religious Experience* counsels against what he describes as "Stoic insensibility and Epicurean resignation."

> The Epicurean said: "Seek not to be happy, but rather to escape unhappiness; strong happiness is always linked with pain; therefore hug the safe shore, and do not tempt the deeper raptures. Avoid disappointment by expecting little, and by aiming low; and above all do not fret." The Stoic said: "The only genuine good that life can yield a man is the free possession of his own soul; all other goods are lies."[12]

---

[12] William James, *Varieties of Religious Experience* (New York: Longmans, Green, and Co., 1917), 140.

"Each of these philosophies," argues James, "is in its degree a philosophy of despair in nature's boons. Trustful self-abandonment to the joys that freely offer has entirely departed from both Epicurean and Stoic; and what each proposes is a way of rescue from the resultant dust-and-ashes state of mind."[13] There is, says James, a certain dignity in both forms of resignation; both represent "distinct stages in the sobering process which man's primitive intoxication with sense-happiness" must undergo.[14] And yet neither the Stoics nor the Epicureans describe a philosophy of life that allows us to face death without diminishing either life's joys or our responsibilities to others. This seems a poor bargain.

Heidegger and Being-towards-Death

We discussed above the importance of the admonition "Know yourself." Can we really "know ourselves" if we ignore the inevitable reality of our own death? Is this not refusing to live in truth? Others have thought so, convinced that a culture that ignored death would not know how to live.

An influential modern thinker who believed we should not ignore death was the German philosopher Martin Heidegger (1889–1976). Developing ideas from Max Scheler's *Death and Survival*, Heidegger argued that, whereas classical and medieval men and women every day faced the possibility of death, modern man has suppressed death from his awareness.[15] Death is something that happens to people, but this is not the same as admitting that it will happen to me. Death is perceived as someone else's business,

---

[13] Ibid.

[14] Ibid.

[15] For Heidegger's discussion of death, see Martin Heidegger, *Being and Time*, trans. Joan Stambaugh (Albany: State University of New York Press, 1996), div. 2, ch. 1.

something that affects others; it is not yet conceived as a real possibility for me. It is an indefinite something which we know (at the back of our minds) must at some point arrive, but it is not yet present-at-hand so not a present reality for me here-and-now.

To live this way, thought Heidegger, is to live in falsehood and thus "inauthentically." Only in facing up to the unavoidable reality of death can a person realize his or her full humanity as mortal rather than indulging the illusion of a kind of deathless divinity that our present awareness gives us; only in this way does man transcend his biological limitedness. I have been "thrown into the world," said Heidegger, at a time and place and in circumstances not of my choosing. Similarly I cannot entirely control the circumstances of my exit, nor will I exist any longer after my death to manage the consequences. What I can do is simply face the realities of the world as I find it, and these include the reality that at some point I will cease to exist.

Heidegger's proposal, that my way of being in the world should be a Being-towards-death, requires that I dismiss any possibility of something beyond death. To bask in the illusory comfort of an afterlife would be another way to live "inauthentically," he thought. Man's greatness, rather, is precisely in the refusal to give in to the illusion of immortality and to face his mortality. We are not gods; we will not live on, so we had better live our lives now with a clear sense of that fact. To live for an indeterminate future in this life or for a future after death, as though this life were only a dry run for another life, would be to live in falsehood. Better to choose to live fully now.

What should characterize this "Being-towards-death," thought Heidegger, is care for the world. The daily recognition that my life is limited and that all my plans to achieve a kind of immortality by means of the accumulation of wealth or power or technical prowess will in the end amount to nothing should cause me to conclude that an authentic human life is one characterized by care for the world and for others.

Is Being-towards-Death Conceivable? Is It Authentically Human?

There are elements of this view one can admire, just as we could admire the Epicurean recognition that death can come at any time and their determination to make as much as possible of life each day. Christians can admire elements of both views while also recognizing that the two give opposing advice about how to deal with death. Epicureans advise ignoring it; Heidegger advises facing it every day. And, as with certain aspects of the Epicurean view so with Heidegger's view, there are limitations and potential problems. The first is simply that it is difficult if not impossible to conceive of my own non-being. When I am thinking about it, I still exist, so there is a falseness to my thinking. More likely, I am, as if from a divine height, looking down upon a world in which I am absent. But on Heidegger's view, this is a vision I could never have since I would not exist. While I am conceiving of a world without me in it, I am still thinking, reflecting, and envisioning, so I am not really conceiving of my "non-being." Given this impossibility, it is difficult to conceive of what Being-towards-death really is, especially for creatures such as we are, who look to the future in an open-ended way. I think about what I will do with my friends tomorrow and the next day and next year even though I know I might not live to do any of it. I imagine the future for my family and my city, even though I know I won't be alive when the possibilities present now come to fruition years from now.

Man is by nature a creature that looks to the future—not only his own but that of his children and grandchildren and that of his city. So, too, man by nature searches for truths that transcend the limitations of time, place, and culture. Are these desires not themselves a kind of desire for immortality—a desire to have one's efforts "live on" in the lives of others? Do we not find within our self a desire to bring our mind into contact with truths that transcend the limitations of the body?

Indeed, it was precisely these elements of the human spirit that caused thinkers such as Plato and Cicero to conclude that there is something in man that transcends the death of the body. Indeed, it was Cicero who wrote, "No one would ever have exposed himself to death for his country without good hope of immortality."[16] Would we be willing to characterize this statement as an "inauthentic" expression of our human finitude? Or could we not, rather, see it as a basic fact of life and an authentic expression of the universal human longing for an existence that transcends the boundaries of death.

Men have always known that, in the order of nature, things were born, grew to maturity, diminished, died, and decayed. But precisely because they knew that they *knew* this—that is to say, precisely because they possessed a self-awareness and power of knowing not tied to the material order (animals do not think about their thinking, nor is self-awareness a material thing)—they concluded that this power might transcend the limitations of the physical body even after the death of the body.

---

[16] Cicero, *Tusculan Disputations*, trans. J. E. King, Loeb Classical Library, vol. 141 (Cambridge, MA: Harvard University Press, 1927), 1.15.

Should We Sacrifice Our Lives for a World That Will Not Last?

As much as we might hope that, contrary to Cicero's judgment, people would exhibit a Heideggerian care for the world absent any hope in personal immortality, it is hard to see how we could get people to care about the future good of their community and rest their hopes on it when so many events in the twentieth century have put the lie to all such vain hopes. People were promised immortality as members of the Third Reich, which was to last for a thousand years. People of other polities were promised a kind of immortality as part of the great socialist revolution, which would bring about the final stage of history, the rule of the proletariat. And of course, these are just two of many such movements to which people gave their lives and entrusted their identities. Even the hopes that science would bring about a great utopia have been dashed, given the human destruction (e.g., the Holocaust and the atomic bomb) and the environmental damage that science has helped to bring about. With the increasing breakup of families, the frequent in-fighting over the wealth and legacy of parents, and the crumbling of what were once thought to be solid institutions, we have to wonder whether there is anything lasting to which one might devote oneself.

As philosopher Bernard Schumacher has argued: "The tragedies of the twentieth century ended up killing this desire for immortality in immanence, obtained by human strength alone, that the philosophers of progress and the prophets of the earthly city had promised."[17] Schumacher notes that contemporary German philosopher Thomas Macho expressed a not-uncommon

---

[17] Bernard N. Schumacher, "The Desire for Immortality at the Dawn of the Third Millennium: The Anthropological Stakes," *Nova et Vetera*, vol. 17, no. 4 (Fall 2019): 1228.

skepticism when he wrote: "In the past few decades the last remaining substitutes for hopes of immortality were shattered. We have no more reason to expect to live on in our children or in our works; we have no more reason to trust in the 'everlasting life' of the human species or in the development of the 'world spirit.'"[18] If nothing will come of what I am striving for now, why should I care about anything beyond taking care of myself now? Perhaps Cicero was right, then, when he admonished, "No one would ever have exposed himself to death for his country without good hope of immortality."

Isn't the desire to sacrifice for future generations based, at least in part, on the illusion that I can see past my death? I think of the future good of my family or my city as though I were looking down on it from above—as though I will be able to see it, know it, and enjoy it, at least in some sense. I envision myself as part of it or as connected to it—as, for example, in the *Aeneid,* the gods allow Aeneas to see the future glory of Rome that will come after his death. We will have more to say about the importance of this connectedness to the living in chapter 3.

Old Age Has the Last Word . . . or Does It?

In contrast to those who, like the Epicureans, would prefer not to let the prospect of death burden their thoughts, it is William James again who warns against taking refuge in a simple-minded refusal to face the problem. To all this talk about death, a not uncommon response has been: "Forget all this nonsense, you just need to get out into the sun and enjoy life," or (to use James's example): "Cheer up, old fellow, you'll be all right erelong, if you will only

---

[18] Thomas Macho, *Todesmetaphern*, translated and quoted in Schumacher, "Desire for Immortality," 1228.

drop your morbidness!" To all such remarks, James replies: "But in all seriousness, can such bald animal talk as that be treated as a rational answer? To ascribe religious value to mere happy-go-lucky contentment with one's brief chance at natural good is but the very consecration of forgetfulness and superficiality. Our troubles lie indeed too deep for that cure."[19]

"Old age has the last word," writes James, and "the purely naturalistic look at life, however enthusiastically it may begin, is sure to end in sadness." Indeed, "this sadness," says James, "lies at the heart of every merely positivistic, agnostic, or naturalistic scheme of philosophy."[20]

> Let sanguine healthy-mindedness do its best with its strange power of living in the moment and ignoring and forgetting, still the evil background is really there to be thought of, and the skull will grin in at the banquet. In the practical life of the individual, we know how this whole gloom or glee about any present fact depends on the remoter schemes and hopes with which it stands related. Its significance and framing give it the chief part of its value. Let it be known to lead nowhere, and however agreeable it may be in its immediacy, its glow and gilding vanish. The old man, sick with an insidious internal disease, may laugh and quaff his wine at first as well as ever, but he knows his fate now, for the doctors have revealed it; and the knowledge knocks the satisfaction out of all these functions.

---

[19] James, *Varieties*, 137.
[20] Ibid., 138.

They are partners of death and the worm is their brother,
and they turn to a mere flatness.[21]

Thus we need a life, claims James, "not correlated with death, a
health not liable to illness, a kind of good that will not perish, a
good in fact that flies beyond the Goods of nature."[22]

False Immortality Systems and the Denial of Death

Since Christians believe that there is life after death, they are not
faced with the same challenge as those, such as the Epicureans and
Heideggerians, who don't believe. Christians are, however, faced
with the challenge of how best to conceive of that life-after-death
so as to avoid the problems from which other views suffer. A few
words are in order on that score.

Ernest Becker (1924–1974), professor of anthropology at
the University of California, in his Pulitzer Prize-winning book
The Denial of Death, describes what he takes to be "an impossible
paradox" that characterizes man's existential condition: "The fear
of death must be present behind all our normal functioning, in
order for the organism to be armed for self-preservation. But the
fear of death cannot be present constantly in one's mental functioning, else the organism could not function."[23] What Professor
Becker describes as "the denial of death" is not mere forgetfulness,
a simple letting go of care; it is, rather, "a constant psychological effort to keep the lid on."[24] Measurements such as galvanic
skin responses strongly suggest that "underneath the most bland
exterior lurks the universal anxiety" about death, which we seek

---

21 Ibid.
22 Ibid., 137.
23 Ernest Becker, *The Denial of Death* (New York: Free Press, 1973), 16.
24 Ibid., 17.

to repress by various means.[25] However much the Stoics and Epicureans imagine they have put behind them their fear of death, the likelihood is that, in reality, they have not. And perhaps this is a good thing.

One way of coping with the "existential paradox of constantly being faced with one's own mortality," writes Becker, is "to allow it to happen and go with it," giving oneself over to the bodily passions in order to numb one's sense of ultimate futility and the seeming meaninglessness of life. As author Dennis Ford notes in *The Search for Meaning: A Short History*:

> Several, ultimately futile possibilities exist on both the individual and social levels for at least temporarily denying meaninglessness and its associated depression. One strategy is to return to our primary instincts. The pioneering sociologist Émile Durkheim describes the failure of culture as *deculturation*, a state, he said, that reduces its victims to the animal level of chronic fighting or fornication. If I find direction or meaning neither in culture nor in more self-conscious attempts to answer the *why* questions, then I may find solace in my body, emotions, and pure, unmediated experience. From the perspective of these strategies, meaninglessness is not the problem; thinking self-consciously is the problem. Avoid or deny the questions, concede that you are nothing more than an instinctual animal in an indifferent universe, and you've solved the problem. Alcoholism, drug addiction, sexual obsessions, and adventurousness— in which meaning remains, but only while engaged in

---

[25] Ibid., 21.

extreme and risky activities, including violence—have all been attributed to misguided and finally self-destructive attempts to suppress the question of meaning by drowning in instinctual behavior.[26]

Hence, as Becker would argue more forcefully in a subsequent book, *Escape from Evil*, the attempt to repress the knowledge of our inevitable extinction leads to violence and a host of other ultimately disastrous pathologies.[27] Man, says Becker," is "the only animal conscious of death and decay, and so he engaged in a heightened search for powers of self-perpetuation."[28] Ultimately, claims Becker,

> All power is in essence power to deny mortality. Either that or it is not real power at all, not ultimate power, not the power that mankind is really obsessed with. Power means power to increase oneself, to change one's natural situation from one of smallness, helplessness, finitude, to one of bigness, control, durability, importance.[29]

But most of all, writes Becker, if it is to be real power, power must be "accumulated and passed on" so that it "radiates even after one's death, giving one a semblance of immortality as he lives in the vicarious enjoyments of his heirs that his money continues to buy,

---

26 Dennis Ford, *The Search for Meaning: A Short History* (Berkeley: University of California Press, 2007), 14–15.

27 Ernest Becker, *Escape from Evil* (New York: Free Press, 1975).

28 Ibid., 107.

29 Ibid., 81.

or in the magnificence of the art works that he commissioned, or in the statues of himself and the majesty of his own mausoleum."[30]

When humans recognize that they lack this power and that all their individual efforts will fail to achieve it in the end, they turn to collective entities to provide this sense of immortality for them, trying as it were "to avoid the natural plagues of existence by giving themselves over to structures" which embody "immortality power."[31] "If it is no longer the clan that represents the collective immortality pool," writes Becker, "then it is the state, the nation, the revolutionary cell, the corporation, the scientific society, one's own race. Man still gropes for transcendence, but now this is not necessarily nature and God, but the SS or the CIA." To whichever group one turns, however, the "stake is identical—immortality power—and the unit of motivation is still the single individual and his fears and hopes."[32]

Since there really is "no secular way to resolve the primal mystery of life and death," all secular societies promising this sort of redemption, says Becker, are lies.[33] And as with all lies, there are consequences.

If culture is a lie about the possibilities of victory over death, then that lie must somehow take its toll of life, no matter how colorful and expansive the celebration of joyful victory may seem. The massive meetings of the Nazi youth or those of Stalin in Red Square and Mao in Peking literally take our breath away and give

---

[30] Ibid., 81–82.

[31] Becker, *Denial of Death*, 93.

[32] Becker, *Escape from Evil*, 119. Becker includes in his critique groups that offer what he calls "experiential transcendence," which he describes as "the intense experience of a feeling state which, for a little while anyway, eliminates the problem of time and death." Ibid., 120.

[33] Ibid., 124.

us a sense of wonder. But the proof that these celebrations have an underside is in Auschwitz and Siberia.[34]

When people have invested a human system with ultimate meaning, they will do whatever they must to protect themselves against the exposure of that system as just one mortality-denying system among others. A far too common way of insulating oneself and one's select group from this sort of devastating critique is to attack and degrade—sometimes even kill—the adherents of other mortality-denying systems that threaten the truth of one's own. This battle might be Protestants vilifying Catholics (or vice versa), Muslims vilifying Christians (or vice versa), or good students of the Enlightenment demonizing religion (and vice versa). The list could be expanded indefinitely. The problem is not only in the self-comforting delusion that one has embraced something lasting, some ultimate meaning—and what kind of authentic life can be built on an illusion? Presenting even greater problems are the attempts people make, sometimes violent attempts, to insulate themselves from anything that might threaten the immortality system by which they feel they have transcended their own, inevitable mortality. "The thing that makes man the most devastating animal that ever stuck his neck up into the sky," writes Becker, "is that he wants a stature and a destiny that is impossible for an animal; he wants an earth that is not an earth but a heaven, and the price for this kind of fantastic ambition is to make the earth an even more eager graveyard than it naturally is."[35]

It is unclear whether Becker himself ever thought he had found a satisfactory answer to the problem; in March of 1974,

---

[34] Ibid., 121.
[35] Ibid., 96.

at the age of 49, he died of colon cancer.[36] However there is an interesting chapter in his book *The Denial of Death* on the Danish Christian philosopher Søren Kierkegaard. Kierkegaard, he believed, had engaged in an "extremely difficult and unbelievably subtle exercise . . . to be able finally to conclude with authority what a person would be like *if he did not lie*"[37]—that is to say, if he could escape from the prison he had painstakingly built up to deny the truth about himself and his own creatureliness. To be authentically human is to be true to one's existence as a creature. And only when all the illusions of our own immortality are cast aside can we face up to the truth about ourselves: we did not create ourselves or the world, and so we are not and cannot be in complete control of either.

This ultimate renunciation of control, which is a renunciation of one's very self, is something we experience as a kind of death—a "death to self" (see Rom 6:6–7). "The self must be brought down to nothing," writes Becker, "in order for self-transcendence to begin."[38] Only then can the self "begin to relate itself to powers beyond itself." Only when a person "links his secret inner self, his authentic talent, his deepest feelings of uniqueness, his inner yearning for absolute significance, to the very ground of creation" does his life acquire an "ultimate value in place of merely social and

---

[36] There is much in Becker's books, in fact, that many readers may find problematic and with which they will likely disagree. My use of his work here is not meant to be an endorsement of his entire intellectual project, especially in its relationship to the major intellectual currents in psychology with which he saw himself in dialogue in the early 1970s. He does offer, however, to my mind, an interesting and important challenge to our culture's "denial of death" and the propensity of human beings to take refuge in false and facile "immortality projects."

[37] Becker, *Denial of Death*, 85. Italics in original.

[38] Ibid., 89.

cultural, historical value."[39] Faith, writes Becker, is the belief that despite one's "insignificance, weakness, death, one's existence has meaning in some ultimate sense because it exists within an eternal and infinite scheme of things brought about and maintained to some kind of design by some creative force."[40]

The "horror and anguish which death inspires in us," writes Nicolas Berdyaev, "prove that we belong not only to the surface but to the depths as well, not only to temporal life but also to eternity."[41] If this is so, then we must not deny the reality of death, but we must face and embrace the truth of it as something that can point to an ultimate meaning beyond ourselves and what are often our own superficial concerns with things like money, power, and status. As philosopher John D. Morgan has written:

> Life is a gift from God that places on the individual the obligation to return the gift lovingly by the acceptance of death. *Death ultimately is the proof that no matter what powers we as humans have or develop, we still are not God.* . . . Death reminds us that we are good, but not absolutely so. Death does not mean that life is without meaning; indeed death give meaning to our lives because it is that by which we understand the importance of what we do and that by which we render homage to God, the task for which we were born.[42]

---

[39] Ibid., 91.

[40] Ibid., 90.

[41] Nicolas Berdyaev, *The Destiny of Man* (London: Geoffrey Bles, 1937), 250.

[42] See John D. Morgan, "Miguel de Unamuno and Ernest Becker: The Human Person as Mortal," in *Images of the Human: The Philosophy of the Human Person in a Religious Context*, ed. Kennedy, Brown, et al. (Chicago: Loyola Press, 1995), 610–611. I am much indebted to Prof. Morgan's chapter in this volume for introducing me to the work of Ernest Becker.

"Authentic faith," writes philosopher Glenn Hughes, "affirms enduring meaning in the context of an open if anxious acceptance of mortality."

> And so one must conclude that there are two opposites to authentic faith. One is the dogmatic clinging to an immortality project; and the other is the equally dogmatic insistence that enduring meaning is an illusion. Both of these are denials of our real human situation, making up two sides of the same counterfeit coin.[43]

If this is an accurate (if yet still incomplete) picture of faith, then contrary to what is often assumed, anxiety and dread are not alien to faith. Rather, they are part of the mystery of faith. The paradox that faith must embrace is that although we are creatures made in the image of God, we are fallen. Because we are made in the image and likeness of God, we perceive within ourselves the seeds of immortality. But because we see in ourselves and all around us the evidence of our fallenness, we also recognize that we are destined to die. It is the jarring contradiction between these two that faith must resolve.

The question we must face is how we can "live in the truth" concerning our inevitable death without living in its shadow and how we can *care* for the world while remaining aware of the limitations of our actions and interventions on behalf of others. On the Christian account, this paradox of our creatureliness can be resolved only by the victory of the Cross, when Life Itself accepts death in order that our death can be made life. Death, then, is

---

[43] Glenn Hughes, "The Denial of Death and the Practice of Dying," posted October 1, 2014 on the Ernest Becker Foundation website, https://ernest-becker.org/becker-in-the-press-test-2/.

the ultimate loving release—the ultimate release by which I surrender myself into the loving hands of the Creator. There can be no Resurrection without the Cross, nor the Cross without the Resurrection and Christ's Ascension to the Father and the sending of the Holy Spirit.

Transhumanists of the world unite—we have immortality to gain and only biology to lose.

Nikola Danaylov, "The Transhumanist Manifesto"

In us organic life has produced Mind. It has done its work. After that we want no more of it. We do not want the world any longer furred over with organic life, like what you call the blue mould—all sprouting and budding and breeding and decaying. We must get rid of it. . . . For the moment, I speak only to inspire you. I speak that you may know what can be done: what shall be done here. This Institute—Dio meo, it is for something better than housing and vaccinations and faster trains and curing the people of cancer. It is for the conquest of death: or for the conquest of organic life, if you prefer. They are the same thing. It is to bring out of that cocoon of organic life which sheltered the babyhood of mind the New Man, the man who will not die, the artificial man, free from Nature. Nature is the ladder we have climbed up by, now we kick her away.

C. S. Lewis, *That Hideous Strength*

All our human problems, with their intolerable sufferings, arise from man's ceaseless attempts to make this material world into a man-made reality . . . aiming to achieve on earth a "perfection" which is only to be found in the beyond . . . thereby hopelessly confusing the values of both.

Otto Rank, *Beyond Psychology*

Millions long for immortality who don't know what to do with themselves on a rainy Sunday afternoon.

Susan Ertz, *Anger in the Sky*

Chapter 2

TRANSHUMANISTS AND THE IMMORTALITY PROJECT

Historically, most of the ways of dealing with death were based on the notion that death is inevitable, that there are natural limits to human life, and that all efforts to overcome this limit would indulge a false hope and lead to frustration and unhappiness. And yet there have been those throughout history who have sought to transcend death not by an escape to some afterlife but by escaping death itself and maintaining this life. Most of these efforts are embodied in legends in which a person drinks a magic elixir or, having asked it of a god or demon, is "blessed" (or cursed) to live on forever and ever.

Modern advances in science and technology have revived, among some, the hope for unending life. Increasing numbers of people in the modern world imagine that technological progress will soon allow us to nullify the negative effects of aging and extend the human lifespan, and that such an extension will be an unmitigated blessing. This group of theorists—which includes both scientists and philosophers—is often collectively referred to as the "transhumanists" because they theorize a time when human beings will be able to "transcend" the current limited nature of their humanity. They argue that death is not a necessary part of life. So, for example, as French sociologist Edgar Morin (b. July 1921; still alive in 2022 as this book goes to press) claims: "Biology discovered *that death was not a necessity of organic life*. . . . Only accidental death is natural."[1]

This use of the term "natural" in this context is a bit odd, however; we might even call it somewhat unnatural. Customarily, a natural event is thought to be contrary to an "accidental" event. Thus if a death was said to be accidental, it was not natural, and if the death was due to natural causes, then it was not accidental. Even in a so-called "accidental" death, death itself is "natural" to human beings. As we have moved into the twenty-first century, however, people increasingly ask, even at the deaths of very old adults, "How did he die?" as though death were something for which one always has to give an account. The notion that sometimes people just die—that this is simply the natural course of human life—is becoming more and more difficult for us to admit. And so, too, for transhumanists, old age and death are considered mere disturbances; they are illnesses for which we can find a cure. As University of Montreal sociologist Céline Lafontaine has stated: "Viewed through the biomedical prism of pathology, even ageing looks like a disease."[2] She sums up our current cultural condition thus:

---

[1] Edgar Morin, *L'Homme et la mort* (Paris: Seuil, 1976), 331: "La biologie a découvert *que la mort n'était pas une nécessité de la vie organique*. . . . Seule la mort accidentelle est naturelle."

[2] Céline Lafontaine, "The Postmortal Condition: From the Biomedical

The endless health advice presented in the media and in public-health campaigns attests to the ever-increasing importance of biomedical science in our societies. Deferring death, addressing its causes, altering its boundaries, controlling all of its parameters and understanding its process in order to prolong life as long as possible or even surpass the temporal limits of human existence—such is the objective that the scientific and political authorities are pursuing so doggedly that health has become one of our societies' major concerns. . . . As death becomes increasingly medical and biomedical devices become increasingly technical and perfected, the definition of death is seen as malleable and historically constructed. . . . Far from being an inevitable and irreversible phenomenon that formerly bore witness to the passing of time, death has become multiple and plural, subject to indefinite extension.[3]

One of the most prominent proponents of "transhumanism" or "posthumanism" is the director of engineering at Google, Ray Kurzweil, author of *The Age of Spiritual Machines* (1999) and *The Singularity Is Near* (2006). In an interview corresponding with the launch of the latter work, Kurzweil spoke about "three great over-lapping revolutions that go by the letters 'GNR,' which stands for genetics, nanotechnology, and robotics."[4] Each, Kurzweil assures us, will provide a dramatic increase to human longevity—and eventually immortality—as developments in genetics allow us to

---

Deconstruction of Death to the Extension of Longevity," *Science as Culture*, 18:3 (2009): 298.

[3] Lafontaine, "Postmortal Condition," 297–298.

[4] The interview can be found at https://www.kurzweilai.net/singularity-q-a. The quotations in this paragraph are taken from that interview.

perfect our biological cells and advances in nanotechnology allow us to "capture the intelligence of our brains in a machine." Within several decades, he predicts, "We'll ultimately be able to scan all the salient details of our brains from inside, using billions of nano-bots in the capillaries. We can then back up the information. Using nanotechnology-based manufacturing, we could recreate your brain, or better yet re-instantiate it in a more capable computing substrate."[5] The point at which machine intelligence and humans merge completely is what Kurzweil calls "the singularity."

Other prominent experts in modern technology, such as Microsoft co-founder Paul Allen, have disputed whether the developments Kurzweil promises are in the offing. But whether the singularity is near or not, or even possible at all, one question we should ask is, even if it were possible, would it be advisable—or even desirable. And for guidance here, we might turn to some ancient sources for wisdom.

Classical Warnings against Immortality

Most of the stories from the ancient world, in fact, warn against indulging the hope of immortality. A good example would be the famous prophetess of Apollo known as "the Sibyl of Cumae," with whom, in Virgil's tale, Aeneas is said to have made his journey into the underworld and the land of the dead. In some legends, the Sibyl is said to have asked the gods to grant her everlasting life, which they did. She forgot, however, to ask for everlasting youth. As the years went by, she grew older and became so shriveled that she fit into a bottle that hung from the roof of her cave, increasingly mis-erable and yearning for death. The epigraph to T. S. Eliot's poem *The Wasteland*, a passage from Petronius's *Satyricon*, is based on

---

[5] Ibid.

the Sibyl. Translated into English, it says: "I saw with my own eyes the Sibyl at Cumae hanging in a jar, and when the boys said to her, 'Sibyl, what do you want?' she replied, 'I want to die.'"

So, too, in earlier Greek mythology, we find a similar story about Tithonus, the mortal lover of Eos, also known as Aurora, goddess of the Dawn. When Eos asked Zeus to grant Tithonus immortality, he granted her wish. But since the goddess forgot to ask for eternal youth as well, Tithonus grew old and decrepit, like the Sibyl, begging for death. Eos's progressive disenchantment with her beloved once he shows the signs of aging is truly heart-rending.

> So while he enjoyed the sweet flower of life he lived rap-
> turously with golden-throned Eos, the early-born, by the
> streams of Ocean, at the ends of the earth; but when the
> first grey hairs began to ripple from his comely head and
> noble chin, queenly Eos kept away from his bed, though
> she cherished him in her house and nourished him with
> food and ambrosia and gave him rich clothing. But when
> loathsome old age pressed full upon him, and he could
> not move nor lift his limbs, this seemed to her in her heart
> the best counsel: she laid him in a room and put to the
> shining doors. There he babbles endlessly, and no more
> has strength at all, such as once he had in his supple limbs.[6]

This story is told to Anchises by Aphrodite after she has spent the night with him and become pregnant with his child, whom she

---

6   Homeric Hymn 5, "Hymn to Aphrodite", in Anonymous, *The Homeric Hymns and Homerica*, trans. Hugh Evelyn-White, Loeb Classic Library (Cambridge, MA: Harvard University Press, 1914), lines 225–45. Also available online at https://homer.library.northwestern.edu/html/application.html.

says will be named Aeneas. Because she loves Anchises, she does not want the same fate for him Tithonus suffered. "I would not have you be deathless among the deathless gods," she tells him, "and live continually after such sort." If he could but "live on such as you now are in look and in form," then all would be fine. She would call him her husband. "But as it is," she tells him, "harsh old age will soon enshroud you—ruthless age which stands someday at the side of every man, deadly, wearying, dreaded even by the gods."[7]

The question many are asking is whether our recent advances in medical science have merely extended old age. In a culture that valued the wisdom and gifts of the elderly, the extension of old age would not be considered so "deadly, wearying, and dreaded" as it is now. But unfortunately, too often this is not the case. Those who roam the earth as gods, who have "kicked away the ladder of Nature," will likely look upon whatever diminishment comes with aging as worthy of contempt, as a lower form of existence, even unnatural, just as aging was considered unnatural among the Greek gods. Even now, we treat aging as an embarrassment to look upon.

As we enter further into a post-Christian age, and as more people return to what are essentially pagan views of the world untouched by Christian sensibilities, an age in which we are more and more intent on "kicking away the ladder of Nature," we can expect this pagan dread of old age to return, as in many ways it already has. We can expect more of what we are already seeing: an apotheosis of youth and youthful beauty and an increasing contempt for the diminishing powers of the elderly. Increasingly, the elderly must look and act youthfully or be shut in a room somewhere to "babble endlessly," no longer possessing strength such as once they had in their supple limbs.

[7] "Hymn to Aphrodite," lines 235–45.

Perfect Bodies

Oddly, the transhumanist project encourages at the same time both a disdain for the body and a preoccupation with its perfection as great as any in the culture of classical Greece. While, on the one hand, saying that the body is only accidental to the human person, transhumanists obsess over its perfection. Bernard Schumacher has highlighted the problem. The goal, as Schumacher points out, is "to free oneself from the limits of one's body, from the limits imposed by nature, from all laws imposed from outside, including the ultimate limit to the subject's autonomy, which is the mortal, suffering, vulnerable body,"[8] to construct for oneself, instead, "a perfect body, free of all imperfections, failings, and vulnerabilities."[9]

So, for example, French sociologist David Le Breton in his 1990 book *L'Adieu au corps* declares that "the body is the endemic illness [*la maladie endémique*] of the mind or of the subject"; it is the "rough draft to be corrected" (*le brouillon à corriger*), until one obtains "final perfection" (*la perfection ultime*).[10] Understood in this way, as "ontologically distinguished from the subject" (*ontologiquement distingué du sujet*), the body is no longer to be identified with the person and becomes merely "an object available on which one acts in order to improve it" (*un objet à disposition sur lequel agir afin de l'améliorer*).[11] To attain "technical purity," says Le Breton, the body must be "dedicated to innumerable revisions to escape its precariousness and its limits" (*voué aux innombrables*

---

[8] Bernard N. Schumacher, "The Desire for Immortality at the Dawn of the Third Millennium: The Anthropological Stakes," *Nova et vetera*, vol. 17, no. 4 (Fall 2019): 1225.

[9] Ibid., 1223.

[10] David Le Breton, *L'Adieu au corps* (Paris: Éditions Métailié, 1999), 10.

[11] Ibid., 9.

biffures pour échapper à sa précarité, à ses limites) so that it may be made, at last, "a really flawless machine" (*une machine réellement impeccable*).[12]

Such views, though based on the soul-body dualism popularized by thinkers such as René Descartes, go far beyond anything Descartes or his contemporaries could have envisioned in its obsession with creating the perfect body. We might wonder, therefore, whether it is healthy for a society to have as its goal a "perfect body," envisioned as a "flawless machine." Don't contemporary men and women already get that message too often as people try to "sell" them on a more "perfect" body or persona, something that requires more makeup, more diets, more workout regimens, more liposuction, more breast implants, more Botox? Can some of these interventions have beneficial, therapeutic uses? In some cases, yes. But that's not the question. The question is whether the transhumanists, rather than helping society by encouraging people to be at home with their bodies, foster in human beings instead a greater discontent with their imperfect bodies, thereby rendering them more vulnerable to manipulation and abuse by marketers who make a great deal of money selling products that are supposed to lead to just such "perfect" bodies.

The presumption of the transhumanist project is that a lost hand, arm, or leg will be able to be repaired or replaced. Without this promise, one would be condemned to living one's endless life damaged or disabled in a world where the standard has become a "perfect body." Whether or not each person's body could be repaired to "like new" condition after any damage would likely affect a person's decision whether to choose lengthening his or her years without any guarantee of a vibrant, active life. But in

---

[12] Ibid., 11.

addition, one might wish to ask: How much would it cost? Companies don't give away life-saving drugs for free. Doctors don't do surgery for free. Who imagines companies would give away new bodies for free? Does anyone expect companies to give this technology away for free? What modifications will these companies make to the new bodies they sell to ensure that they will continue to remain highly profitable? Tech companies work very hard to ensure that consumers will keep coming back to them and not to their competitors, and they work very hard to ensure that consumers need to keep coming back to them to update their technology every eighteen months or so. Once you have purchased the new Legs 4.0, how long before those legs are outmoded and no longer serviced by the company with the advent of Legs 6.0.

Let us say, for the moment, that the transhumanists were successful in extending human life. In order to avoid the curse of the Sibyl, it would be necessary not only to extend life but also to extend youth. But then the question is, would society have enough money to keep all of us eternally young or only the rich and successful? How long would it take and how hard would a person have to work at a low-end job to be able to afford a new arm that was blown off in an accident? Would those with money be able to afford the "best," most "up-to-date" bodies and body repairs while those among the "lower" classes would have to satisfy themselves with second-rate "used" bodies and body parts? In the television science fiction show "Altered Carbon," characters can transfer their consciousness to a new body. The show reveals in certain ways the horrible consequences of this system; it takes account, for example, of the different results for "rich" and "poor." The rich switch bodies ("alter carbon") more easily and into more desirable bodies. The transfer does not generally make them any less craven or selfish. One imagines such a system could only make them more so since their continued existence in "good" bodies depends on their remaining far ahead of their fellow competitors for new bodies. Given the difficulties we have had spreading the blessings of current technology widely among all sectors of society, rich and poor, it is hard to imagine we will do much better with technologically "perfected" bodies. Does anyone imagine we will really be able to insist that poor children in Africa have access to the same quality bodies as the rich children in Beverly Hills, California?

Unanswered is just how are the "benefits" of the immortality project to be shared—or marketed? The technologies of human perfection are not inexpensive, and the problem of the increasing divide between the rich and poor becomes ever more pressing as the benefits of technological advances in medical science are not shared equally by all. Even now, the costs of medical care for the aging are becoming an increasing concern. Sociologist Céline Lafontaine warns, "The constantly increasing public burden of health-care costs is at the heart of the political and economic concerns of 'postmortal' society. The unlimited extension of biopower that results from the right to health care places biomedical knowledge at the very core of social regulation. In other words, in view of the deconstruction of death, 'nothing nowadays is external to medicine.'"[13] When perfect bodies become the most desired market item and supplying them to meet an unlimited demand becomes essential to people's survival, then it will become one of society's most pressing concerns. Even now, argues Lafontaine, "aiming to control individuals and make them aware of their responsibilities for their own health" has become "one of the major challenges faced by Western states"—one that is "at the heart of contemporary biopolitics."

---

[13] Lafontaine, "Postmortal Condition," 298.

As maintained by the largest international organizations, such as the World Bank and the International Monetary Fund, the notion of an "old-age crisis" falls within the context of capitalist globalization, in which ageing is perceived both as a collective burden and as a risk for which individuals should be given personal responsibility. Thus, according to the logic of the commodification of health care, individuals must make a financial investment in order to ensure their longevity.[14]

The question is whether poor people in a transhumanist society would ever get the same level of medical care as do the rich. Although we all *say* we want the poor to be "taken care of," most people are not willing to surrender any of their precious freedom-to-do-whatever-they-want-to-do—the freedom to create the perfect me I want to be—in order to provide everyone else not only sufficient benefits, but equal benefits. Whatever sentimental attachments our modern individualistic society may harbor concerning the poor or the elderly, when push comes to shove or when resources run short, as they always do in a society constantly engaged in repeated self-creations and in which more is thought to be better, people will quickly come to believe that they simply don't have enough money to spare. Everyone becomes that teenager who insists about the latest fad or fashion, "But mom, I *neeeed* it." A culture based on the project of self-creation would never produce citizens who think of themselves as having enough—and certainly not enough with an excess left over—to provide for others in need. This is increasingly true even now in our materialist, consumerist culture. The technology of transhumanism could

---

[14] Ibid.

only worsen the problem and the divide between the haves and the have nots.

The Lesson of Gulliver and the Struldbruggs

The elderly are not unaware of the dangers they face by extending their lives indefinitely. In a 2013 Pew Research Center survey of more than two thousand adults, sixty percent reported that they did not want to live past the age of ninety. Thirty percent did not want to live past eighty. These results were no different for those who had lots of money. Nor were they different for people who did not believe in an afterlife.[15] What seems to be driving people's misgivings about extending their lives is uncertainty about what kind of lives they would be living.

One reporter's question about the Pew survey, however, revealed a great deal. "Would medical progress keep us feeling young?" he wondered, "or would it only stretch out our declining years?"[16] To ask the question in this way, however, is to betray a definite bias: namely, that "feeling young" is essential to human flourishing and that aging can be characterized as "our declining years" rather than as "years of wisdom" or "years devoted to prayer and contemplation." Characterizing aging as "decline" is so common now we hardly recognize it. Undoubtedly the reporter thought he was merely repeating a commonplace, not making a

---

[15] Pew Research Center, "Living to 120 and Beyond: Americans' Views on Aging, Medical Advances and Radical Life Extension," Pew Research Center's Religion and Public Life Project, Aug. 6, 2013, https://www.pewforum.org/2013/08/06/living-to-120-and-beyond-americans-views-on-aging-medical-advances-and-radical-life-extension/.

[16] William Saletan, "Fear of Immortality," *Slate*, August 6, 2013, https://slate.com/technology/2013/08/aging-polls-and-life-extension-why-dont-americans-want-to-live-longer.html.

statement. But the fact that we don't question this view of aging makes a statement of its own.

Diminishing physical prowess is one thing, bad enough for many people but acceptable to those who value other human gifts and accomplishments more than merely the physical. Often, however, the greatest fear harbored by the elderly is the problem of dementia and the loss of memory; to lose one's ability to reason and any connection with our loved ones or even memory of them—this is a truly terrifying fate.

We might consider prophetic in this regard the tale of the Struldbruggs recounted in Jonathan Swift's 1726 satire *Gulliver's Travels*. Swift describes how Gulliver comes upon the Struldbruggs and finds that some of them would live very long lives, centuries in some cases. Gulliver is envious at first and imagines all the knowledge and learning he could accumulate over the centuries if his lifetime were extended in this way. What he discovers instead, however, is that these long-lived Struldbruggs are considered by their fellow citizens to be the most wretched of their race. As they aged, they would start to forget things, eventually forgetting even their spouses, their children, and their own names. Gulliver comes to the realization that his previous envy was a mistake.

So, too, if Professor Kurzweil's biogenetic revolution extending human life arrives long before the technological innovations he thinks are possible to keep the body and brain young, an increasing number of people may find that a mere extension of life is not always the blessing it is purported to be. The statistics are not comforting. According to the Alzheimer's Association, there was an eighty-nine percent increase in deaths due to Alzheimer's between 2000 and 2014, and by 2025, the number of people aged sixty-five and older with Alzheimer's disease is expected to reach 7.1 million people, a twenty-seven percent increase from the 5.6

million aged sixty-five and older in 2019. Currently, one in nine people age sixty-five and older (11.3 percent) has Alzheimer's dementia although it is estimated that only one in four people with Alzheimer's disease have been diagnosed. Of Alzheimer's cases, eighty-two percent involve people seventy-five or older; only four percent are in persons sixty-five or younger.

It is hard to avoid the conclusion that, as medical science has extended human life beyond the median age of sixty-five to seventy, we have opened the doors to a new, terrifying human malady. This may be one of the reasons why so many respondents in the Pew survey were unwilling to vote an overwhelming "yes" to extending their lives past age seventy-five or eighty. The prominence of "Do Not Resuscitate" orders and medical directives suggests that many people are choosing to forgo the "blessings" of more life that medical technology might offer them. Indeed, increasing numbers of people are opting for suicide instead of extended life and demanding that their physicians kill them instead of continuing to treat them. A culture devoted to extending life has become a culture increasingly captivated by the lure of suicide. Like the Sibyl, more and more people are responding to the question, "What do you want?" with the answer: "I want to die." In a culture devoted to control and mastery over nature, this is, for an increasing number of people, the last act of the self-assertion of the will over nature and human nature.

Mastery over Nature?

Although Christians should not wish to stand in the way of the authentic benefits of modern science and technology—they should be considered, in the words of Pope St. John Paul II, "a wonderful product of a God-given human creativity"—we might still ask some important questions about the consequences and unintended side effects of the mastery over nature being proposed here, just as we ask serious questions about nuclear bombs, coal-fired power plants, toxic chemicals, and billions of automobiles spewing carbon into the atmosphere.[17] Experience shows that once we see ourselves as the technological masters of nature, we soon become slaves of our own technology and/or slaves of those who control the technology. C. S. Lewis has argued: "Man's power over Nature turns out to be a power exercised by some men over other men with Nature as its instrument."[18] Mastery belongs to those who actually have technological control.

Will those who have this technological mastery use this power altruistically? Whether that is their intention or not, the more basic problem is that, as a society, we will have no basis for judging what "altruism" would be once the guidance of human nature and natural human flourishing are erased or ignored. We know that it is a good thing to restore a disabled child's ability to walk and run and jump like other children. But can we be sure it is similarly a good thing to enhance a child's ability to run 40 mph faster than any of his peers or to punch harder than any other child on the playground? And yet, it is hard to understand on what basis we would resist the temptation to make these enhancements if the

---

[17] See Pope St. John Paul II, "Address to Scientists and Representatives of the United Nations University," Hiroshima, Wednesday, Feb. 25, 1981, §3: "Criticism of science and technology is sometimes so severe that it comes close to condemning science itself. On the contrary, science and technology are a wonderful product of a God-given human creativity, since they have provided us with wonderful possibilities, and we all gratefully benefit from them. But we know that this potential is not a neutral one: it can be used either for man's progress or for his degradation. Like you, I have lived through this period, which I would call the 'post-Hiroshima period,' and I share your anxieties."

[18] C. S. Lewis, *Abolition of Man* (New York: HarperOne, 1944), 55.

goal of science is control and the great scandal is any kind of weakness or vulnerability.

A related difficulty arises from the transhumanists' unreflective use of the modern notions of "freedom" and "mastery" as the basic principles of their project. They hold the very common modern notion of freedom: namely, freedom from all constraint on one's will, even from characteristics inherent in one's own nature. Cardinal Robert Sarah has warned: "The West refuses to receive, and will accept only what it constructs for itself. Transhumanism is the ultimate avatar of this movement. Because it is a gift from God, human nature itself becomes unbearable for Western man." "Our contemporaries are convinced," says Sarah, "that, in order to be free, one must not depend on anybody. There is a tragic error in this. Western people are convinced that receiving is contrary to the dignity of human persons. But civilized man is fundamentally an heir, he receives a history, a culture, a language, a name, a family. . . . Because he refuses to acknowledge himself as an heir, man is condemned to the hell of liberal globalization in which individual interests confront one another without any law to govern them besides profit at any price."[19]

We might keep Cardinal Sarah's warning in mind as we contemplate the costs of all this life-extending technology. When the sweet-sounding promises of individual freedom and autonomy are ringing in our ears, it is appealing. But does this siren song cause us to forget our duties and connectedness with our loved ones? When I think of myself as autonomous and free from all external

---

[19] Cardinal Robert Sarah, "Cardinal Sarah: 'We Must Rebuild the Cathedral . . . We Do Not Need to Invent a New Church,'" *Catholic World Report*, Dec. 29, 2019, https://www.catholicworldreport.com/2019/12/29/cardinal-sarah-we-must-rebuild-the-cathedral-we-do-not-need-to-invent-a-new-church/.

constraints, will I really be able to commit myself selflessly to others? Or will other people become for me a threat to my autonomy or just another thing to be manipulated? When this happens, I deny myself the internal goods that can come only from honest, selfless, self-giving relationships with others, in which neither party is using the other for his or her purposes. Transhumanism turns the subject of work, the worker, into the object of work; it turns the person who should be treated with the dignity due a subject into an object, a resource, material for transformation.[20]

The most common notion of freedom is freedom *from external constraint*.[21] But if we embrace the idea that freedom is freedom from external constraint, even the constraints of my own nature, then it seems my will should exert command over both my body and my emotions. But should my will really be "free" from the constraints provided by emotions such as empathy, sorrow, and guilt? Would I (or any engineer) be able to know in advance which of these emotions to "engineer" in the right way or to the right extent? To think of freedom as merely the removal of all constraints is to fail to see that we are often our own worst enemies; that our willfulness can sometimes cause us to do things we should not do and that are not good for us. It can even cause us to ignore

---

[20] For more on the distinction between the "subject" and "object" of work, see Pope St. John Paul II, On Human Work *Laborem Exercens*, Sept. 14, 1981, esp. §§5 and 6, https://www.vatican.va/content/john-paul-ii/en/encyclicals/documents/hf_jp-ii_enc_14091981_laborem-exercens.html.

[21] See, for example, the famous passage in Thomas Hobbes, *Leviathan* (London: Penguin, 1968), 64: "By LIBERTY, is understood, according to the proper signification of the word, the absence of externall Impediments: which Impediments, may oft take away part of a mans power to do what hee would; but cannot hinder him from using the power left him, according as his judgement, and reason shall dictate to him."

basic realities. Should I be free from the limitations imposed on my will by others, by the duties of love?

And if I habituate myself to thinking of freedom in this way, why would I curb my will if I desire to intervene in nature in other ways? Why would I stop at thinking of just my own body as material to be formed by the power of my will? Why not the natural environment? Why not other people? Why not engineer the next generation of children, for example?

And yet, if we are fallen human beings—and even the transhumanists admit that human nature as it exists now is fundamentally flawed, or why else would we need to spend billions to "perfect" it—then on the basis of what wisdom and from what source or standard are we to propose engineering the "perfection" of the species? Would it not be more likely that we would simply be passing on to those whom we are attempting to engineer many of the worst features of our fallen human nature—those features associated with our baser instincts and our will to dominate and control others? Mastery and control are, after all, the goals that drive the transhumanists engaged in the immortality project.

The Film *Ex Machina* and the Machines of Fallen Humanity

A contemporary movie that hits upon many of these issues dramatically is the 2014 science fiction film *Ex Machina*, in which a programmer (Caleb Smith) is invited by the legendary founder and CEO (Nathan Bateman) of the tech company for which he works to come to his remote yet highly tech-heavy house in the wilderness to test whether a humanoid robot he has made can be considered conscious. Is it actually thinking?

But Nathan is not only interested in thinking, as is common among researchers in the area of artificial intelligence; he is curious also about his creation's emotional and bodily responses as well, especially those concerned with sex and sexuality. Nathan wonders, for example, about the centrality and importance of the sexual drive and the powerful passions and emotions that accompany it. "Can you give an example of consciousness at any level, human or animal, that exists without a sexual dimension?" he asks Caleb Smith. "What imperative does a gray box have to interact with another gray box? Can consciousness exist without interaction?"[22]

And indeed we might admit that Nathan, though unhinged in many ways, is at least on to something here. When we put a plug into a wall socket, we do not think of it as "sexual," except perhaps metaphorically. If the sexual act were as mechanical as a plug inserted into a wall socket, we would be unlikely to call it "sex," and even if we did, it would still not be the thing people yearn for when they desire *sex*.

The problem for Nathan Bateman, which will eventually destroy both him and Caleb Smith, is that he has designed "Ava," his humanistic android robot, in his own image. It becomes clear as the movie proceeds that Nathan wants to create a robotic sex partner who will not merely be a "grey box" computer but will mirror his own passions, desires, and intelligence. And yet, since Nathan is creating Ava merely to use her to achieve his own goals, both for fame (as the first man to create an intelligent machine) and for sexual pleasure, to the extent that he is successful in creating the kind of "conscious" being he intends, how could it not result in a being that views both Caleb and Nathan merely as *things* to be used? Caleb risks a great deal to help Ava escape her

---

[22] *Ex Machina*, directed by Alex Garland (2014, Orlando: Universal Studios, 2015), DVD, 108 minutes.

prison in the belief that she will love him. But her reaction is not gratitude; this is a human emotion Nathan could not program into her because he does not understand or value it himself. She has become no more than what she was created to be: a being concerned with achieving her own individual goals, willing to use and manipulate others as much as needed, which is the only range of emotions her designer was able to give her.

And of course, Nathan has designed Ava with perfections he lacks but foolishly wishes her to have. Ava is young, beautiful, and sensual, and we have no reason to think that she will age. In fact, the emptiness of her life becomes apparent in one of Caleb's first interviews with Ava. She tells him her age is "one."

> "One what?" he asks. "One year or one day?"
> "One," is all she replies.[23]

As Charles Rubin notes in a fascinating essay on the film, "We have no evidence that she would enjoy eating or drinking, and without an organic metabolism, she would never age or put on weight. In sum, even though [Ava] convinced Caleb that she fears her dissolution, Nathan has not given her the thousand little moments of mortality that form human consciousness."[24] We might wonder, then, whether she would or even could make any sense of the meaning of her life. She has only goals to achieve but not any sense of the meaning of her life as a whole of the sort Pope St. John Paul II speaks of in the first paragraphs of *Fides et Ratio*. How could she? She was created to be used for the pleasure of her creator-master, not to have freedom, meaning, and purpose of her own. She does

---

[23] *Ex Machina*, dir. Alex Garland.
[24] Charles Rubin, "Mind Games," *The New Atlantis*, 51 (Winter 2017): 109–27, https://www.thenewatlantis.com/publications/mind-games.

not seem capable of feeling sorrow over the deaths she causes, nor, more crucially, can she even ask whether she should. Has Nathan Bateman created a more perfect human—that "really flawless machine" (*une machine réellement impeccable*) David Le Breton hoped for? Or is Ava merely an expression of Nathan's own fallen humanity? Or perhaps something even more insidious: a powerful machine without human emotions or a human conscience?

What Would You Include in the New You? What Would You Leave Out?

Nathan Bateman's dream of creating a machine with "artificial intelligence"—a machine that can teach itself, that can learn new concepts, that can think and understand and become self-aware the way humans are—is one shared by many of the most prominent proponents of transhumanism. The sooner we can make true humanoid robots, they believe, the sooner we will be able to engineer replacement bodies for ourselves. And yet the question is, how will we engineer these replacement bodies, replacement "selves"—with what wisdom or what blindness? Those responsible for engineering our future technological selves are likely to be as poor a judge of their own motives as Nathan Bateman and, worse yet, blind to the limited range of human capacities they would choose to engineer into our future selves.

So, for example, if you could program your future android "self" any way you choose, would you include sorrow? Would you? Wouldn't programming a machine to feel sorrow be condemning it to the kind of pain we wouldn't wish on anyone? If I were a Stoic, I might allow a little sorrow but not much. If we were following an Epicurean ethic of avoiding all pain and suffering, then programming pain into a machine would seem highly unethical.

Indeed, it would be hard for anyone to blame you for wanting to avoid pain and suffering.

But isn't the ability to feel sorrow the root of all compassion? And if we eradicate sorrow, won't we also eradicate compassion? Do we really want a host of human androids, pure "thinking things," walking around with intellectual processing power magnified a hundredfold but lacking the capacity for compassion? Put that way, the answer is likely to be no. But how many mistakes of this sort would technicians be likely to make if they decided to try to engineer our future "selves"? Not only are mistakes of this sort highly likely, they are also likely to have grave consequences to the extent that transhumanists are operating in their work with an incomplete, overly simplified picture of human nature and the human mind.

On the first pages of his biography of Pope St. John Paul II, *Witness to Hope*, author George Weigel writes that John Paul II

> gradually came to the conviction that the crisis of the modern world was first of all a crisis of ideas, a crisis in the very idea of the human person. History was driven by culture and the ideas that formed cultures. Ideas had consequences. And if the idea of the human person that dominated a culture was flawed, one of two things would happen. Either that culture would give birth to destructive aspirations, or it would be incapable of realizing its fondest hopes, even if it expressed them in the most nobly humanistic terms.[25]

In a similar way, however nobly humanistic the professed goals of the transhumanists, they will give birth to destructive aspirations

---

[25] George Weigel, *Witness to Hope* (New York: Harper, 1999), 7.

or be incapable of realizing their fondest hopes and promises if they are based, as they seem presently to be, on a flawed idea of the human person. Since our technological advances have been blessings in many cases but not in all, we need to proceed carefully lest we end up cursing those we profess to want to help.

What Would Be the Social Consequences of the Immortality Project?

And yet, it might still seem irrational to refuse immortality. How can it be rational for a thinking, self-aware being to agree to the cessation of its own thinking and self-awareness? Is it reasonable for a being of reason to agree to the complete loss of its reason? At present, there is nothing we can do about our expiration date. But if we could, shouldn't we?

The problem is, our focus may be too narrow. The promise of individual immortality could be blinding us to certain unavoidable social consequences. Too often, when people are thinking about making "reasonable" choices, their perspective is too individualistic; they consider only what a single individual desiring to maximize his or her preference-satisfaction would choose to do. It is often necessary, though, if we are to make a truly rational choice, to broaden our perspective. Many individuals independently make "rational" choices that, together, bring about "irrational" results. At 5 p.m. every day, thousands of workers in our major cities make an entirely rational choice to go home. And yet the consequence of everyone making that choice at the same time is gridlock on the highways.

So, too, we can predict that, were human life and youth extended, many human beings would make the entirely rational choice to continue to have children. The aggregate consequence of those rational choices, however, would be grave. If no one dies, and new humans are constantly being added to the world, pretty soon the overcrowding would make today's traffic jams look tame by comparison. The only solution, it seems, would be strict enforcement of a "one-child" or, eventually, a "no child" policy. It is difficult enough for today's young adults to refrain from engaging in potentially reproductive acts for several years. How much more difficulty would society be likely to have if it asked sexually-capable adults to refrain from acts that might produce more children for the foreseeable future. No sex for the next four hundred years? Or will we require sterilization? One of the consequences of death, whether in plants, animals, or human beings, is that it clears the way for new growth. If no one dies, then it is hard to see how we could continue to allow the birth of new life. Choosing to act against the order of nature usually brings either chaos or tyranny or both. Considered in this light, the choice for immortality seems less and less rational.

Perhaps not everyone would gain this coveted immortality but only a select few. Would a rational person refuse the chance then? And yet, if I am one of the few who gets immortality, then I will have to watch all my relatives and loved ones age and die while I remain young and vibrant. Would that be a desirable outcome? And would my choice still be a rational choice?

And if our bodies were to become entirely subject to our will and were increasingly taken to be expressions of our own self-creation, then we would be faced with other questions. At what age, for example, would I stop the aging process and with what body? The body of a fifty-year-old man? Or a twenty-year-old woman? With what body should I greet my grandchildren? The body of a thirteen-year-old? Would husbands pressure their wives to look younger? And would children push back against this desire? How many teenage boys want their mother to look just like the teenage girls they are dating? How would they feel if one of their best friends started looking yearningly at their teenage-looking mother?

Would I have to re-think my relationship to others every time they switched bodies? Wouldn't I wonder whether this is still really my wife, my son, or my brother if he or she doesn't have the same smile, the same body language, the same way of moving? Note again how we have diminished the importance of the body. In this transhumanist utopia, the body is not *me*; it is merely a coat I wear. But just like coats I wear and eventually throw away, having just the right coat acceptable to the group to which I want to belong can become overwhelmingly important. And of course those who can will switch coats fairly often, precisely to distinguish themselves from those who can't. Having considered the numerous difficulties, perhaps we should conclude that this is not an entirely healthy way to think about persons—persons who live an embodied existence in relationships with and often dependent upon others.

Does Death Make Life Meaningful?

The problems arising from choosing immortality are highlighted in a notable opera by Czech composer Leoš Janáček entitled *The Makropulos Affair* (or sometimes *The Makropulos Case*). We have been examining the question of whether it would be irrational to refuse immortality. A related problem we have been examining since the beginning of this book is that if death is an ultimate end, it can seem to make meaningless all that we have done and experienced in our lives. In our consideration of *The Makropulos Case* we will find the idea that it is death that makes life meaningful.[26]

---

[26] Philosopher Bernard Williams wrote a famous essay entitled "The Makropulos

The story of Elina Makropulos is, in its own way, a modernization of the story of the Sibyl. But instead of the curse of old age, Elina Makropulos has taken a potion that keeps her permanently at the age of forty-two. Immortality, however, has made her life dull, lonely, and meaningless. She has had to witness multiple lovers and multiple children age and die. She has experienced this pain over and over again and can only look forward to experiencing it again and again in the future. Elina Makropulos has had all the experiences of a forty-two-year-old woman over and over. But she has denied herself the experiences she might have had as a seventy-five-year-old grandmother with five grandchildren. Her unending life has become incredibly dull, and her emotions have become cold and indifferent. She sees in the two young lovers of the story, Kristina and Janek, emotions she can no longer feel. What is she living for? Simply to go on living? To experience more pain and suffering, more loss and grief at the death of loved ones, more forgetting of things and people she knew decades ago? To know more loveless relationships to which she cannot commit herself completely? Immortality has made her life empty and meaningless, and like the Sibyl, she yearns for death. Is death, then, in its own way, a blessing?[27]

Case: Reflections on the Tedium of Immortality," which appeared originally in his *Problems of the Self* (Cambridge: Cambridge University Press, 1973), but which can also now be found several places online, including https://www3.nd.edu/~pweithma/Readings/Williams/Williams%20on%20Immortality.pdf.

[27] See also Nicolas Berdyaev, *The Destiny of Man* (London: Geoffrey Bles, 1937), 249: "Death is the most profound and significant fact of life. . . . The fact of death alone gives true depth to the question of the meaning of life. Life in this world has meaning just because there is death; if there were no death in our world, life would be meaningless. The meaning is bound up with the end. If there were no end, i.e., if life in our world continued for ever, there would be no meaning in it. Meaning lies beyond the confines of this limited world, and

No Death, Endless Evil

Perhaps, then, there is some wisdom to be gained from the Genesis story according to which, after Adam and Eve had succumbed to the serpent's temptation to "become like gods" by eating the fruit of the tree of the knowledge of good and evil, after they had presumed to be gods who create good and evil by their choices rather than being the faithful servants of the moral law with which the Creator had imbued his creation, and after they had in this way introduced evil into themselves and into the world, God providently kept them from eating from the tree of life, thus preventing them from living forever (Gen 3:22). Rather than seeing merely a punishment, might we not view this restriction as a great act of mercy? Man's sin has introduced death into his soul. To be condemned to living a fallen, sinful existence forever is not a blessing; it is a curse.

There are some workaholics in our society who, if they were to live for four hundred years, would still never take a day off. Is God not doing them a certain kindness by forcing on them a certain rest after eighty or ninety years? What evil could we and would we be tempted to do to one another if we lived forever? Think of the tortures one could devise. In the movie *Interview with the Vampire*, a group of vampires condemns another vampire to "eternity in a box." They chain him in a coffin, which they wall up with bricks, intending that it never be found. He, being deathless, would survive in this little hell forever. His only hope would be that the

---

the discovery of meaning presupposes an end here." And again, 250: "Life is noble only because it contains death, an end which testifies that man is destined to another and a higher life. Life would be low and meaningless if there were no death and no end. Meaning is never revealed in an endless time; it is to be found in eternity." And finally, 251: "The meaning of death is that there can be no eternity in time and that an endless temporal series would be meaningless."

building would burn so completely that he would be incinerated. Like the Sibyl and like Elina Makropulos, he is left yearning for death.[28] For fallen beings, is immortality a heaven on earth or a recipe for a life of hell?

The Immortality Project: Alluring but Inhuman

However alluring the prospect of immortality may seem, rational examination reveals it to be based on a host of false promises. So, too, the transhumanist project reveals itself to be based on a too-limited vision of the human person, one that holds out hope for certain elements of the human experience but not all of them or even necessarily the most essential ones. That project and the cultural consequences that result from it will lead us astray because it is based on (a) a failure to appreciate the intrinsic relationship between the body and the soul, including the important role of the emotions and the irreducible character of the virtues; (b) an incomplete notion of freedom as mastery and self-sufficiency; and (c) a failure, in my vision of my "self," to take account of my own nature and end and accord proper respect to the natures and ends of other beings with whom I share the world. So, too, the transhumanist immortality project's concern for mastery and control would appear to diminish our appreciation of our life and the lives of others as a precious gift. As Harvard's Michael Sandel has written:

> To acknowledge the giftedness of life is to recognize that our talents and powers are not wholly our own doing, nor even fully ours, despite the efforts we expend to develop

---

[28] *Interview with the Vampire*, directed by Neil Jordan (1995, Los Angeles: The Geffen Film Company, 1995), DVD, 122 minutes.

and to exercise them. It is also to recognize that not everything in the world is open to any use we may desire or
devise. An appreciation of the giftedness of life constrains
the Promethean project and conduces to a certain humility. It is, in part, a religious sensibility. But its resonance
reaches beyond religion.[29]

Readers should ask themselves whether they find the transhumanist vision of human beings with perfect bodies, complete mastery
over nature, and everlasting life superior to the vision of humanity proposed to us in the lives of people like St. Francis of Assisi,
St. Mother Theresa of Calcutta, St. Damien of Molokai, and
St. Martin de Porres, or in the life of your endlessly kind and loving
grandmother or grandfather. Whose values and goals would you
prefer to emulate?

Jesus Christ and the Full Realization of Our Humanity

But transhumanists might object, asking, "Don't Christians claim
to be interested in human perfection? Aren't Christians told in the
Book of Genesis to 'subdue' the earth and 'have dominion' over
every living thing (see Gen 1:28)? Aren't Christians also eager to
embrace 'eternal life'? Aren't Christians and transhumanists moti-
vated by similar goals: human perfection and the domination
of nature?

The words may be similar, but what is being signified by those
words is different because Christian notions of nature and human
nature fundamentally differ from those of the transhumanists.

---

[29] Michael J. Sandel, "What's Wrong with Enhancement," paper presented to the
President's Council on Bioethics, December 2002, https://bioethicsarchive.
georgetown.edu/pcbe/background/sandelpaper.html

Christians claim that human beings are fallen and imperfect, but they do so with a particular sense of what a perfected human nature would be. That idea of a perfected human nature is based in the first place upon reflection on the person of Jesus Christ. The Christian vision, though based on a "perfect" human person, does not lead to the same diminishment of "imperfect" human nature that the transhumanist project does. We are, each of us, according to Christian revelation, made in the image of God, which image lends to each of us an infinite dignity. Certainly human beings are beings who change and develop. They are works in progress. But Christians do not claim, as the transhumanists appear to do, that human beings, in and of themselves, are "incomplete" humanity. On the Christian account, human nature, even in its incompleteness and with its imperfections, is still made "in the image of God" and thus still has dignity and is worthy of respect.[30]

So, too, the Christian project of personal development is not entirely open-ended, based solely on extending the power of human will. Rather, it emphasizes a moral renewal and love and respect for others and for the natural world. So, too, the Christian project of "renewal" respects the whole human person in ways the transhumanist project does not. The Christian project of renewal respects the dignity and meaningfulness of both body and soul; it includes a coherent vision of the relations among reason, will, the passions, and human choice.

Our analysis of the transhumanist project should have

---

[30] Although there are some differences between Catholics and Protestants on how much damage has been done to human nature by the Fall—indeed, those differences sometimes arise within Catholic and Protestant traditions as well as between them—yet no magisterial Christian tradition has claimed that the damage is so great that human beings are no longer called upon to respect the dignity of other human beings as created and loved by God.

provided us with several important insights. First, it should give us an increased appreciation of the fact that our embodiment is an essential element of our humanity. We are not minds trapped in a body from which we yearn to break free. And second, it should help us come to terms with the fact that our goal cannot be merely more of the same: more bodies to choose from, more will-to-power over nature, and more of the same of the life we have now. "Old men ought to be explorers," proclaims the poet T. S. Eliot.

> We must be still and still moving
> Into another intensity
> For a further union, a deeper communion.[31]

Christian thinkers talk about the inherent "dignity" of every human person while also distinguishing two other senses of the word. We might say that dignity is something we have, but it is also something in accord with which we must act. And it is something we are called upon to achieve by the way we live our lives. The Christian vision of the development of the human person is based on the notion that we are, at least in one sense, trying to restore an integral human nature that has been damaged by the Fall. And yet we must also remain open to a gift that transcends that integral state of nature. Why? Because Christian revelation tells us that our state before the Fall was itself meant for a higher completion. It, too, would have been perfected by being taken up into a deeper union and more intimate communion with God. So it is not enough that we merely return to the pre-lapsarian state of our first parents. To be truly restored means to become fully open

---

[31] T. S. Eliot, "East Coker."

once again to this deeper communion with God, which is what God had in store for our first parents before they fell.

On the Christian view, our liberation from the reign of sin-and-death from which we currently suffer requires us to "die to self" and "live in Christ" (see Rom 6:6–8). That project of dying to self and entrusting ourselves fully "to others and to God" is one that begins now but can be completed only in our final, faithful embrace of Christ in our actual, physical death. The promise is that God's faithfulness and God's love will raise us up—as God raised up his Son—into a "further union, a deeper communion" with him and with our loved ones.

[Man] rightly follows the intuition of his heart when he abhors and repudiates the utter ruin and total disappearance of his own person. He rebels against death because he bears in himself an eternal seed which cannot be reduced to sheer matter. All the endeavors of technology, though useful in the extreme, cannot calm his anxiety; for prolongation of biological life is unable to satisfy that desire for higher life which is inescapably lodged in his breast.

Gaudium et Spes §18

Chapter 3

INTIMATIONS OF IMMORTALITY: REFLECTIONS ON CERTAIN PAGAN VIEWS OF LIFE AFTER DEATH

Although it is not universal, the sense that there is something in human beings that transcends the boundaries of death has been exceedingly common throughout history and across cultures, and not merely among those who are "religious." The Roman orator and philosopher Cicero once wrote: "If I err in my belief that the souls of men are immortal, I gladly err, nor do I wish this error which gives me pleasure to be wrested from me while I live."[1] This conviction that there is something about human life that will outlive our physical death has several sources. Some people have noticed that we have "outlived" the particular "stuff" of our organic body many times over as it has changed over

---

[1] Cicero, *De senectute, De amicitia, De divinatione*, trans. William A. Falconer (Cambridge, MA: Harvard University Press, 1923), 85.

the years, suggesting that our identity—what makes you *you* or me *me*—is not tied solely to the material stuff of which we happen to be composed physically at any particular moment. Others have concluded that our intellects are not solely physical—you cannot "divide" a thought the way you can slice a cake—and this leads them to the conclusion that the intellect is not tied to the body and therefore may survive the death of the body. Still others have the sense that the reality of a person is not ultimately limited by or contained within his or her bodily frame, especially when we find a person who has severe physical disabilities whose mind and spirit seem to surpass the limitations of his or her body. All these arguments, and others like them, are based on the judgment that there is something essential about human beings that is not limited to a physical body.

In the works of Cicero, for example, we read:

Moreover, I had clearly set before me the arguments touching the immortality of the soul, delivered on the last day of his life by Socrates, whom the oracle of Apollo had pronounced the wisest of men. Why multiply words? That is my conviction, that is what I believe—since such is the lightning-like rapidity of the soul, such its wonderful memory of things that are past, such its ability to forecast the future, such its mastery of many arts, sciences, and inventions, that its nature, which encompasses all these things, cannot be mortal; and since the soul is always active and has no source of motion because it is self-moving, its motion will have no end, because it will never leave itself; and since in its nature the soul is of one substance and has nothing whatever mingled with it unlike or dissimilar to itself, it cannot be divided, and if it cannot be divided it cannot perish.[2]

It is, of course, still possible for people to doubt that anything survives death; Cicero jokes that even if those who argue against him turn out to be right, at least they won't be able to mock him about his error. "But if when dead I am going to be without sensation (as some petty philosophers think)," he says, "then I have no fear that these seers, when they are dead, will have the laugh on me!"[3]

It's a good line, but Cicero may have missed something. He will not be mocked if he is preparing now for an afterlife that will never come, unless there is another sort of afterlife for which he should have been preparing instead. If a man has devoted his life to killing the enemies of Rome in the belief that he will be rewarded for that after his death but, in fact, he will be punished eternally for that, then he will suffer mockery—or something much worse. Thus it is not enough to affirm that there is an afterlife; it is important to consider what kind of afterlife I expect and how my aspiration to reach that ultimate goal affects—or fails to affect—the way I live my life now.

Views of the Afterlife that Undermine Visions of the Good Life

Consider, for example, this classic story from the ancient world in which an author recounted a picture of the afterlife that was at odds with—indeed, it may have been a purposeful critique of—the notion of human excellence held by his society. In Book 11 of the *Odyssey*, one finds the story of Odysseus's trip to Hades, the

---

[2] Ibid., 78.
[3] Ibid., 85.

land of the dead. In Hades, Odysseus meets his mother and several of his companions from the Trojan War, all of whom are ghost-like shades. The afterlife pictured in Homer's Hades is not a place of freedom or joy; far from being a place of liberation for the soul, as Socrates would later claim in the *Phaedo*, it is a dark, dreadful abode, where the light of the sun never shines. Furthermore, even the most glorious and renowned of the Greek heroes end up there. Odysseus sees the shade of his dead mother, but when he attempts to embrace her, his arms pass right through her body. She admonishes him that, since she has no body, embraces are impossible now. Later, Odysseus sees the shade of the illustrious Achilles, whom he assures that "no man, before or after, is more blessed than you, Achilles, for we Argives valued you alive as equal to the gods, and you now again wield great power, among the dead, since you're here. So don't at all be sorry that you're dead." But Achilles tells him, "Don't console me about death, brilliant Odysseus. I'd rather be a hired farmhand, slaving for another, for a landless man who hasn't much substance, than rule all the dead who've perished."[4] This is not a happy place where the souls roam freely.

Homer's account of the afterlife in the *Odyssey* would seem to be at odds with the valorization of heroic prowess and courage that characterized ancient Greek society, evidence of which can be found in many Greek sources. No source, though, was more well-known among the Greeks themselves than the *Iliad*. In the *Iliad*, the presupposition of the characters seems to be that the way to achieve immortality (of a sort) is to gain glory that will be

---

[4] *Odyssey* 11.482–91. All English translations of the *Odyssey* are quoted from the translation by James Huddleston available at Northwestern University's on-line resource, "The Chicago Homer," https://homer.library. northwestern.edu/.

everlasting by doing great, heroic deeds, even if this means dying bravely in battle.

We might think in this regard of the heart-rending scene in the *Iliad* in which Hector stands on the walls of Troy with his wife Andromache and their child looking out over the battlefield where so many of his countrymen have been slain. Hector holds their child tenderly, but he predicts his own coming death and the consequent destruction of Troy. His wife, he predicts, will become the concubine of a Greek warrior. His wife begs him to stay behind and leave the fighting to others, to avoid this fate if possible. But he tells her he cannot shirk his duty; he must be in the forefront of the fighting as always, defending their city regardless of the outcome. We might admire his courage but question his wisdom. If he really thinks he cannot save his city, would it not be better to run away, to escape to another town and live out his days with less glory but a longer life? Some might call him a coward for doing so, but he would be alive, and so would his wife and child. Those of us who have read the *Odyssey* and know the grim future that awaits Hector in the afterlife would likely question his decision even further.[5]

How, then, should we understand the story of Achilles in the underworld? The lesson of this story for young Greek warriors would seem to be that it would be better to stay home and live a pleasant life for as long as they can rather than sacrificing themselves in battle because death is a miserable state to be kept at bay for as long as possible. The Epicureans would agree with the latter conclusion even though they would have disagreed with the

---

[5] *Iliad* 6.390–502, esp. 440–65. All English translations of the *Iliad* are quoted from the translation by Richard Lattimore available at Northwestern University's online resource, "The Chicago Homer," https://homer.library. northwestern.edu/.

underlying presupposition about the afterlife. "No need to fear," they would have added, "because there *is* no afterlife. You don't go to a place of misery; you just cease existing." Given Achilles's speech in the *Odyssey*, however, it is hard to understand why anyone would venture to risk his or her life for his or her city. Perhaps this is one reason why Socrates was so critical of Homer's stories: they provided no support for living a just and courageous life.

There is a similar paradox in book 9 of the *Iliad.* An embassy of Achilles's friends comes to his tent to offer him prizes meant as a penance from Agamemnon for having violated Achilles's honor. Achilles rejects them, saying that riches he can always win, but once his life is lost, he cannot get it back.[6] Furthermore, he says, his mother Thetis has revealed to him his two possible fates. Either he can stay in Ilium and die there but his "glory shall be everlasting," or he can return home, where he would live a "long life" but "the excellence of his glory" would be gone.[7] He has decided to choose the latter, a long life, he tells his friends. Although this choice would make a great deal of sense to most of us in the modern world since many of us, like the transhumanists, seek to prolong life as long as possible, Achilles's choice here was a scandal to his fellow Greeks. Indeed, his announcement causes an explosion of anger and rejection by his friends.

Challenging Facile Notions of Immortality

If, having heard the legendary stories of the great Greek heroes of the Trojan War, one were to conclude that the life of a famous hero is the best and happiest life for human beings, a perceptive reading of the lives of the famous heroes in the *Iliad* and the afterlife of

---

[6] Ibid., 9.405–9.
[7] Ibid., 9.410–16.

Achilles in the *Odyssey* should disabuse that person of any facile notions about the rewards the hero can expect, either in this life or the next. In particular, the account of Odysseus's meeting with Achilles in the underworld should challenge any reader who imagines that the way to heavenly bliss in the afterlife is to die gloriously in battle. Even those who think that such a sacrifice can sometimes be a glorious thing might wish to push back against the cheapening of human life that can result from such a view. Should the goal of such a sacrifice be personal glory? Or is the glory, rather, simply in the willingness to sacrifice for the good of others? We might wonder whether this isn't Achilles's problem: that he is focused too narrowly on his own personal glory and renown and not enough on simply serving the good of his comrades.

Bringing these various stories together in the way the author or authors of the *Iliad* and the *Odyssey* have presents to the reader a question much like the one Glaucon and Adeimantus pose to Socrates in Book 2 of *The Republic*. Should a man really be considered just if he lives a just life merely for the sake of a reward of some pleasantries after his death? And yet, if there is no reward in the afterlife for living the just life, would anyone still choose it? There was little respect among the Greeks for those who shirked their military duties or for those who preferred the soft, easy life at home when others were incurring the hardships of life in camp with other brave warriors.[8] It is unlikely, then, that these same

---

[8] That prowess and endurance in battle were admired among the Greeks is clear from many sources (see, for example, Herodotus, *The Persian Wars* 1.7.4, 3.11.3, 6.101.28, 12.2), but it is manifested with a special poignancy by the fact that one of the characteristics that distinguished the philosopher Socrates among his peers was his outstanding behavior in battle. In the *Symposium*, Alcibiades stresses that Socrates at war was "a sight worth seeing" (*Symposium* 220e). He stresses Socrates's extreme capacity for "endurance" (καρτερία), noting his ability to endure the extreme cold, "wearing nothing but his same

people would respect a warrior who engaged in heroic deeds not for the deeds' own sake but merely to enjoy an afterlife of soft, pleasurable activities for which in life they would have had contempt.[9]

Cicero may have been right when he claimed, "No one could ever meet death for his country without the hope of immortality."[10] But Homer's portrayal of the afterlife in the *Odyssey* forces the reader to ask whether he or she would ever freely choose to risk death if immortality was like the sad immortality suffered by Achilles and the other shades in the underworld. If so, wouldn't it make more sense, as the Epicureans thought, simply to live safely and pleasantly for as long as possible?

But what if a pleasant form of immortality were possible, such as the one offered by the transhumanists? We've discussed some of the troubling social consequences. But could one choose personal immortality if it meant abandoning one's duties and obligations to one's family and fellow citizens? This is the question posed for us in Book 5 of the *Odyssey*, when Odysseus is offered immortality by the nymph Calypso if he agrees to stay with her. He refuses, choosing instead to return home to his wife, Penelope, and his son, Telemachus, and resume his duties as ruler of Ithaca. When Odysseus recounts this story to King Alcinous, he has already been

---

old light cloak" and that even "in bare feet he made better progress on the ice than the other soldiers did in their boots" (*Symposium* 220b). And Alcibiades says that when he himself was seriously wounded, Socrates "just refused to leave me behind" and "single-handedly saved my life"—indeed, both his life *and* his armor (*Symposium* 220e). See Plato, *Symposium,* trans. Alexander Nehamas and Paul Woodruff (Indianapolis, IN: Hackett, 1989).

9   It is noteworthy that Socrates, for example, did not think that souls in the afterlife would be enjoying physical pleasures denied to them in this life. Rather, they would be continuing the life of contemplation for which they would have been preparing themselves during this life. See Plato's *Phaedo* 114c–15a.

10 Cicero, *Tusculan Disputations*, trans. J. E. King, Loeb Classical Library, 141 (Cambridge, MA: Harvard University Press, 1927), 1.15.

to the realm of the dead where he had seen Achilles, so he would not have been unaware of what awaited him after his own death and hence what he was giving up by leaving Calypso's island. More noble than achieving personal immortality and living comfortably with Calypso would be for him to return home and purge his house and his land from the plague of the suitors so that a just rule might be restored, his wife and father might be saved from debasement and humiliation, and his son's life might be saved from the suitors plotting his murder. Odysseus will then "live on" in the life of his son and other descendants. Isn't the lesson here that we should forsake the desire for the personal immortality proper only to the gods and seek instead the immortality we get by living virtuous lives and passing on good things to future generations?

Is It a Good Idea to Try to Live On in the Memories of One's Descendants?

Although there is undoubtedly something noble about Odysseus's sacrifice of his chance at individual immortality so that he can help re-establish the proper order of justice in the land and for the people who raised him and others to whom he has pledged his life and service, we might still wonder: *How long will the Kingdom of Ithaca last? How long will Odysseus's descendants remember him? And even if they do, will they remain worthy of his sacrifices?* The numerous examples of the foolish children of famous men in history and the ephemeral nature of nearly all human kingdoms could easily cause us to conclude that such sacrifices are not worth giving up what might be the only life we have.

Indeed, we might question whether it would be healthy for Odysseus or anyone else to think about their own immortality in terms of "living on" in and through their children and their children's children. Children often do not live up to their parents' expectations. Nor are dutiful parents always fondly remembered. Some children resolve to define themselves precisely in opposition to everything represented by their parents. And yet, in some cases, this is exactly right. Children cannot be made the clones or proxies of their parents. The goal of parents must be to help nourish in their children the virtues and capacities to handle whatever challenges they will face, not to try to dictate in advance how they will handle them.

So, while it is true that, if I have been given the gift of being born into wealth, I will have certain responsibilities for the community into which I have been born that others may not—responsibilities especially for the poor and disabled—and I will, moreover, have good reasons to try to instill a sense of those responsibilities in my own children, I must not attempt to make decisions for them in advance that should be left to their prudential judgments. It is one thing to raise one's son or daughter with a sense of their obligations to the community; it is quite another to try to dictate in advance the life you want them to live so as to properly represent you in the future; to say, for example: "First, I want you to attend my prestigious alma mater, then take this job at the company, then take over the company and build it into the richest, most dominant company in the business."

For these reasons among others, conceiving of "immortality" as "living on" in the lives and memories of one's children can be unwise.[11] Children cannot help but disappoint us because they are not us. And because they are not us, they will not make precisely

---

[11] Nicolas Berdyaev, *The Destiny of Man* (London: Geoffrey Bles, 1937), 259, warns: "However flourishing the life of the new generations may be, it does not remedy the unendurable tragedy of the death of a single living being." He describes the view by which one achieves "endless life through child-bearing" as a kind of "sexual pantheism."

the prudential judgments we would have made and in the ways we would have made them. By the same token, we know, or should know if we were to reflect for a bit, that if they *did* do things in exactly the way we have instructed them, we would consider them "yes men," incapable of making their own, independent judgments. So undoubtedly it would be best to train them as best we can in the virtues and then offer them up to the care of "the gods" or God, who cares for them with greater love and wisdom than we possess, both now and after our death.

Therefore, concerning each of the Homeric notions of immortality—the immortality of the soul in the land of the dead or the immortality that involves "living on" in one's descendants—we are led seriously to question whether it could adequately support the vision of the "best life for man" that the author wishes to instill in his reader. Would a sensible person make Achilles's choice to die bravely in battle if the consequence was eternity among the dark shades in the underworld? Would a sensible person make Odysseus's choice to forego personal immortality if the result was a short life trying to shore up a dying political regime?

Both Socrates and Plato found Homer's account of the gods and the afterlife inadequate, and each of them searched for an understanding of immortality that would more adequately serve the purposes of moral exhortation with which they were concerned. Plato, for his part, may have entertained the possibility that souls were reincarnated although scholars dispute this.[12] At

---

[12] See, for example, the *Meno*, 81b; *Cratylus*, 400b–c; *Phaedo*, 70c, 81c–e; *Timaeus*, 90e–91e; *Laws*, 870d–e, 872e, 881a, 904a. For a nice overview of the arguments for and against the view that Plato believed in reincarnation, see the arguments and bibliography in John S. Uebersax, "Did Plato Believe in Reincarnation?" John Uebersax, PhD (website), accessed March 24, 2021, https://john-uebersax.com/plato/plato4.htm.

first glance, reincarnation might seem to resolve two problems. First, as to the question of whether the soul dies when the body dies, the proponent of reincarnation answers, no. The soul continues on in different bodies since our current body is merely a "shell" anyway. And second, as to the question of moral exhortation, such proponents of reincarnation as Plato and classical Hindus answer that how we live now will determine how we are reincarnated in the future. Living a good life results in a more favorable reincarnation; living a bad life means a less favorable one, even a punishing one. Since there is some dispute about Plato's settled views about reincarnation, we will turn next to later Roman sources—first Virgil and then Cicero—in whose works the potential difficulties with reincarnation are often clearer and more manifest.

Reincarnation: Aeneas in the Underworld

In a famous scene in Book 6 of Virgil's *Aeneid*, Aeneas is given permission by the gods to go to the underworld to visit with the soul of his dead father, Anchises. While there, Aeneas discovers that the souls of those who have lived lives of duplicity and evil are punished in everlasting torment in Tartarus while those who have lived noble lives, like his father, are sent to Elysium, a paradise of lovely fields and meadows in the sun. On the grassy fields of Elysium, Aeneas sees some of the spirits exercising, competing in Olympic sports, and wrestling.[13] Why would these souls be in training? Their lives are over. One reason is simply because this was considered an important part of "the best life" for man. To be denied the pleasures of such competitions was to live a diminished

---

[13] See *Aeneid* 6.642–643. All English quotations of the *Aeneid* have been taken from the translation by A. S. Kline, *Poetry in Translation*, accessed July 16, 2021, https://www.poetryintranslation.com/PITBR/Latin/VirgilAeneidVI.php.

existence. But another reason comes into view a little later, when Aeneas sees a large group of people in a secluded grove huddled around the River Lethe, the "river of forgetting." When Aeneas asks who these people are and why they are there, his father replies that they are spirits who are "owed another body by destiny" and who, once they have crossed the River Lethe, will "with a desire to return to the flesh," be reincarnated and live new lives.[14] Anchises is eager to point out the souls in this group who will, once they are reincarnated, become the great Roman heroes and statesmen of the future. The sight of these great-men-to-come is meant to inspire Aeneas for the difficult task that lies ahead of him, the founding of Lavinium, the city that will eventually become Rome.

Although Virgil shares with the Platonists the notion that death involves the "liberation" of the soul from the body, there is obviously less concern here in Virgil's account that one should remain "freed" from the body. Although the souls slated for reincarnation have gone through a long and arduous purgation, they are still eager to return to the material realm to do further service to Rome, for to be able to do service to Rome as one of its greatest heroes and statesmen seems to be the highest goal to which one can aspire, greater even than one's personal comfort and happiness in Elysium.

One gets the sense that any soul that stayed back and lacked the requisite eagerness to return and do service to Rome would be considered second rate and lacking something, as would any soldier in the Roman army who did the same. A really heroic soul would want to return to fight the good fight for Rome. The connection between Virgil's vision of the afterlife and his vision of what he thinks is the best life for man is clear. He thinks Romans

---

[14] Ibid., 6.703–21, 751.

should be noble, do their duty, and devote themselves to the future glory of Rome by fighting bravely in battle and ruling wisely with prudent laws.

Consider for a moment how an Epicurean would view all this. None of it would be relevant in the slightest. Since the Epicureans did not believe there is anything after this life, they naturally concluded that a person would be foolish to seek certain things or avoid other things based on the expectation of a reward or a punishment after this life. The wise person, they thought, would realize, rather, that the best life for man is not one given over to the pains and frustrations of entangling oneself in the political machinations of the city but is a life in which the person has lived a moderate life in which he has maximized his simple pleasures and minimized the pains and frustrations that beset so many others. Virgil clearly promotes a notion of the afterlife that will undergird a sense of moral duty among his fellow Romans.

And yet even those who accept that there is life after death might conclude, upon reflection, that Virgil's view of reincarnation is neither reasonable nor appealing. So what, you just keep coming back over and over again as someone else so that you can keep dying again and again for Rome? And in the interim between lives, you get to walk around in some pleasant woods—that is, unless you happen to have made a mistake, done something unworthy of Rome, and end up tortured forever in Tartarus? Virgil's literary vision may be unsurpassed in its beauty, but an Epicurean philosopher would undoubtedly have found it foolish to think that one should sacrifice one's life now on the remote chance that one might enjoy a bit of uncertain and impermanent happiness in the afterlife. Better to be free of such illusions; they only serve to enslave you. Indeed, many contemporary atheists, especially those of a Marxist bent, are convinced that the promise of "glory" in the afterlife is one of the methods the ruling classes throughout history have used to convince the working classes to sacrifice their freedom and well-being now for some purported "higher good" to come in the afterlife.

It is hard to claim such critics would be entirely wrong in Virgil's case. As great a poet as Virgil was, we might question whether he overvalued his singular devotion to Rome. If a person is good enough in his devotion to Rome, it seems, he or she is rewarded with the pleasures of the Elysian Fields. Carthaginians would likely have been far less impressed than Virgil's Roman audience with Virgil's vision of paradise with all the great and noble Romans who pillaged Carthage and murdered so many of its citizens. Christians of the first four centuries would undoubtedly have noticed that some of the future "great" Roman leaders, who so impressed Aeneas on the shores of Lethe waiting to be reincarnated, were men who would persecute and kill Christians.

So although Virgil's account of the afterlife might have seemed reasonable and desirable to his Roman audience, it could scarcely be so for Christians and not merely because it glorifies Romans who persecuted Christians. What Christian revelation teaches is that all are God's people and that we should not be overly concerned with our political divisions. For as St. Paul says, "There is neither Jew nor Greek, there is neither slave nor free, there is neither male nor female; for you are all one in Christ Jesus" (Gal 3:28). And although we are to render to Caesar the things that are Caesar's—Christians should be good citizens in the earthly city—yet we must render to God the things that are God's (see Mark 12:17). Our true home is the heavenly city. The only truly "eternal city" is not Rome or Constantinople or any other earthly city; it is the heavenly Jerusalem.[15] A Christian vision of the afterlife that was based on serving the glory of a single political entity would, therefore, be contrary to the Gospel message. Christian revelation bids us to care for our communities but in such a way that we do not implicate ourselves too deeply in our own earthly, political rivalries and entanglements. Christians who would interpret the Gospel message about Christ going to prepare a place for us in such a way that heaven would be only for Jews or only for Greeks or only for free and not slave, or only for Aryans and not Jews, would be affirming a view contrary to the clear teaching of the Gospel.

A Higher Perspective: Cicero's Dream of Scipio

Quite frankly, Virgil's tale is so clearly directed at motivating a Roman audience to be willing to sacrifice for Rome that not only Christians but even a thoughtful Roman might find its perspective too narrow. There were some Romans, even very devoted Romans, who understood the limits, both moral and physical, of the Roman Empire. The great orator and philosopher Cicero, for example, was as faithful a Roman as one could wish, serving devotedly both in the Senate and as consul. But he was also a philosopher. And as a man who had both worked within the state as a politician and reflected on it as a philosopher, he sought to understand how one could sustain one's devotion to a particular people, place, and country while also acknowledging their relative smallness when viewed from a broader, more cosmic perspective.

In Book 6 of Cicero's *De republica*, for example, in a section which has come to be known simply as "The Dream of Scipio,"

---

[15] The best discussion of the relationship (or lack thereof) between the heavenly city and the earthly city is still to be found in St. Augustine's monumental *City of God*.

Cicero's main character in the dialogue, Scipio Aemilianus, recounts for his friends the story of a dream he had in which he saw and spoke with his grandfather, the great Scipio Africanus, the Roman general who defeated Carthage in the Second Punic War. His grandfather assures him that for all his service to Rome, his grandson will be rewarded after his death.

> [F]or all who have preserved their fatherland, furthered it, enriched it, there is in heaven a sure and allotted abode, where they may enjoy an immortality of happiness. For nothing happens in the world more pleasing to that supreme Deity, who governs all the universe, than those gatherings and unions of men allied by common laws, which are called states. From this place [the highest sphere of heaven] do their rulers and guardians set out, and to this place do they return.[16]

And yet, after having been assured of this rich reward, the younger Scipio notices something that troubles him. At the height of heaven from which he and his grandfather look down upon the earth, the earth appears very small—so small, in fact, that the younger man is grieved to think that the Roman Empire covers no more than "a point, as it were, of its surface."[17]

Seeing his distress, his grandfather scolds him: "How long will your mind be chained to the earth?"[18] If he keeps his mind on celestial things, he will no longer worry about the affairs of men. People in vast swaths of the earth will never hear of him, and even those

---

[16] *M. Tulli Ciceronis Somnium Scipionis*, trans. W. D. Pearman (Cambridge: Deighton, Bell, 1883), sec. 5.

[17] Ibid.

[18] Ibid., sec. 9.

in Rome who know of him and his great deeds, "How long will they talk? Why, even if those generations of men to come should care to hand down, in succession from father to son, the glory of each one of us; yet, still, owing to the deluges and conflagrations of the earth, which must happen periodically, we cannot acquire a lasting, much less an eternal renown."[19]

And so, rather than staking his hope "on the rewards of men" or enslaving himself to "the rumors of the rabble," says the elder Scipio, the younger man should continue to fix his gaze solely on his eternal home with the blessed.[20] "Virtue must draw you by her own attraction to true glory," says the elder man, which can be found only above, not "in the forgetfulness of posterity."[21]

It is worth noting, however, how the view Cicero expressed here in *The Dream of Scipio* challenges the one we saw in the *Odyssey* wherein Odysseus refused individual immortality with Calypso, preferring instead to return home and resume his duties to his family and the people of Ithaca. What would most of us conclude about Odysseus's decision to leave Calypso's island if, in the *Odyssey*, Odysseus and his son Telemachus had died fighting against the suitors, as Hector died fighting bravely against the Greeks? Would we still consider wise his choice to leave Calypso? Although we might admire Odysseus's bravery and devotion to his wife and son, we might still question the wisdom of his choice to give up immortal life and youth, enjoying sex with an eternally beautiful woman, to go and fight against overwhelming odds in a battle he might lose, with his eventual death a certainty either way.

The fact that many readers throughout history have admired

---

[19] Ibid., sec. 14–15.
[20] Ibid., sec. 17.
[21] Ibid.

his choice as something noble suggests the importance we human beings attribute to living a *meaningful* existence, not merely extending life perpetually, even if it were a life filled with endless physical pleasure. Better to die fighting meaningfully for a noble cause, it would seem, than merely going on endlessly in the pursuit of meaningless pleasures.

And yet, as noble as some of us might find Odysseus's choice to forego personal immortality in order to return home and restore order to Ithaca, perhaps this goal would not, for most of us, justify making the same decision. How many people would sacrifice not only their own lives but also their sole chance at personal immortality on the off-chance that their children (perhaps of dubious character) or their society might benefit? Odysseus has an admirable faith in the continuing fidelity of his wife (even after his twenty years away) and the future wisdom of his son (whom he hasn't raised and hasn't seen in twenty years). But would most of us have the same confidence that what happens after our deaths would really be worth sacrificing a chance at immortality? Will Telemachus become and remain the good and worthy ruler over Ithaca that Odysseus hopes he will become? And even if Telemachus succeeds, will there not likely come a time in the future when Odysseus's descendants no longer deserve that honor or when, like Priam and Hector, they will have that privilege torn away from them by a conquering enemy?[22]

The "view-from-above" we find in Cicero's *Dream of Scipio* forces us to consider how ephemeral and transitory human

---

[22] It is Berdyaev, again, who warns (*Destiny of Man*, 260–61): "Man suffers anguish not only because he is doomed to death but because all the world is doomed to it. . . . There can be no comfort in the thought that we shall be immortal in our children and that our work will last for ever, for the end is coming to all consolations that are in time."

accomplishments in this life can be.[23] Cicero was the one, after all, who claimed, "No one could ever meet death for his country without the hope of immortality."[24] Indeed, for Cicero, it is precisely because human renown and glory are so tenuous and short-lived that humans must be sure of something more significant and everlasting after their death—something more significant and everlasting, perhaps, than merely the restoration of one's son as king of a small Greek island.

Cicero's vision is more convincing than either Virgil's or Homer's on this score since he understands how small Rome (let alone Ithaca) would seem viewed from a cosmic perspective. On his account, earthly glory of the sort with which Virgil seems concerned is largely meaningless. Thus, in his own way, Cicero poses the same challenge to his Roman readers that Glaucon and Adeimantus posed to Socrates. What if the unjust man is considered a hero and the just man is considered a villain? What if a just man like Cicero is executed as a criminal (as he was) and criminals are rewarded with honors and high offices? The lesson of "the dream of Scipio" is that one must not listen to the crowd or depend on the opinions of the ignorant. Rather, the just man acts for the good of the state whether he is rewarded for it or not and even if he is fated to suffer punishment. For doing so, he will win his reward with the blessed after his death. In the end, the only reliable judges of the just man are the gods. They will see and

---

[23] See James 4:13–16: "Come now, you who say, 'Today or tomorrow we will go into such and such a town and spend a year there and trade and get gain'; whereas you do not know about tomorrow. What is your life? For you are a mist that appears for a little time and then vanishes. Instead you ought to say, 'If the Lord wills, we shall live and we shall do this or that.' As it is, you boast in your arrogance. All such boasting is evil. Whoever knows what is right to do and fails to do it, for him it is sin."

[24] Cicero, *Tusculan Disputations*, 10.

respect the sacrifices of the just man and reward him accordingly even when a man's fellow citizens do not.

Such a view presumes that the gods themselves are just, that they do not fight among themselves nor show unwarranted favor or disfavor to particular human beings or cities. As we know from Homer's *Iliad* and *Odyssey*, this was not a view shared among most of the ancient Greeks, nor is it a view that has been shared by most of the polytheistic religions throughout history. When there are multiple gods, they fight, and human beings align themselves with one or the other in order to win favor, whether that favor is earthly power and pleasure or some reward in the afterlife. Either way, one's relationship with the gods or God becomes a *quid pro quo*. I do something now in accord with the will and desires of the gods or God *in order that* I can attain something I want later. We might wonder about the wisdom of Odysseus giving up his chance at immortality, but at least his choice was admirably selfless. He didn't leave Calypso in order to make a better deal with an even more powerful and beautiful goddess later on down the line. In Odysseus's sacrifice, there was at least some prospective glimpse at the eternal meaningfulness of selfless love.

The Dream of Scipio and the Preparation for Death

On Cicero's account in the "Dream of Scipio," the life of the just man is, as it was for Socrates, a preparation for death, and this in two ways. For Cicero, as for Socrates, one "prepares for death" by not being tied to the body so that the soul can more easily be liberated from the body after death. But on Cicero's account, one also "prepares for death" by doing good service for the city because serving one's city faithfully is what is most pleasing to the gods. Indeed, these two goals—liberation from the body and service to the city—are united in Cicero's account, perhaps even more so

than in Plato's *Phaedo*. "Exercise your soul in the noblest activities," Cicero has Scipio Africanus tell his grandson.

> Now the noblest are cares and exertions for our coun-
> try's welfare. And the soul which has been enlivened
> and trained by these will speed more fleetly to this its
> resting-place and home. And this will it do more readily if,
> even while still imprisoned in the body, it strains beyond
> it, and, surveying that which lies outside it, as much as
> possible, endeavors to withdraw itself from the body.[25]

But why then, the younger Scipio wishes to know, do we "linger
on earth"? Why not hurry up and get to heaven? "It is not as you
think," Scipio's grandfather tells him. "For unless that God, to
whom all this region that you can see belongs, has released you
from the keeping of your body, the entrance to this place cannot
be open to you. For men were created subject to this law, to keep
to that globe, which you see in the centre of this region and which
is called the Earth."[26] And so, Scipio and all good men, his grandfather tells him, "must allow the soul to remain in the keeping of
the body" and not abandon their human life, lest they "appear
to have deserted the post assigned to men by God."[27] While alive,
then, they should "follow justice and natural affection" in service
to their parents and kinsfolk but most of all to their fatherland
because such is the life "that leads to heaven"[28] and the company of
those who have "soared away from the bonds of the body, as from

---

[25] Cicero, *Somnium Scipionis*, sec. 21.
[26] Ibid., sec. 7.
[27] Ibid.
[28] Ibid., sec. 8.

a prison-house," in comparison to which this present life, "as it is called, is really death."[29]

But Why Come Back?

Christians can admire Cicero's conviction that life is something given, something that brings with it duties and obligations, and thus there is no "checking out" without the permission of the One who gave us this life, but an important question remains. If this life, "as it is called," is really death, then why must human souls keep coming back? Cicero's only answer seems to be that this is a punishment for past sins. Although good souls, such as Scipio Africanus, ascend to the company of the blessed, the souls of those who have given themselves over to the passions and done evil deeds are condemned to "go grovelling over the face of the earth"; they do not "return to this place," says Scipio Africanus, "except after many ages of wandering."[30]

So, on this view, heaven's response to mankind's earthly suffering would consist in sending back to earth only the worst souls, keeping the best and most virtuous out of the earthly struggle for justice. Even as a Roman, indeed perhaps especially as a Roman, one might find this view wanting. Would anyone consider a Roman general either wise or just if he took his best and bravest soldiers out of the battle and fought with only the cowards and shirkers, those whom he knew in advance were likely to give in to their fears and greed?

More problematic is the fact that the afterlife envisioned by Cicero and Virgil does not offer the best and happiest life for mankind; rather it seems to afford a lesser form of human

---

[29] Ibid., sec. 6: "vestro vero, quae dicitur, vita mors est."
[30] Ibid., sec. 21.

existence, one involving no risk, no noble struggles, and no chance to exhibit bravery, courage, or justice. It should be little wonder, then, that such souls would crowd along the banks of the River Lethe eager for another chance to live an embodied life wherein such virtues and great deeds were once again possible.

From the Christian perspective, the Ciceronian heaven sounds very much like what theologian Oliver O'Donovan would call a redemption *from* the world rather than a redemption *of* the world.[31] Certain elite souls who have earned their reward are rescued from the world and taken off to a better place, leaving the rest behind to fend for themselves and struggle until perhaps one day (or one reincarnation in the future) they, too, will merit rescue from this valley of tears. Moreover, Cicero's depiction of the elite in heaven makes them sound suspiciously like the Roman elite who ordered members of the Roman underclass off to Rome's many wars over and over again, preaching to them their duty to Rome while remaining home enjoying luxuries in their palaces like the gods. In the end, therefore, Cicero's heaven seems to be at odds with Cicero's own view of justice and the importance of service to the common good of Rome.

Both Cicero and Virgil were animated by an admirable sense of commitment to their community. But neither man could meet

---

[31] See, for example, Oliver O'Donovan, *Resurrection and Moral Order: An Outline for Evangelical Ethics*, 2nd ed. (Grand Rapids, MI: Eerdmans, 1994), 14: "It might have been possible, we could say, before Christ rose from the dead, for someone to wonder whether creation was a lost cause. If the creature consistently acted to uncreate itself, and with itself to uncreate the rest of creation, did this not mean that God's handiwork was flawed beyond hope of repair? It might have been possible before Christ rose from the dead to answer in good faith, Yes. Before God raised Jesus from the dead, the hope that we call 'gnostic,' the hope for redemption *from* creation rather than for the redemption *of* creation, might have appeared to be the only possible hope."

the challenge of envisioning an afterlife that was entirely reasonable and consistent. And in the end, that lack of rational consistency could not help but undermine their efforts to inspire in their fellow citizens the determination to sacrifice for the common good all they had wished. Men will sacrifice for the hope of an immortality they cannot be certain of achieving, but they will not sacrifice for a fable they have good reason to suspect is false.

Reincarnation and the Meaningless Life

We should distinguish what I am calling the *classical* view of reincarnation, however, such as is found in classical Hinduism—what we might also call the *moral* view of reincarnation—from certain popular modern views that exhibit little or no concern for the moral character of a person's life and in which a person moves on easily and happily from one life to the next without much concern for the moral development that is preeminent in all classical views, whether Hindu, Greek, or Roman.

Why is the possibility of living multiple lives alluring to some people? In the chapter "The Amnesiac Self" in his book *Lost in the Cosmos*, author Walker Percy considers the popularity of stories involving characters who wake up with no memory of who they are.[32] Are the stories popular because "[t]he times are such that everyday life for everybody is more or less intolerable and one is better off wiping out the past and starting anew"?[33] Is the source of the delight "the certified and risk-free license to leave the old self behind and enter upon a new life"? Percy's subtitle for this chapter is "Why the Self Wants to Get Rid of Itself." Has a certain modern, Western notion of reincarnation become popular for similar

---

[32] See Percy, *Lost in the Cosmos: The Last Self-Help Book* (New York: Farrar, Straus, & Giroux 1983), 17–19.
[33] Ibid., 18.

reasons? Because it seems to offer a chance to "start over" with a "clean slate"? Is it a way of "getting rid of" the self you no longer want to be and of absolving yourself of responsibility for it?

This is not what Socrates had in mind when he said we should be preparing for death. Nor is it what classical Hindus have had in mind either. For each, reincarnation has a serious moral dimension that is missing from the common, easygoing, modern Western view.

On the classical views of reincarnation, one's life is lived with a clear sense of some serious repercussions that might follow after one's death. Those who think the notion of hell is cruel should consider the possibility of being reincarnated as a snake or a slug. One doesn't always get reincarnated as a beautiful ingénue in Paris or a daring James Bond type. One might be reincarnated as a drug addict or a serial killer. Or as an earthworm.

On the classical view, you live with certain burdens now because of sins you committed in your past lives. And sins you commit now will condemn you to a later reincarnation further down the hierarchy and more distant from your ultimate goal, which is nirvana and freedom from the repeating cycle. One imagines most westerners would find a system in which a person is being condemned now for acts he or she committed in some previous life—acts they don't even remember doing—to be unfair. In the West, people get themselves off the hook all the time for bad things they have done by saying things like, "I was a different person then"—as though this really absolves them of responsibility. One imagines it would be even more difficult to take personal responsibility for things one had done if one really was a different person and had done these bad things in a past life.

There are a number of issues here having to do with memory, identity, and responsibility. It is essential to every notion of reincarnation that the soul, before coming back into a new body, must pass through a process whereby the soul forgets everything about its previous life. In Virgil's vision, the souls must cross over the River Lethe. This forgetting is essential for obvious reasons since none of us readily remembers things we did in past lives. Even those who claim to have recovered past lives commonly claim to remember only the sparsest details. But the forgetting is precisely the problem. Not only am I responsible for things I did in a past life that I do not remember, worse yet, I cannot really learn from those mistakes since I cannot remember any of them. Whatever wisdom I might have gained in the past was lost when "I" crossed the river of forgetfulness—if I can even use the pronoun "I" as though the person I am now is really the same person I was before, even though I have no knowledge of who that person was.

Not only would I have lost my knowledge of the wealth of experiences I had, I would have lost my memory of all the people I had known and loved. And for most people, this loss of their relationships with others is the thing they fear most about death: they do not want to lose the people they love. Reincarnation does not hold hope that you won't lose the people you love; it promises only that you won't care that you've lost them. You just won't remember them. If we said to most people living a healthy, loving life, "We are now going to wipe your memory clean of all your friends and family," they would consider this a horrible punishment, not a promise of hope. It is one of the fates that makes people so fearful of succumbing to Alzheimer's. Thus, for people with family and friends they love, reincarnation could hardly be a consolation in the face of death.

There is in this Western, "non-moral" view of reincarnation a danger of viewing this life as a kind of dry run; if I get bored with this life or if I make some bad life choices, I will just chuck this life and see whether I can get it right next time. The temptation is to treat our present life as if it were one of the "lives" you get in a video game. But on this view, none of my actions are lastingly meaningful nor, indeed, is life itself. I shed all of this when I shed my memory and become a new "person."

As Walker Percy's reflection on the popularity of the "Amnesiac Self" suggests, perhaps this ersatz, non-moral view of reincarnation has become popular in the West precisely because it fits nicely with certain modern Western attitudes about living life "flexibly": I change my clothes; I change my body; I change my self. I constantly recreate myself and, in the process, leave behind all the messy attachments to people and responsibilities I had before.

In the *Odyssey*, at least there is a continuity and permanence to personal identity; Odysseus's mother is still his mother. And in Virgil's account of Aeneas and his father Anchises in the underworld, it is essential that Anchises has not yet crossed Lethe to prepare for reincarnation. Had he already done so, he would no longer remember his son and would have no particular care or concern for Aeneas. Nor would he possess the wisdom he is pictured as imparting to Aeneas. Once across Lethe, he would have left behind all he had learned and all he had loved in order to become someone else. He would be "clearing the slate," preparing to become someone else's father or mother or son or daughter, with obligations to them, not to Aeneas. Virgil's introduction of reincarnation into the story undermines the connection between the two characters on which the story itself depends.

The horror of Ibsen's Peer Gynt at the threat that the Button Molder would melt him down and recast him as another button would not be changed if he had been offered reincarnation: the fear of being swallowed up and of losing all that makes you *you*. It won't be *you* in a new body; it's not really *you* at all. You might as well have been melted down by the Button Molder and re-cast; it comes to the same thing in the end. For the reincarnated Anchises to enter upon his new "life," his previous self must be dissolved, and at that moment, his previous life becomes meaningless to him.

Reincarnation and Our Attitude toward the Body and Relationships

Reincarnation teaches people that the body and soul are two separate entities and that people can change their bodies the way they change their coats. This view would be congenial to the proponents of transgenderism, as it would be to many contemporary transhumanists, but it could never be so to Christians, who believe in the integral relationship of the body and soul. We discussed some of the potential difficulties with this sort of mind-body dualism in chapter 2.

At the heart of the problem is a failure to understand the body as essentially *relational* and *sacramental*. We express ourselves and communicate with others in and through the body. And yet, it is important that we distinguish this view from one that encourages people to view the body as merely an expression of the self the way some modern artists view their art as an expression of the self. If I view the body as essentially a resource for my self-expression, then I treat it like a canvas on which I paint and then re-paint, or like the clay that I mold into one shape and then another. The body, on this view, is merely something to be manipulated in accord with my will, not an essential part of an integral identity I am called upon to respect.

And if I view my own body this way, as merely a resource for my own self-expressive will, then how will I be able to resist viewing all of nature that way, including my relationships with other persons? If I change bodies, would I have the same relationships with my spouse, my children, and my friends? And if not, will I demand that they accept the new me or clear out? If even my own body is not essential to who I am, then why would I consider friends and loved ones essential to the self-expression of my identity? Perhaps these friends worked well when I was in my "blue period," but now I have moved on to my cubist phase or surrealism and the blue just isn't me anymore, so they need to go. Sadly, this is the way increasing numbers of people in our society view even their most intimate relationships. Perhaps it is no mystery, then, why they seem increasingly willing to discard their bodies—indeed, in reincarnation, their very lives—in order to put on a new, potentially more exciting identity. Because the self perceives itself as a kind of nothing, it strives to become somebody else, almost anybody else, rather than to continue suffering the meaninglessness of simply remaining the same old me.[34]

In *Sickness unto Death*, Søren Kierkegaard identifies the ultimate form of despair as the inability to rid oneself of oneself. This sort of despair, says Kierkegaard, is at the heart of suicide. To become a true self, then, to be true to oneself, one must not only be conscious of the self but also be conscious of being grounded in the love that created and sustained oneself. When a person denies either this self or the power that creates and sustains himself or herself, he or she falls into despair, the "sickness unto death." What is needed, then, to root out despair is *faith*, the state whereby "in relating to itself and in willing to be itself, the self rests transparently in the power that established it."[35]

We might contrast the modern creation of a *self*, only accidentally related to others and for whom others are potentially

---

[34] On this, Walker Percy, "The Self as Nought," in *Lost in the Cosmos*, 23–26.
[35] See Søren Kierkegaard, *Sickness unto Death*, trans. Howard and Edna Hong (Princeton, NJ: Princeton University Press, 1980), esp. 14, 49, 131.

disposable resources depending upon my current constitution of the self, with the kind of friendship we find between two saints of the Church, St. Gregory Nazianzen (ca. 329–390) and St. Basil of Caesarea (ca. 330–379). Gregory once wrote about his great friend, "We seemed to be two bodies with a single spirit." What united them so profoundly?

> Our single object and ambition was virtue, and a life of hope in the blessings that are to come; we wanted to withdraw from this world before we departed from it. With this end in view we ordered our lives and all our actions. We followed the guidance of God's law and spurred each other on to virtue. If it is not too boastful to say, we found in each other a standard and rule for discerning right from wrong. *Different men have different names, which they owe to their parents or to themselves, that is, to their own pursuits and achievements. But our great pursuit, the great name we wanted, was to be Christians, to be called Christians.*[36]

Since, as St. Paul assures us, there are in the Body of Christ many members, all of whom play their roles according to their diverse gifts (see 1 Cor 12:12–26), these two men could (and did) strive

---

[36] These lines are quoted from a sermon by Saint Gregory Nazianzen used in the Roman Office of Readings for January 2, the feast of Saints Basil the Great and Gregory Nazianzen. The text has been slightly edited here. For the original, see Oratio 43, *Funeral Oration on the Great S. Basil, Bishop of Caesarea in Cappadocia,* in Philip Schaff and Henry Wace, ed. *Nicene and Post-Nicene Fathers, Second Series,* vol. 7, trans. Charles Gordon Browne and James Edward Swallow (Buffalo, NY: Christian Literature Publishing Co., 1894.), rev. and ed. for *New Advent* by Kevin Knight, *https://www. newadvent.org/fathers/310243.htm.*

to "die to self"[37] in order to become "one in Christ"[38]—a unity that did not diminish either their distinct gifts or their identities. Rather, in the image of the Triune God, their lives became a selfless gift of self to each other.

Release from the Cycles: The Drop of Water Returning to the Ocean

In classical Eastern views of reincarnation, the goal of reincarnation is not to continue being reincarnated in new and different lives—something more likely to appeal to a wealthy, middle class westerner bored with his or her middle class life—but to live nobly in order to gain freedom from the repeated cycles of reincarnation. Unlike the ersatz Western views of reincarnation we have been discussing, the classical view of reincarnation is concerned not primarily with individual human satisfaction but with the accomplishment of a larger, more cosmic moral order over time. Indeed, for many such forms of Eastern thought, it is precisely our human tendency to indulge the illusion of human individuality and separability from others and from nature that is the root of all suffering.

One way of picturing the escape from the cycle of reincarnation is to say that our ultimate goal is to "become one" with the universe: that we are like a drop of water returning to the ocean. It is a lovely image, but a moment's reflection would bring the realization that once the drop of water has returned to the ocean, the individual drop disappears; it is simply absorbed into an indistinct mass. This is not unlike Peer Gynt's horror of being melted down by the Button Molder into an indistinguishable mass. Now, for

---

[37] See *Gal 2:20; Eph 4:22–24; Rom 6:11, 12:1–2.*
[38] See *Gal 3:28.*

those who hold that all individuality is an illusion to be rejected, this fate would not be as horrific as it is for Peer Gynt. Ibsen clearly did not believe that our individuality is a terrible illusion that we need to reject. For him, recognizing and affirming our individuality was a strength, not a weakness.

Where would Christians fall on this spectrum that extends from the evisceration of individuality to its exaltation? Christian revelation has always affirmed both the value of the individual and the communal nature of human persons.[39] In the Triune God, we find three distinct Persons whose diversity does not diminish their unity and whose unity does not obliterate their diversity. So, too, in the Body of Christ, there are many members, each of whom has a distinct character and role. In both the Trinity and the Body of Christ, we find a unity in diversity and a diversity in unity. In the Old Testament, God often addresses himself to a "people." But he also speaks in and through individual persons, each with a very distinct character. There is no sense with figures such as Abraham, Moses, Elijah, or Hosea that their individual characters were standing in the way of their missions. Quite the contrary; if they

---

[39] For an example from a contemporary analysis of the value Christianity places on the individual and individual creativity and ingenuity while also affirming each person's social connectedness and relationality, see Pope St. John Paul II, *Laborem Exercens*, e.g., §6: "Man has to subdue the earth and dominate it, because as the 'image of God' he is a person, that is to say, a subjective being capable of acting in a planned and rational way, capable of deciding about himself, and with a tendency to self-realization." And §15: "But here it must be emphasized, in general terms, that the person who works desires *not only* due *remuneration* for his work; he also wishes that, within the production process, provision be made for him to be able to *know* that in his work, even on something that is owned in common, he is working *'for himself.'* This awareness is extinguished within him in a system of excessive bureaucratic centralization, which makes the worker feel that he is just a cog in a huge machine moved from above, that he is for more reasons than one a mere production instrument rather than a true subject of work with an initiative of his own."

had not been so distinctive and different, they would have failed to be and to do what God willed. And of course, the climax of God's self-revelation comes in the person of Jesus Christ, the Son of God, one of the Persons of the Triune God, who became incarnate as an individual person at a very particular time and place. Human individuality is not the problem; human selfishness is.

Christians, no less than classical Eastern proponents of reincarnation, see the goal of death and resurrection as the restoration and fuller realization of a cosmic moral order. The two differ in their teachings on the necessity (or not) for evisceration of individuals and their individual identities, characters, and particular relationships to people and places. Classical accounts of reincarnation hold that the reincarnated soul *must* let go of all those particular relationships of the old self in order to clear the way for the new self. Christian accounts have no such requirement.

Common Beliefs, False Hopes

Faith, says the Letter to the Hebrews, is "the assurance of things hoped for, the conviction of things not seen" (Heb 11:1). And yet, although there are matters of faith that transcend the grasp of reason, especially with regard to the afterlife, the Catholic intellectual tradition has always held that faith will not *contradict* reason—nor, of course, will it contradict itself. In this regard, Christians face challenges similar to those we have been examining and serious questions about the relationship between this life and the next. So, for example, the Christian affirmation about the ultimate goodness of creation and human life contradicts any notion of the afterlife that would diminish the meaningfulness of this life.[40] And yet, Christians should also avoid concluding that

---

[40] For the best modern statement on the infinite value of human life, see Pope

the afterlife consists in activities which are, from the perspective of Christian faith, fundamentally meaningless or that the afterlife lacks some important good we enjoy in this life, such as the enjoyment of friends, physical comfort, or love. And since the "good news" Christianity proclaims to the world is ultimately about the salvation of the world, Christians cannot understand the afterlife as an escape from the problems of this world into some other realm or as an abandonment of the world to the evils that plague it.

Each of the views we have been examining in these first three chapters has been popular throughout history: (a) the conviction that there is no afterlife, so we must either live without care (Epicureans) or live "towards-death," caring for the world (Heidegger); (b) the hope that we can somehow extend life forever; (c) the belief that there is some life after death that entails punishment for the wicked and rewards for those who are good; or (d) the hope that life can be extended by reincarnation in other lives.

The goal of our analysis is clarification. We want to understand how Christian revelation about the afterlife can help us to avoid the problems that arise with other conceptions; in a related vein, we want to make sure that our interpretation of Christian revelation does not lead us to embrace any of those mistaken notions. We should also acknowledge the degree to which these common popular views of the afterlife remain tempting even for Christians, especially Christians who lack a fuller understanding of the richness of the Gospel promise.

As humanity has done throughout the centuries, we perceive within ourselves something that participates in what is eternal.

St. John Paul II's 1995 encyclical On the Value of Human Life *Evangelium Vitae*. Any view of the afterlife that causes Christians to de-value this life would contradict firm Catholic teaching.

The desire to live on and avoid personal obliteration is, on the Christian view, neither unhealthy nor unnatural. Christian revelation tells us that it is a deep spiritual yearning placed in our hearts by God. We know that things in nature are born, live and grow, then decay and die. But Christian revelation confirms something many people throughout history have felt deeply: that somehow human beings avoid that fate, that we have something in us that transcends other things in nature. So on the one hand, it makes sense for people to yearn for immortality.

And yet, some serious reflection on what a mere extension of this present life would mean, both for us and for our children and grandchildren, should allow us to recognize that this is a false promise, one that could never fulfill the desire for the fullness of life that God has put into our hearts. If, for example, we love our children and are willing to sacrifice for future generations; if we recognize that for new life to arise and flourish, old life must move on; if we recognize that aging appropriately while remaining in relationship with our children and grandchildren (not seeking to remain young forever) is the best way of loving them and serving as a model for their future; if we realize that reincarnation necessitates forgetting and giving up all my loving relationships in this life—then these realizations can, one hopes, clear away those false allurements and open us up to the true promise contained within Christ's victory over death, his Resurrection from the dead and Ascension to the right hand of the Father.

Although the mystery of death utterly beggars the imagination, the Church has been taught by divine revelation and firmly teaches that man has been created by God for a blissful purpose beyond the reach of earthly misery. In addition, that bodily death from which man would have been immune had he not sinned will be vanquished, according to the Christian faith, when man who was ruined by his own doing is restored to wholeness by an almighty and merciful Saviour. For God has called man and still calls him so that with his entire being he might be joined to Him in an endless sharing of a divine life beyond all corruption. Christ won this victory when He rose to life, for by His death He freed man from death. Hence to every thoughtful man a solidly established faith provides the answer to his anxiety about what the future holds for him. At the same time faith gives him the power to be united in Christ with his loved ones who have already been snatched away by death; faith arouses the hope that they have found true life with God.

Gaudium et Spes §18

For I delivered to you as of first importance what I also received, that Christ died for our sins in accordance with the Scriptures, that he was buried, that he was raised on the third day in accordance with the Scriptures, and that he appeared to Cephas, then to the Twelve.

1 Corinthians 15:3–5

For if the dead are not raised, then Christ has not been raised. If Christ has not been raised, your faith is futile and you are still in your sins. Then those also who have fallen asleep in Christ have perished. If for this life only we have hoped in Christ, we are of all men most to be pitied. But in fact Christ has been raised from the dead, the first fruits of those who have fallen asleep.

1 Corinthians 15:16–20

Chapter 4

TO THE FATHER, THROUGH THE SON, IN THE HOLY SPIRIT: RESURRECTION AND THE BODY OF CHRIST

The most common image of Jesus depicts him on a cross. Some images portray him as he was in death, hanging lifeless on the Cross. Other images, usually more in the style of an icon, portray him on the Cross yet risen: eyes open and arms outstretched as if inviting all to come to him. Both images are attempts to capture the twofold truth that Christ truly died and is truly risen. He was truly man and did not merely feign death, and yet he has truly risen to the right hand of the Father. Both affirmations have always been at the heart of the Christian creed. Scholars tell us that one of the earliest creeds is contained within this passage of Paul's First Letter to the Corinthians.

> Now I would remind you, brethren, in what terms I preached to you the gospel, which you received, in which you stand, by which you are saved, if you hold it fast— unless you believed in vain. For I delivered to you as of first importance what I also received, that Christ died for our sins in accordance with the Scriptures, that he was buried, that he was raised on the third day in accordance with the Scriptures, and that he appeared to Cephas, then to the Twelve. Then he appeared to more than five hundred brethren at one time, most of whom are still alive, though some have fallen asleep. Then he appeared to James, then to all the apostles. Last of all, as to one untimely born, he appeared also to me. (1 Cor 15:1–8)

There are some minor disagreements between scholars over which phrases here are parts of this early creed. Some suggest only verses 3 and 4 ("For I delivered to you . . . then to the Twelve") while others think it includes everything but the first and last sentences. But most agree that this is a creed in use from the earliest Church—from the period before Paul converted. Paul says he has "delivered" (*paredoka*)—some translations have "handed on"—"as of first importance" what he himself received: namely, that Christ died, that he was buried, and that he rose on the third day, and that he appeared to the disciples. If in fact, as St. Paul proclaims a little further on (v. 20), "Christ has been raised from the dead, the first fruits of those who have fallen asleep," then we can understand something of what is in store for us by attending closely to what Christ has revealed in his death and Resurrection.

One thing that should be clear right away is that the Christian promise of eternal life is not the same as the transhumanist goal of immortality. It is not a promise that Christians will never die.

Christ died; so, too, will we. Nor does Christ's Resurrection suggest that our souls will be "liberated" from the prison of our bodies. Christ rose in the flesh.

Although there are many religious and philosophical traditions that look upon death as a "release" or a "liberation," the Scriptures overwhelmingly speak of death negatively, as a violation of the divine order. "God did not make death," we are told in the Book of Wisdom, "and he does not delight in the death of the living. For he created all things that they might exist" (1:13–14). Life is associated with God; sin and the rejection of God, who is the Source of Life, are what bring death into the world. "God created man for incorruption," says the Book of Wisdom, "and made him in the image of his own eternity, but through the devil's envy death entered the world, and those who belong to his party experience it" (2:23–24).

In the Scriptures, "sin and death" go together verbally the way "ham 'n eggs" do in English, and they are not a kindly or benevolent pair. The Scriptures, far from valorizing death as something "blessed" or a great "freedom," as something we can look forward to as a great relief from our sufferings, instead picture death as the enemy that needs to be defeated. St. Paul calls death "the last enemy to be destroyed" (1 Cor 15:26). Indeed, the good news of the Gospels is precisely this: that this enemy has been defeated at long last by Christ.[1] As St. Paul writes: "When the perishable puts

---

[1] For more, see Alexander Schmemann, *For the Life of the World: Sacraments and Orthodoxy* (Yonkers, NY: St. Vladimir's Seminary Press, 2018), 116–21. He who argues that "to 'comfort' people and reconcile them with death by making this world a meaningless scene of an individual preparation for death is also to falsify it. For Christianity proclaims that Christ died for the life of the world, and not for an 'eternal rest' from it" (116). "What pains Plato took in his *Phaedo*," says Fr. Schmemann, "to make death desirable and even good, and how often he has since been echoed in the history of human belief

on the imperishable, and the mortal puts on immortality, then shall come to pass the saying that is written:

> 'Death is swallowed up in victory.'
> 'O death, where is thy victory?
> O death, where is thy sting?'

The sting of death is sin, and the power of sin is the law. But thanks be to God, who gives us the victory through our Lord Jesus Christ" (1 Cor 15:54–57).

Images of Heaven

So what sort of hope does the Christian teaching about the resurrection of the body and the communion of saints hold out for us? To answer this question, we must first distinguish between what revelation teaches and what later artistic representations have sometimes led people to imagine.[2] We begin by putting out of our

---

when confronted with the prospect of release from this world of change and suffering!" (117). Christianity, on the other hand, claims Schmemann, "is not reconciliation with death. It is the revelation of death, and it reveals death because it is the revelation of Life. Christ is this Life. And only if Christ is Life is death what Christianity proclaims it to be, namely the enemy to be destroyed (1 Cor 15:26), and not a 'mystery to be explained.' Religion and secularism, by explaining death, give it a 'status,' a rationale, make it 'normal.' Only Christianity proclaims it to be *abnormal* and, therefore, truly horrible. . . . To accept God's world as a cosmic cemetery which is to be abolished and replaced by an 'other world' which looks like a cemetery ('eternal rest') and to call this religion, to live in a cosmic cemetery and to 'dispose' every day of thousands of corpses and to get excited about a 'just society' and to be happy!—this is the fall of man" (120–21).

2   CCC, §1027: "This mystery of blessed communion with God and all who are in Christ is beyond all understanding and description. Scripture speaks of it in images: life, light, peace, wedding feast, wine of the kingdom, the Father's house, the heavenly Jerusalem, paradise: 'no eye has seen, nor ear heard, nor

minds pictures of people with halos standing on fluffy clouds. This is not to fault those pictures any more than we would wish to fault Renaissance paintings of the birth of Christ or of the Last Supper even though we know that these paintings idealize the scenes in various ways and are not meant to be taken as if they were snapshots of the original historical event. Artworks of this sort were meant to bring out a certain meaning of the event and to inspire wonder, awe, and ultimately worship. Modern artists, too, are not usually painting as though they were trying to do what we do when we take a simple photograph. Van Gogh did not paint "Starry Night" the way he did because he thought it would do the work a photograph would do. He wanted his viewers to see something new, something beyond the everyday. So, too, when Renaissance and Baroque artists painted saints on the clouds, they wanted people to look up at the clouds they saw above them every day and imagine that they were in the presence of God and the saints.

To be honest, we have very little idea what heaven is like. The most common image we get in the Scriptures is of a heavenly city, built with walls and buildings that gleam like precious stones.[3] This image is meant to signify a reality beyond our comprehension, but what we can discern from this image and from other parts of revelation is that heaven is not a lone existence; it is a communion of persons. This view of the afterlife suggests that we should prepare for death by continually perfecting our ability to enter into a communion of persons with God and with others. This communal understanding of the afterlife is reaffirmed, as we will see, by the Trinitarian character of our union with God, who is both One and Three, and by the doctrine of the communion of the saints. What

---

the heart of man conceived, what God has prepared for those who love him' [1 Cor 2:9]."

[3] See esp. Ezek 40–48 and Rev 21–22.

would entering into this communion of persons entail? Many things, obviously, but among them, the reduction of selfishness and all those dispositions that lead us to sin against others and the development of virtues that perfect our ability to unite with others without losing ourselves in a collectivist mass, such as happened so tragically in the twentieth century with Nazism, Fascism, and the communism of Lenin, Stalin, and Mao.[4]

Speculations about what heaven will be like—whether there will be flowers, dogs, meadows, trees, or ice cream—are probably pointless. We are not told. But we can be certain, in faith, that there is nothing good in this world that could possibly be lacking in God, who is the Source of all Being, Goodness, and Beauty in creation. Whatever there is that is good in flowers, dogs, meadows, trees, and ice cream not only will be present there but will be present even more fully. To experience them in their Source, as contrasted with the way we experience them now, is like the difference between reading a letter from your beloved, which can bring a certain, undeniable joy, and being present *with* your beloved. We would consider it odd if a person preferred only reading letters and never wished to be present with his or her beloved.

What we call "heaven" is a name Christians give to our union with God after death, when we will enjoy the beatific vision—that is to say, when we will share with God so great an intimacy that it is said we will see God "face to face," the way lovers stare into each

---

[4] For a wonderful (and very funny) critique of the mob mentality passions of such collectivist movements, see Eugene Ionesco's absurdist comedy Rhinoceros, in which a simple, timid man named Bérenger watches helplessly as all the inhabitants of his small, provincial French town, including his friends and fellow workers, choose one by one to become destructive rhinoceroses rather than human beings.

other's eyes.[5] This fuller union and deeper communion is made possible by our union with the Body of Christ.

That great saint and doctor of the Church St. Thérèse of Lisieux, who early in her life had such a clear sense of the beauty of heaven and who found it hard to believe that there were people who denied the existence of heaven, was later struck by her own "dark night of the soul." Shortly after Easter, she writes, Jesus "permitted my soul to be invaded by the thickest darkness, and that thought of heaven, up until then so sweet to me, became no longer anything but the cause of struggle and torment. This trial was to last not a few days or a few weeks, it was not to be extinguished until the hour set by God himself and this hour has not yet come." All Thérèse's lovely images of heaven as a place, along with the consolation they had given her, were stripped away, and all that was left was simply her faith in the person of Jesus Christ.[6]

Heaven in and through Christ

Let me suggest, then, that, in addition to the images of the heavenly city we get in the Scriptures, the clearest and most definitive revelation of what "heaven" is has been given to us *in the person of*

---

[5] See 1 Cor 13:12: "For now we see in a mirror dimly, but then face to face. Now I know in part; then I shall understand fully, even as I have been fully understood." And Rev 22:4: "They shall see his face, and his name shall be on their foreheads." CCC, §1023: "Those who die in God's grace and friendship and are perfectly purified live for ever with Christ. They are like God for ever, for they 'see him as he is,' face to face [1 John 3:2; cf. 1 Cor 13:12; Rev 22:4]." CCC, §1024: "This perfect life with the Most Holy Trinity—this communion of life and love with the Trinity, with the Virgin Mary, the angels and all the blessed—is called 'heaven.' Heaven is the ultimate end and fulfillment of the deepest human longings, the state of supreme, definitive happiness."

[6] See Thérèse of Lisieux, *Story of a Soul: The Autobiography of Saint Thérèse of Lisieux*, trans. John Clarke, O.C.D. (Washington, DC: ICS Publications, 1996), esp. 333.

the risen Christ. As we have seen, St. Paul describes the proclamation that Christ has risen from the dead as "of first importance." For him, this is the heart of the good news: that Christ "has indeed been raised from the dead" and is "the first fruits of those who have fallen asleep" (1 Cor 15:20). Hence it is no accident that each of the four Gospels should culminate in the story of Christ's death and Resurrection. In John's Gospel, soon after Jesus has washed the disciples' feet, he says to them: "In my Father's house are many rooms; if it were not so, would I have told you that I go to prepare a place for you? And when I go and prepare a place for you, I will come again and will take you to myself, that where I am you may be also. And you know the way where I am going" (John 14:2–4).

From this statement alone, we might imagine that Jesus is saying that he is going to a place and will later show the disciples how to get to that place. The Apostle Thomas shows that this is the way he has interpreted Jesus's statement when he asks: "Lord, we do not know where you are going; how can we know the way?" (v. 5). Christians know, from centuries of biblical tradition, that there is a subtle play on words here. Jesus *is* "the way." So when he says, "And you know the way," he means, "You know me, and I am the way." Indeed, this is precisely the answer he gives to Thomas: "I am the way, and the truth, and the life; no one comes to the Father, but by me. If you had known me, you would have known my Father also; henceforth you know him and have seen him" (vv. 6–7).

But now the image has shifted, from "a place" that Christ is preparing —"many rooms" in the Father's house—to one in which Christ is "the way" *to* the Father (union with him) and the way to *know* the Father. But union with the Father seems like a lot to ask, perhaps too much, so Philip says to Jesus: "Lord, show us the Father, and we shall be satisfied" (other translations have, "and that will be enough for us"). To this Jesus replies: "Have I been with you so long, and yet you do not know me, Philip? He who has seen me has seen the Father; how can you say, 'Show us the Father'? Do you not believe that I am in the Father and the Father in me?" (vv. 9–10).

Note the important series of associations here. Christ is preparing a place for us "in his Father's house" and showing us the way. But he is the way. So in showing us himself—revealing himself in his life, death, and Resurrection—he is showing us the way to the Father's house. But since he and the Father are one, to be united to Christ is to be united to the Father.

Toward the end of Mark Twain's comic tale "The Diary of Adam and Eve," Adam, who had at first been resistant to Eve, this new creature who has invaded his personal space, laments at Eve's grave, having realized, "Wheresoever she was, there was Eden." Twain's "Diary" is a comic love story, not theology. But it poses the important question: Is paradise a place or a person? As Christians, we are called upon to recognize that paradise is not merely a place but a Person, and that Person is Christ, who sends the Holy Spirit so that God's love may be "poured into our hearts" (Rom 5:5), uniting us with the Father as the Son is united to the Father. The way for us to be united with the Father is to be united with his incarnate Son, who has been sent by the Father and returns to the Father. Hence we come to the Father and know the Father by uniting ourselves to the crucified and risen Body of Christ.[7] Thus Christians should be wary of thinking about heaven

---

[7] Sometimes when we say "the Body of Christ," we are referring to the Church. In other circumstances, we might be referring to the Eucharist. But it is important to remember that both the Eucharist and the Church are sacramental embodiments in the here-and-now of the *one* crucified-and-risen, glorified Body of Christ. The Church is spread throughout the world and has many members, as St. Paul teaches (1 Cor 12:1–31), but all are "one in Christ Jesus" (Gal 3:28). The Eucharistic sacrifice is celebrated time and again across the world

primarily as just a very nice place, like the Elysian Fields in Virgil's *Aeneid*, where it is Jesus rather than Aeneas's father, Anchises, who will meet us. Nor should we imagine the main difference between Virgil's story and Christian revelation is that Christians, like Dante, picture heaven up in the sky whereas Virgil, like Homer before him, pictured the "realm of the dead" under the ground.[8]

Etymologically, the word "heaven" is derived from the Old English *heofon*, meaning "home of God." Like the German *Himmel*, the Latin *caelum*, and the Hebrew *šāmayim*, *heofon* referred originally to the visible sky, the "heavens." But when the word eventually came to be associated with the state of bliss we

---

and throughout history, but each makes present Christ's singular sacrifice on Calvary, for as Hebrews 10:10 teaches: "we have been sanctified through the offering of the body of Jesus Christ *once for all*" [emphasis added]. In the pages that follow, when I speak of the "crucified and risen Body of Christ," I will be referring to the glorified Body of Christ, risen and "seated at the right hand of the Father" in heaven. Unfortunately, some people do not realize that Christ rose *bodily* to the Father and that his fully human body persists in union with the Father and the Spirit. Perhaps they imagine his body melted away somehow somewhere along the line. This is a very common gnostic temptation: to imagine that only something *spiritual* can survive death, not anything physical or *bodily*. From the time of the earliest Church, we see the Fathers and doctors vigorously opposing this gnostic heresy while always affirming the reality of the resurrection of the body. Unfortunately, whenever this gnostic tendency spreads more widely, Christians begin to lose their faith that Christ is *really present* in the Eucharist—as present as he was to the apostles during his life and as present as he was to them in the Upper Room after his Crucifixion—and that he is *really present* in his Church, which is soon taken to be just another human institution, not much different from others. Without faith in the concrete *bodily* character of the Resurrection, people soon "spiritualize" the Church to such an extent that it becomes as thin as the mists. No longer do I take myself to be a member of the Body of Christ, but I start to see myself as someone who "attends religious services at a church."

8 One way of viewing the Elysian Fields in Virgil's *Aeneid* would be to say that they are in a somewhat nicer ante-chamber of hell. Dante seems to view it that way. But Dante shares the view that hell is a place physically under the ground beneath us.

enjoy in union with God, it was no longer identified simply with a place up in the sky. It was, rather, a place that was somehow beyond the sky. Some Old Testament texts refer to the "heaven of heavens" (*shamayi h'shamayim* in Hebrew, *caeli caelorum* in Latin).[9] But whatever term was used—whether "heaven" or "the heaven of heavens" or as in St. Paul, "the third heaven"[10]—it was understood that God was present everywhere in his creation, so what was being signified by the word was a special sort of union with him. For this reason, Matthew can refer in his Gospel to "the kingdom of heaven" whereas the other Gospels use the phrase "the kingdom of God." The kingdom of heaven is the place where we are united with God. And in the context of Matthew's Gospel, the kingdom of heaven is made present with Jesus Christ. It is made present with him and in him. The kingdom of heaven is not merely something that Christ brings; it is something he *is*. He is God's presence with us and for us, *in the flesh*. To enter the kingdom of heaven, then, is to be united to Christ's risen Body.[11]

Resurrection of the Body: The Witness of the Early Fathers of the Church

But we must take care not to interpret what St. Paul says in these passages in a gnostic fashion and thereby do away with the resurrection of the body of all believers. The reality of the bodily

---

[9] See, for example, Deut 10:14; 1 Kgs 8:27; 2 Chr 2:6, 6:18; Neh 9:6; Ps 68:33, 148:4. It is translated "heaven of heavens" in the New King James Version and several others. In the RSV2CE, we find "ancient heavens." There are other instances, however, when the word used is simply "the heavens" (*šāmayim* in Hebrew), which can mean either the sky or the place where God dwells.

[10] 2 Cor 12:2.

[11] CCC, §1025: "To live in heaven is 'to be with Christ' . . . 'For life is to be with Christ; where Christ is, there is life, there is the kingdom' [St. Ambrose, *In Luc* 10.121]."

resurrection—the resurrection of the *flesh*—was something the early Fathers of the Church were insistent upon against the gnostic tendencies of their own day. Two early Fathers of the Church who testified powerfully to their faith in the bodily resurrection were Justin Martyr (AD 100–165) and Irenaeus of Lyons (AD 130–200). Their witness can serve as an important guide for us since they foresaw most of the objections one hears to this day.

Justin Martyr, for example, states very clearly that "the resurrection is a resurrection of the flesh which died."[12] He knows that the Platonists of his day would argue that after death, the incorruptible soul leaves the corruptible body.

> They who maintain the wrong opinion say that there is no resurrection of the flesh; giving as their reason that it is impossible that what is corrupted and dissolved should be restored to the same as it had been. And besides the impossibility, they say that the salvation of the flesh is disadvantageous; and they abuse the flesh, adducing its infirmities, and declare that it only is the cause of our sins, so that if the flesh, say they, rise again, our infirmities also rise with it.[13]

But the revelation of the Incarnation and Resurrection convinced Justin to affirm, to the contrary, a more profound unity between the soul and the body.

---

[12] Justin Martyr, *On the Resurrection*, in A. Robert, J. Donaldson and A. Cleveland Coxe, ed., *The Ante-Nicene Fathers: Translations of the Writings of the Fathers down to A.D. 325*, vol. 1, trans. Marcus Dods (Buffalo, NY: Christian Literature Publishing Co., 1885), ch. 10, rev. and ed. for *New Advent* by Kevin Knight, https://www.newadvent.org/fathers/0131.htm.

[13] Ibid., ch. 2.

But, in truth, He has even called the flesh to the resurrection, and promises to it everlasting life. For where He promises to save man, there He gives the promise to the flesh. For what is man but the reasonable animal composed of body and soul? Is the soul by itself man? No; but the soul of man. Would the body be called man? No, but it is called the body of man. If, then, neither of these is by itself man, but that which is made up of the two together is called man, and God has called man to life and resurrection, He has called not a part, but the whole, which is the soul and the body.[14]

Christ clearly reveals in his own bodily Resurrection that this is what is in store for all the faithful. Because, argues Justin, if Christ had no need of the flesh, why did he heal it? Why did he raise his own flesh from the dead? "Was it not to show what the resurrection should be?"

How then did He raise the dead? Their souls or their bodies? Manifestly both. If the resurrection were only spiritual, it was requisite that He, in raising the dead, should show the body lying apart by itself, and the soul living apart by itself. But now He did not do so, but raised the body, confirming in it the promise of life. Why did He rise in the flesh in which He suffered, unless to show the resurrection of the flesh? . . . And when He had thus shown them that there is truly a resurrection of the flesh, wishing to show them this also, that it is not impossible for flesh to ascend into heaven (as He had said that our

---

[14] Ibid., ch. 8.

dwelling-place is in heaven), He was taken up into heaven while they beheld (Acts 1:9), as He was in the flesh.[15]

So, too, we find similar strong affirmations and arguments in Irenaeus's monumental work *Against Heresies*. Arguing against the "secret doctrines" of the Gnostics, Irenaeus affirms that the entire Church believes in "the resurrection from the dead, and ascension into heaven in the flesh of the beloved Jesus, our Lord."[16] And he makes clear repeatedly that he does not take the phrase "in the flesh" metaphorically or spiritually, whether we are referring to Christ's Resurrection or the general resurrection of all the faithful.

> In the same manner, therefore, as Christ did rise in the substance of flesh, and pointed out to His disciples the marks of the nails and the opening in His side (now these are the tokens of that flesh which rose from the dead), so shall He also, it is said, raise us up by His own power (1 Corinthians 6:14). And again to the Romans he says, "But if the Spirit of Him that raised up Jesus from the dead dwell in you, He that raised up Christ from the dead shall also quicken your mortal bodies" (Romans 8:11).[17]

Like Justin, Irenaeus understood that the Christian revelation of the Incarnation and the resurrection of the body meant affirming a more holistic unity between the body and the soul than was

---

[15] Ibid., ch. 9.

[16] Irenaeus, *Against Heresies*, in Alexander Roberts, James Donaldson, and A. Cleveland Coxe, ed., *The Ante-Nicene Fathers: Translations of the Writings of the Fathers down to A.D. 325*, vol. 1, trans. Alexander Roberts and William Rambaut (Buffalo, NY: Christian Literature Publishing Co., 1885), 1.10.1, https://www.newadvent.org/fathers/0103.htm.

[17] Ibid., 5.7.1.

customary among many philosophers and other religious traditions of his day.

> What, then, are mortal bodies? Can they be souls? Nay,
> for souls are incorporeal when put in comparison with
> mortal bodies; for God breathed into the face of man
> the breath of life, and man became a living soul. Now the
> breath of life is an incorporeal thing. And certainly they
> cannot maintain that the very breath of life is mortal.
> Therefore David says, "My soul also shall live to Him"
> [Ps 21:31, Vulg.], just as if its substance were immortal.
> Neither, on the other hand, can they say that the spirit
> is the mortal body. What therefore is there left to which
> we may apply the term mortal body, unless it be the thing
> that was moulded, that is, the flesh, of which it is also said
> that God will vivify it?[18]

There was a saying among later Fathers of the Church: "What has
not been assumed has not been redeemed."[19] The phrase seems to
have been inspired by Athanasius of Alexandria, but one finds
something similar in the writings of Gregory of Nazianzus,
among others.

> For that which He has not assumed He has not healed;
> but that which is united to His Godhead is also saved. If
> only half Adam fell, then that which Christ assumes and
> saves may be half also; but if the whole of his nature fell,

---

[18] Ibid.
[19] One also finds the translation, "What has not been assumed has not been
healed."

it must be united to the whole nature of Him that was begotten, and so be saved as a whole.[20]

It is worth noting that in this particular instance, Gregory was arguing against the claim of Apollonius and his followers that Christ had a normal human body but a divine mind instead of a regular human soul. Against all these attempts to split the human person in two and divide mind or soul against body, the Fathers of the early Church insisted upon their incarnational unity.

But how, we might wonder, could God give heavenly, eternal life to a body? Answer: If Christ has assumed it, he has redeemed it. But Fathers of the Church like Irenaeus also pointed to God's original act of creation, asking whether the God who gave life to the human bodies we have now would find it impossible to give heavenly life to those bodies after we die. Rather, in the Resurrection, "the power of him who is the bestower of life is made perfect in weakness," says Irenaeus, "that is, in the flesh."[21] He taunts those who deny that God can do this:

> Let them inform us, when they maintain the incapacity of flesh to receive the life granted by God, whether they do say these things as being living men at present, and partakers of life, or acknowledge that, having no part in life whatever, they are at the present moment dead men. And if they really are dead men, how is it that they move about, and speak, and perform those other functions

[20] Gregory of Nazianzus, *Letter 101 (To Cledonius)*, in Philip Schaff and Henry Wace, ed., *Nicene and Post-Nicene Fathers*, second series, vol. 7, trans. Charles Gordon Browne and James Edward Swallow (Buffalo, NY: Christian Literature Publishing Co., 1894), 101.5, https://www.newadvent.org/fathers/3103a.htm.

[21] Irenaeus, *Against Heresies*, 5.3.3.

which are not the actions of the dead, but of the living? But if they are now alive, and if their whole body partakes of life, how can they venture the assertion that the flesh is not qualified to be a partaker of life, when they do confess that they have life at the present moment?[22]

But if, in fact, as is obvious, they have life in their bodies now, why would they deny that it is possible for them to have life in their bodies when they are more fully united to God?

But if the present temporal life, which is of such an inferior nature to eternal life, can nevertheless effect so much as to quicken our mortal members, why should not eternal life, being much more powerful than this, vivify the flesh, which has already held converse with, and been accustomed to sustain, life? For that the flesh can really partake of life, is shown from the fact of its being alive; for it lives on, as long as it is God's purpose that it should do so. It is manifest, too, that God has the power to confer life upon it, inasmuch as He grants life to us who are in existence. And, therefore, since the Lord has power to infuse life into what He has fashioned, and since the flesh is capable of being quickened, what remains to prevent its participating in incorruption, which is a blissful and never-ending life granted by God?[23]

---

22 Ibid.
23 Ibid.

This insistence on the reality of the bodily resurrection of all believers has persisted up to the present day.[24]

The Real Presence of the Risen Christ

In a conversation once with a friend about the Eucharist, I asked whether she believed in "the Real Presence of Christ" in the Eucharist. "Well," she replied, "I believe Christ is *spiritually present*." I had heard those words before, but I wasn't quite sure what they meant. I'm still not. But instead of asking her to explain herself, I asked my question a slightly different way, one that I thought might get us to the heart of the matter. "Do you believe that Christ is as present to us in the Eucharist as he was to Mary Magdalene in the garden after she found the tomb empty, as present as he was to the disciples on the road to Emmaus, and as present as he was to the disciples when he appeared to them in the Upper Room? And do you believe that Christ was as present to the disciples in that Upper Room as he had been at the Last Supper before his death? Because if you simply don't believe that Christ was as present to the disciples in the Upper Room after his Crucifixion as he was before his Crucifixion at the Last Supper—if you think that he was present merely "spiritually" or in their fond memories of him—then you need to understand that this is not now and has never been the faith of the Church."

St. Paul proclaims and the Gospel accounts tell us that Christ is really present in the Resurrection—as present to them after his death as he was during life. Indeed, he was in some ways even more

---

[24] CCC, §1052: "We believe that the souls of all who die in Christ's grace . . . are the People of God beyond death. On the day of resurrection, death will be definitively conquered, when these souls will be reunited with their bodies." This passage cites the firm affirmation of the same doctrine in Pope Paul VI's *Credo of the People of God*, §28.

present to them since he was no longer subject to the limitations of time and space, and so he was even more capable of being with them when they needed him in spite of any obstacles, like locked doors and windows. After his Resurrection, Jesus's bodily existence does not suffer the same limitations as ours. We are limited by time and space. But Christ transcends these limitations. He can be present at the times and places of his choosing with those who need him at that moment. But note, he is not conjured up like a demon or a ghost. He appears when and where he chooses. He is now even more fully revealed as Love Incarnate, a love so strong, so divine, that it can transcend even death on a Cross. After the Resurrection, Christ can be present not only with them but in them and above them: in their hearts and minds supporting their connection to the Father and with each other.

This encounter with the risen Christ requires faith. We do not capture him cognitively as a simple object of experience or a mere datum of history. It is not merely a question of seeing; it is a matter of seeing and believing, of seeing and being transformed by what one has seen, of seeing and accepting the gift offered in the encounter. Even before his death and Resurrection, people did not always see Christ fully. They might have seen a man—if they even noticed him at all in the crowd as they hurried along during their busy day, but rarely did people see him as Love Incarnate, as the culmination of all their hopes and the fulfillment of that for which they had been yearning their whole lives. For that, one had to look more deeply. One had to look with the eyes of faith, hope, and love. Even seeing the miracles did not convince many people that God was present with his people. Most people were frightened by an alien power; some even wanted to kill him. Only a few recognized him as Love Incarnate and believed that he was the promised Anointed One, the Messiah who would redeem mankind.

And this was true even before the Crucifixion and Resurrection. At the Last Supper, Christ tells his disciples that he must go away, but he will send the Holy Spirit to help and guide them after he has gone. And he does "go away"—eventually. But after his death on the Cross, he makes a stop on his way back to his Father (so to speak) to spend some extra time with the disciples. Why? Hasn't he told them everything they need to know? Hasn't he shown them "the Way"? They have the evidence of the empty tomb of his Resurrection from the dead. Perhaps one or two Resurrection appearances are needed to convince the Apostles that he still lives. But he stays with them for a full forty days and comes to them multiple times. Why?

Jesus was never given to bouts of histrionic miracle-making to reveal his power during his life on earth. And if he had simply wanted to show himself as "God," he could have "come down off the Cross," as his antagonists taunted him to do. Indeed, if he had wanted to "prove" that he was God, he could have jettisoned fifty feet into the air and shot laser beams out of his eyes. But (a) Christ did not choose to do this even though the Apostles likely would have been highly relieved if he had, and (b) if he had done this, what kind of god would he have been revealing himself to be? The kind of pagan god everyone expected him to be? The kind of god to whom people give sacrifice so that they can gain power?

But what if the God he was revealing himself to be wasn't asking for human sacrifice but was willing to make himself the sacrifice? How else than by dying would he reveal his message that we have to die to self and to selfishness in order to rise in life? How else would he show mortal, suffering human beings, whose life is, as Martin Heidegger claims, a "life towards death," that he would be with them at the moment of their deaths? How else to demonstrate to suffering, mortal human beings that he understands our suffering and was not asking of us anything that he himself had not suffered? How better to show them that death need not be, as it so often seems, a final obliteration but might be, in union with his death and Resurrection, a purgation and beginning of a new resurrected life. But what sort of life would this be?

Christ, the "First Fruits"

If, as St. Paul claims, Christ is the "first fruits" of what the faithful departed will enjoy in the general resurrection, what do his Resurrection appearances reveal to us about our resurrected life? Two things in particular, I suggest. First, his death has not, as it might have seemed, cut him off from the Father; rather, he shares fully in the Father's glory, which is revealed more fully now that he has risen from the dead. But second—and this is equally important—the person before them is still the Jesus they knew and loved. We sometimes say that Christ's presence among the Eleven in the Upper Room was a glorified presence, but this does not mean he was any less present to them than he was during life.[25] They were

---

[25] In *Jesus of Nazareth: Holy Week* (San Francisco, CA: Ignatius, 2011), Pope Benedict writes this about the risen Christ: "In this remarkable dialectic of identity and otherness, of real physicality and freedom from the constraints of the body, we see the special mysterious nature of the risen Lord's new existence. Both elements apply here: he is the same embodied man, and he is the new man, having entered upon a different manner of existence" (266). And again: "On the one hand, Jesus has not returned to the empirical existence that is subject to the law of death, but he lives anew in fellowship with God, permanently beyond the reach of death. On the other hand, it is important that the encounters with the risen Lord are not just interior events or mystical experiences—they are real encounters with the living one who is now embodied in a new way and *remains* embodied" (268). For more, see also, Fr. Roch Kereszty's wonderful introduction to Christology: *Jesus Christ: Fundamentals of Christology*, rev. ed. (New York: Alba House, 2002). E.g., "The risen Christ for Paul is clearly identical with Jesus of Nazareth. The resurrection does not change his personal identity" (37). "The resurrection of Jesus does not mean for Paul

still able to touch him, talk to him, and eat with him.[26] So much so that years later, the Apostle John would write:

> That which was from the beginning, which we have heard, which we have seen with our eyes, which we have looked upon and touched with our hands, concerning the word of life—the life was made manifest, and we saw it, and testify to it, and proclaim to you the eternal life which was with the Father and was made manifest to us— that which we have seen and heard we proclaim also to you, so that you may have fellowship with us; and our fellowship is with the Father and with his Son Jesus Christ. (1 John 1:1–3)

Consider, for a moment, if the account had been different; if, rather than Jesus himself appearing to the disciples, a divine being made of pure light, glowing like gold, had appeared to calm their fears, saying, "Be not afraid. I am the divine being who existed in

---

Jesus' return into our physical life, but rather his exaltation to the state of the Lord. In this state he shares the glory, power, and dignity of Yahweh. . . . The risen Lord and Jesus of Nazareth, however, are one and the same person" (41). "The risen Christ is not a "re-animated body" returning into our world, like Lazarus or the daughter of Jairus. . . . He is no longer subject to the limitations of our spatio-temporal universe. Yet the risen Christ—in spite of his transcendent status—is the same person as the crucified Jesus of Nazareth" (44).

[26] Strictly speaking, only the Gospels of Luke and John depict Jesus eating with the disciples after the Resurrection although Mark speaks of Jesus coming to the disciples as they sat at table. See Pope Benedict, *Jesus of Nazareth: Holy Week*, 270–71, on "the three elements that characterized the time spent by the risen Jesus in the company of his disciples: he appeared to them, he spoke to them, and he sat at table with them." Benedict says of the repeated reference to Christ eating with the disciples after he has risen that they point to "the risen Lord's new banquet with his followers. It is a covenant-event, and in this sense it has an inner association with the Last Supper."

the man you knew as Jesus. With his death, I have been released, and now I go to be with my Father and your Father in heaven." If that had been the account, this would be the kind of afterlife we would be promised. It would have been the kind of story that a good Neoplatonist or one of the gnostic sects in the early Church would have preferred because it would have reaffirmed their belief that the body is merely a shell hiding an angelic being, and with the death of the body, the angel is released and returns to a higher realm of pure spirit.[27]

But instead, it is clear in the Gospels that the one who appears to the Apostles is the same Jesus of Nazareth who died on the Cross, not some phoenix that has risen from his ashes. In the Gospels of Luke and John, the evangelists go out of their way to insist that it was impossible anyone could have gotten into the room physically: the doors and windows were all locked. So when they saw him, they assumed what most of us would assume: it must be a ghost! But having gone out of their way in one direction, the Gospel writers then go out of their way in the other, insisting that Jesus was, in fact, there *bodily*. He had even preserved in his body the wounds made by the nails and the lance. And yet, having gone out of his way to insist that he was there with them in the room bodily, Luke then shifts gears again and tells the reader that he simply disappeared, leaving the Apostles to wonder again, "Did we just imagine that? Was it a ghost?" Indeed, the Gospel of John recounts the story of the Apostle Thomas: having been absent when Christ came the first time, Thomas is afterwards so

---

[27] Both Pope Benedict XVI and Fr. Roch emphasize that Christ's Resurrection appearances prepare the Apostles for going out on mission to preach the good news and continue Christ's mission establishing the kingdom of God. Thus the Resurrection appearances are not about escape *from* the world, but they are rather meant to put the Apostles on a mission *to* the world.

skeptical about what he is told by the others that he says he will not believe Christ has risen unless he is able to put his hand in the nail marks and in the hole in Jesus's side for himself. And a week later, he does. Jesus still has the wounds from the Crucifixion. So, too, in other Resurrection appearances, Jesus addresses Mary and others in identifiable ways. He calls Mary of Magdala by name (John 20:16); he breaks bread and gives it to them (Luke 23:30–31), or he sends them out for a catch of fish (John 21:6–7).

What is promised to us, then, by the risen Christ, who is the "first fruits" of what we, too, will enjoy, is that—like Christ and with Christ—we can, after death, be united fully with God and share in the eternal communion of love shared between the Father, Son, and Holy Spirit. And yet, in this union with the Triune God, we will not be lost like the drop of water returning to the ocean. Rather, we will become finally and fully who we are meant to be.[28]

Certainly we must "die to self" in order to "live in Christ," as St. Paul tells us, but the Resurrection, as Oliver O'Donovan has argued, implies not a negation of the created order but its perfection. Writes O'Donovan:

> It might have been possible before Christ rose from the dead for someone to wonder whether creation was a lost cause. If the creature consistently acted to uncreate itself, and with itself to uncreate the rest of creation, did this not mean that God's handiwork was flawed beyond hope of repair? It might have been possible before Christ rose from the dead to answer in good faith, Yes. Before God raised Jesus from the dead, the hope that we call "gnostic,"

---

[28] See the full passage (which I quoted partially above, in n11) from CCC, §1025: "To live in heaven is 'to be with Christ.' The elect live 'in Christ,' but they retain, or rather find, their true identity, their own name."

the hope for redemption from creation rather than for
the redemption of creation, might have appeared to be
the only possible hope.[29]

And, in fact, if we look again at the passages in which St. Paul
talks about our death to self, it is clear that he is not talking about
any kind of negation or obliteration of the self or of the body. He
is talking about the newness of life that we can enjoy when our
bodies are no longer enslaved to sin.[30] Clearly this is a necessary
preparation for the life we live in union with Christ in union with
the Father after death. But, as such early Church Fathers as Justin
Martyr and Irenaeus warn us, we must not interpret this passage
in a gnostic fashion and do away with the reality of the bodily
resurrection.

---

[29] Oliver O'Donovan, *Resurrection and Moral Order*, 2nd rev. ed. (Grand Rapids, MI: Eerdmans, 1994), 14.

[30] See Rom 6:1–11: "What shall we say then? Are we to continue in sin that grace may abound? By no means! How can we who died to sin still live in it? Do you not know that all of us who have been baptized into Christ Jesus were baptized into his death? We were buried therefore with him by baptism into death, so that as Christ was raised from the dead by the glory of the Father, we too might walk in newness of life. For if we have been united with him in a death like his, we shall certainly be united with him in a resurrection like his. We know that our former man was crucified with him so that the sinful body might be destroyed, and we might no longer be enslaved to sin. For he who has died is freed from sin. But if we have died with Christ, we believe that we shall also live with him. For we know that Christ being raised from the dead will never die again; death no longer has dominion over him. The death he died he died to sin, once for all, but the life he lives he lives to God. So you also must consider yourselves dead to sin and alive to God in Christ Jesus."

Who Can Look upon the Face of God and Live? Resurrection and the Triune God

What gives us hope that this union with God is even possible? It might seem a complete absurdity to imagine that creatures as small and insignificant as we are could be united to our Creator at all—for "Who can look upon the face of God and live?" as the Scriptures warn us (see Exod 33:20). So, for example, in Rudyard Kipling's wonderful story, "The Man Who Would Be King," two nineteenth-century British regular soldiers, Daniel Dravot and Peachey Carnehan, agree with one another to journey into Kafiristan in the wilds of Afghanistan to find their fortunes and "become kings." In an early battle, Dravot is hit by an arrow but survives seemingly miraculously and is henceforth viewed by the natives as a "god." When Dravot decides, against Carnehan's advice, to marry a local tribal girl and make her his queen, the girl is terrified because she is certain that his kiss, the kiss of a god, will cause her to burst into flames and die. When Dravot bends down to kiss her during the wedding ceremony, she bites him, and he bleeds. Seeing his blood, the priests of the tribe cry out that he is neither god nor devil but a man, and most of the Kafirs in the army turn against Dravot and his friends. The underlying presumption of the Kafiris, common among ancient peoples, is that the gods are simply too much for us, too sacred or too powerful, and as mere humans, we would not survive a direct contact with them. The second presumption is that, since Dravot bleeds, he cannot be a god.

Christians, by contrast, speak of a God who not only bleeds but also dies. To the question "Who can look upon the face of God and live?" Christians answer: Christ, the Son of God incarnate, crucified, and risen. Another answer, equally important, would be: so, too, can all those united to Christ and to one another in the

Body of Christ. United with him, they can look upon the face of God and, at long last, *live*—eternally—with the sort of life that does not run down and run out. Pope Benedict XVI, for example, writes about "the cosmic body of Christ," that "Christ's transformed body is also the place where men enter into communion with God and with one another and are thus able to live definitively in the fullness of indestructible life."[31]

What makes us so presumptuous as to imagine that it is possible to be united with God—that infinite Being beyond all our comprehension—and not be swallowed up like the drop of water in the ocean? That faith is founded upon the revelation that the Father, the Son, and the Holy Spirit can be perfectly united in God as perfectly one and yet not lose their separate personhood. The distinct personhood of each does not make impossible their true union as one God; and yet their unity does not dissolve their distinctness as three Persons. They are a perfect unity in diversity and a perfect diversity in unity. In his life, death, and Resurrection, Christ reveals to us that the love shared eternally by this communion of persons—this perfect unity in diversity and diversity in unity—has been extended to us. Indeed, it has been extended to us *in his Person*. We become "members," St. Paul tells us, of Christ's Body. But there is diversity among the members of the Body.[32] So

---

[31] Pope Benedict XVI, *Jesus of Nazareth: Holy Week*, 274.

[32] First Cor 12:12–20: "For just as the body is one and has many members, and all the members of the body, though many, are one body, so it is with Christ. For by one Spirit we were all baptized into one body—Jews or Greeks, slaves or free—and all were made to drink of one Spirit. For the body does not consist of one member but of many. If the foot should say, 'Because I am not a hand, I do not belong to the body,' that would not make it any less a part of the body. And if the ear should say, 'Because I am not an eye, I do not belong to the body,' that would not make it any less a part of the body. If the whole body were an eye, where would be the hearing? If the whole body were an ear, where would be the sense of smell? But as it is, God arranged the organs in the body,

in Christ's glorified Body, we participate in that unity in diversity and diversity in unity shared between the Father, Son, and Holy Spirit. The foundations of the Christian view of the afterlife must be traced back ultimately, then, to the Trinitarian and Christological faith of the Church.[33]

The Communion of Saints

Not only do we retain our personal identity in union with God, we retain those deep connections of love that made life meaningful and that were our "foretaste" of our final union with the eternal Triune love. In that final union with the Triune God, we do not cease being engaged in meaningful activity. Rather, we continue more fully in the activities that, as Christian tradition understands, make life most meaningful: namely, the love of God and neighbor.

What many people fear in death, whether their own or that of those they love, is the loss of connection with their loved ones. If we think of going to heaven as though it were like going to Cleveland (only better), then we are sad that they or we are "going away," even if we hope it is a "better place." But if heaven is union with the Father in Christ through the Spirit, and if Christ lives and is present to each of us, then we, too, remain connected with our loved ones—even more intimately and fully—in union with Christ's Body and the communion of saints. We believe that Christ lives and that he continues to watch over us, sending his Holy Spirit to guide and strengthen us. When those we love were

---

each one of them, as he chose. If all were a single organ, where would the body be? As it is, there are many parts, yet one body."

[33] CCC, §1050: "'True and subsistent life consists in this: the Father, through the Son and in the Holy Spirit, pouring out his heavenly gifts on all things without exception. Thanks to his mercy, we too, men that we are, have received the inalienable promise of eternal life' [St. Cyril of Jerusalem, *Catech. illum.* 18, 29: PG 33, 1049]."

alive, we sometimes asked them to pray for us, knowing they would precisely because of their love for us. The Christian promise is that this sort of love can never die (see Rom 8:38). It lives on in Christ.

To the extent that our love is selfless and true and directed toward the good of the other person, then it is from God and of God, and, as St. Paul assures us, nothing can separate us from it. And note, we do not love merely with our own imperfect love. Indeed, whatever had been lacking in the justice or goodness of that love is purified in our union with God. We love with God's perfect love, not merely with our own imperfect love. Our descendants need ask only whether what they do is in accord with God's will, not whether it would have been in accord with the limited, imperfect standards we held during life. For if they do God's will, they will be satisfying the perfected love of all those united with God in the communion of saints.

Entering into a heavenly union with God does not mean I can now love only God any more than becoming a Christian means I can no longer love my wife and my children. Those particular embodied connections are a foretaste of the communion of the saints. Christ's Resurrection reveals and makes it possible that those who have died are still connected to us and we to them. We are not merely loving a ghost or a memory. Christ is risen and so are all those who are "members" of his one Body. When we love him, and them in him, we are loving a living person who is now living more truly because he or she is not living a life in the shadow of death; they are not living a life that runs down and runs out. For them, life is not merely the passage of time or mere survival. It is unbounded love, no longer bound by the restrictions of time and space, just as the risen Christ was no longer bound by the restrictions of time and space. He appeared to Apostles bodily in the Upper Room; they touched him and ate with him even though the doors and windows were closed and locked. And he remains just as present to us now, even centuries later.

Catholics believe that they can pray to St. Francis and St. Thomas Aquinas because they believe those saints are still alive in Christ, still loving us and praying for us. The citizens in Italy and Assisi can have a special devotion to St. Francis because his connection to the place of his birth and to the people to whom he was sent has not lessened. He is not less the saint of Assisi now than he was when he was alive. And yet I know that his love, connected as it is through Christ to the Holy Trinity, is now extended to me as well even though I live on another continent centuries after his death. When I embrace the spirit of poverty and refuse to be mastered by my ownership of things, St. Francis is alive in me. When I sit down to write and ask St. Thomas for his guidance, he prays for me. I can participate in the same Spirit of wisdom and love that animated him.

Certain developments in modern science can tempt us into thinking that the universe is empty. More recent research has shown that it is far from empty. Amazing things are happening in that realm we call outer space, which we used to think was cold and empty, So, too, on the Christian account, the universe is full in other ways too, beyond what we can directly observe or measure. It is full of angels and seraphs and the spirits and souls of the just, all of whom are looking out for us, rooting for us, praying for us, and encouraging us. It would not be completely inaccurate to say that we have, each of us, an immensely large cheering section on our side, working and praying for our salvation and well-being. Not only beloved grandmothers and dead uncles but also people we never even knew existed. United with Christ in his risen Body, they are with us, as Christ is with us, in every moment of our lives, especially when we are weak or suffering and in special need of their help and guidance.

We need to pray for them and ask them for their prayers for us. Then we should try to remain aware of all those who are united with God and the saints and look for evidence of their continuing blessings in our lives. We "pray" to them only in the sense that we ask for them to pray for us to the Father, to whom they are united by being united to Christ. We pray, first, because prayer is invaluable for its own sake but also so that we become, even now, persons we hope eventually to become: saints—those who love and pray to the Father in Christ "unto the ages of ages," *in saecula saeculorum,* for the redemption of all mankind and all creation.

We should not think of heaven, therefore, primarily as just a place—as though dying and going to heaven was something like losing your job and having to leave your friends and move to a different city where you don't know anyone. Heaven is a loving communion of persons.[34] You enter into an eternal communion of Trinitarian love. And just as entering into a loving communion of persons here on earth changes you and challenges you to become more than you ever dreamed possible, so too, in union with the Father, Son, and Spirit and the communion of saints in communion with them, you do not love this world less; you love it more, in ways that transcend our current limitations of time and space.

Christianity is a very fleshy religion, a characteristic that has often in history made it seem absurd to those with a gnostic

---

[34] CCC, §1026: "By his death and Resurrection, Jesus Christ has 'opened' heaven to us. The life of the blessed consists in the full and perfect possession of the fruits of the redemption accomplished by Christ. He makes partners in his heavenly glorification those who have believed in him and remained faithful to his will. Heaven is the blessed community of all who are perfectly incorporated into Christ."

spiritualist bent. Christianity, in accord with the Jewish creation account, affirms that the material world is "good," indeed "very good."[35] The Christian creed includes the affirmation that the Word became flesh in the Incarnation of God's Son. And the risen Christ reveals an afterlife in which we will enjoy a bodily resurrection. Properly understood, then, the Christian view of the life after death would not cause one to diminish the value of the human body or, by extension, of our other material connections in this life, especially our connections to other people and the particular communities into which we are born or to whose good we have devoted ourselves.

As St. John Paul II emphasized in his "theology of the body," our communion with others is achieved in and through the body.[36] The Christian teaching about the resurrection of the body assures us that we will not be denied the benefits of our bodily existence after death. As we said above, nothing good in this world could possibly be absent from God, who is the Source of all goodness. The senses are functions of a body. Feeling the softness of skin or the warmth of a hot shower, tasting the sharp, somewhat bitter combination of salt and tequila in a margarita or the musky flavor of some barbequed ribs, smelling the wonderful aroma of cinnamon and apple baking in a pie—all these depend on having a body. Ghosts don't hug (as Odysseus found out when he attempted to embrace his mother) or kiss or eat sizzling fajitas or take hot showers.

But the way we are embodied at present in this life has limits.

---

[35] See Gen 1:1–31: "Good" is the description used after each of the first five days. After the sixth day, we are told, "God saw everything that he had made, and behold, it was very good."

[36] See Pope John Paul II, *Man and Woman He Created Them: A Theology of the Body*, trans. Michael Waldstein (Boston, MA: Pauline Books, 2006).

When we are with our friends in New York, we cannot be with our friends in San Francisco. And when we are with our beloved grandparents, we usually cannot also be with our beloved grandchildren. We are limited by time and space. To be free of those restrictions, but not as a ghost or a memory, is the promise of the glorified body. It is the promise Christ shows us when he reveals himself to the women at the empty tomb and the disciples on the road to Emmaus and to the Eleven in the locked Upper Room. It is the promise realized every day around the world when the one crucified, risen Christ makes himself present in the Eucharist in Chicago and Lima and Tokyo and St. Petersburg and Berlin and Abuja, in cities and hamlets around the world, as he has been doing for centuries and will do until the end of time.

Do We Live on in People's Memories?

One of the great tragedies of people losing their faith in the reality of Christ's Resurrection and his continuing Real Presence in the Eucharist is that they soon lose their hope in the communion of saints and their belief that, in Christ, we can, even in death, remain present to the ones we love. If Christ is not risen, if he was not present to the Apostles as fully as he was during his life on earth, if he is not as present to us now as he was to the Apostles, then neither can any of our beloved dead be present to us.

Indeed, as we move further and further into a post-Christian era, we increasingly hear the claim that our forebears are present to us only in our memories of them. In movies and television, a sympathetic character will be shown bending down to a child who has recently lost a parent and, pointing to her heart, says, "Mommy is alive, right *here*." But as the years go by and those memories fade, what then? How many years has it been since I last thought of my grandmother? If her continued existence (of this diminished sort) depends upon her remaining in my memory, then would my failure to think of her make me complicit in her extinction? Should I feel guilty that I don't think of her more? With my death, there will be no one else left who would remember her at all. And then I might wonder: Is her fate what awaits me? Will anyone remember me? How many people die with no one to remember them?

At what point would we be forced to admit, given this thin view of "living on" after death in the memory of others, that there really is no existence after death. There is nothing. All our memories, all that we have striven for, all our relationships would simply be lost, like a computer memory drive crushed under foot or destroyed in a fire. If you've ever had a computer drive crash and lost months of work along with all your pictures, your email messages, and your contacts, you know how absolutely empty that feeling can be. All that—now *nothing*?

Our parents' and grandparents' continued existence cannot depend entirely upon us. The existence of any one person is simply too limited and ephemeral. If my forebears live and exist, then I am free to have a relationship with them because their existence does not depend on me, it depends on Christ, who has himself transcended death. The only lasting foundation upon which I could base a lasting relationship with my loved ones after death would be a connection to the Creator God, who has taken on my mortal human nature and shown, by dying, that the reign of sin and death is ended. If he were only God, then although I might conclude that *he* is eternal, it would not be clear that I could be. If he were only a man, then even if I thought that *this one man* was saved from death, it would not be evident that anyone else could be. Only if God has taken on our humanity, died, and then risen—not only in his divinity but also in the fulness of his humanity—could a person have faith that death has been conquered for all human persons who are united to his risen Body. [37]

Christ's Resurrection shows us a view of the afterlife that neither negates the value of this life nor proposes that those in the next life would be engaged in an activity that those of us in this life would find essentially empty and meaningless. We discussed this problem in the last chapter, using examples from the writings of Virgil and Cicero. Virtuous Romans who believed that the happy life necessitated activity in accord with virtue would likely have found it less than alluring, perhaps even ignoble, to be told that in the afterlife, they would be sitting around in a green

---

[37] So, for example, Joseph Ratzinger (later Pope Benedict XVI) points out in his *Introduction to Christianity*, trans. J. R. Foster (New York: Crossroad, 1985), 230–232: "Man is a being who himself does not live forever but is necessarily delivered up to death. For him, since he has no continuance in himself, survival, from a purely human point of view, can only become possible through his continuing to exist in another." But Cardinal Ratzinger identifies two mistaken ways of attempting to do this. "First, living on in one's own children." But "when man discovers that in his children he only continues to exist in a very unreal way; he wants more of himself to remain. So he takes refuge in the idea of fame, which should make him really immortal if he lives on through all ages in the memory of others. But this second attempt of man's to obtain immortality for himself by existing in others fails just as badly as the first: what remains is not the self but only its echo, a mere shadow." Perhaps this was what Homer was attempting ultimately to convey by portraying Achilles in the underworld as a shade. "The inadequacy of both ways," argues Ratzinger, "lies partly in the fact that the other person who holds my being after my death cannot carry this being itself but only its echo." Moreover that person, "to whom I have, so to speak, entrusted my continuance, will not last—he, too, will perish." Thus, concludes Ratzinger, if "man has no permanence in himself and consequently can only continue to exist in another, but his existence in another is only shadowy and once again not final, because this other must perish, too,"—if this is so, then the only one who could truly give lasting stability would be "he who is, who does not come into existence and pass away again but abides in the midst of transience: the God of the living, who does not hold just the shadow and echo of my being."

field doing very little but enjoying themselves while Rome and Romans suffered. The Christian notion of human flourishing and the Christian notion of the afterlife involve no such discontinuity. We are commanded in this life to give ourselves over to the love of God and neighbor. It should be no surprise but rather something of a great consolation to find out that the activity in which we are promised we will be engaged in the next life is an even more perfect love of God and neighbor.[38]

We are told to care for the world, especially for the poor and those in need. This is not some "dirty work" we need to do until we are released from the "burden" in the next life, where we will live in condos on the beach and can forget about all those disturbing poor people. The next life is the life of infinite care, when we will be able to see all people with the eyes of divine love, not with the limited perspectives we now have. Christ asks his disciples in the Garden of Gethsemane when he finds them sleeping, "So could you not watch with me one hour?" And then he notes: "The spirit indeed is willing, but the flesh is weak" (Matt 26:40, 41). To have bodies and emotions and an integrated series of dispositions that allow us to "keep awake" with our loved ones during their times of trial: this, too, is the promise of the resurrection of the body.

The hope of entering the communion of saints in union with

---

[38] St. Thérèse of Lisieux is reported to have said on July 17, 1897, shortly before her death: "I feel that my mission is about to begin, my mission of making others love God as I love Him, my mission of teaching my little way to souls. If God answers my requests, my heaven will be spent on earth up until the end of the world. Yes, I want to spend my heaven in doing good on earth." This passage, including the last and oft-quoted sentence, is to be found in the "epilogue" section of the authorized English version of her diary: *Story of a Soul: The Autobiography of St. Thérèse of Lisieux*, trans. John Clarke, 3rd ed. (Washington, DC: Institute for Carmelite Studies Publications, 1996), 263. See also CCC, §1029: "In the glory of heaven the blessed continue joyfully to fulfill God's will in relation to other men and to all creation."

God the Father, Son, and Spirit should not make us less concerned to love and care for our neighbors in this life; it should make us more concerned for them. So, too, the Catholic view of the afterlife does not negate the importance of this life. Rather it encourages us to see that all our actions and all the connections we make in this life can remain eternally meaningful even though the full realization of the ultimate good we are working toward will not come to fruition until Christ's return in glory.[39]

Living Sacramentally as a Preparation for Eternal Life

In the *Phaedo*, Socrates advised that the philosopher should always be preparing for death, which he understands to be the separation of the soul from the body, by encouraging his soul even in this life to be liberated more and more from the body.[40] The Christian view of the afterlife does not require us to prepare ourselves now to shed our bodies later. Rather, the Christian who understood the

---

[39] CCC, §1049: "'Far from diminishing our concern to develop this earth, the expectancy of a new earth should spur us on, for it is here that the body of a new human family grows, foreshadowing in some way the age which is to come. That is why, although we must be careful to distinguish earthly progress clearly from the increase of the kingdom of Christ, such progress is of vital concern to the kingdom of God, insofar as it can contribute to the better ordering of human society' [*GS* 39, §2]."

[40] See *Phaedo*, 64c: "We believe, do we not, that death is the separation of the soul from the body, and that the state of being dead is the state in which the body is separated from the soul and exists alone by itself and the soul is separated from the body and exists alone by itself? Is death anything other than this?" "No, it is this." 64e: "Altogether, then, you think that such a man would not devote himself to the body, but would, so far as he was able, turn away from the body and concern himself with the soul?" 65a: "To begin with, then, it is clear that in such matters the philosopher, more than other men, separates the soul from communion with the body?" See *Plato in Twelve Volumes*, vol. 1, trans. Harold North Fowler, Loeb Classical Library (Cambridge, MA: Harvard University Press; London: William Heinemann Ltd., 1966).

significance of the Resurrection the way St. Paul did would prepare for death by dying to sin and selfishness in order to live in Christ. "Do you not know," writes Paul, "that all of us who have been baptized into Christ Jesus were baptized into his death?"

> We were buried therefore with him by baptism into death, so that as Christ was raised from the dead by the glory of the Father, we too might walk in newness of life. For if we have been united with him in a death like his, we shall certainly be united with him in a resurrection like his. We know that our old self was crucified with him so that the sinful body might be destroyed, and we might no longer be enslaved to sin. For he who has died is freed from sin. But if we have died with Christ, we believe that we shall also live with him. For we know that Christ being raised from the dead will never die again; death no longer has dominion over him. The death he died he died to sin, once for all, but the life he lives he lives to God. So you also must consider yourselves dead to sin and alive to God in Christ Jesus. (Rom 6:3–11)

We put off "the old self" (some translations have "the old man") so that we can live a new life in Christ (see also Col 3:9; Eph 4:22).

So we need to prepare ourselves for death, as Socrates advised, but not in the way Socrates advised. The Christian way is not through a separation of the soul from the body; it is by incorporation into Christ's Body. One way we encounter the risen Christ and become incorporated into his Body is through the sacraments, especially the Eucharist. By partaking of Christ's Body and Blood, we enter into the communion of the heavenly banquet. When we consume earthly food, it is incorporated into our bodies. When we consume the Body of Christ in the Eucharist, we are incorporated into it—or to put this more precisely, into him. But it is important to understand that this is not a "cultic" act like the pagan sacrifice to appease the gods. Nor should it be thought of as an attempt to gain God's favor by engaging in an external show of obedience to divine authority. The sacrifice of the Mass is not ours; it is Christ's. Our salvation is not earned by the sacrifice of bulls and goats. It is won by the Blood of Christ and that alone. We participate in the sacrifice of the Cross, made by Christ, once for all.

So what difference would that make to us now? How would we live differently so as to prepare ourselves for death? One way would be to embrace what has been called a "sacramental" view of creation. One often finds a sacrament defined as an effective sign of God's grace instituted by Christ. Strictly speaking, there are in the Catholic tradition seven sacraments of the Church: Baptism, Eucharist, Confirmation, Reconciliation, Matrimony, Anointing of the Sick, and Holy Orders. But it is important to note that in each of them, there is a physical material that becomes the instrument or embodiment of God's grace, whether it is the water of baptism, the oil of anointing, or the bread and wine of the Eucharist. In marriage, the bride and groom are the material of the sacrament who are sacramentally united as Christ is united to his Church. To use the physical material in this way is not, however, a violation of their created nature. It is, rather, a fuller realization and fulfillment of it because, on the Christian understanding of the creation, all created reality has been created as an instrument or embodiment of God's love and grace. Catholics do not view the bread and wine that become the Body and Blood of Christ with contempt, as material that can be simply thrown away. They are gifts—fruit of the earth and work of human hands—that are good in and of themselves but that can also serve a higher purpose.

When they become instruments of God's grace and love—when they become the Body and Blood of Christ—this is not contrary to their created nature; rather, the gifts realize to the fullest extent the potentialities of their nature. They nourish us in the highest and truest sense possible.

All creation proclaims the glory of God, as the Psalms declare, and all creation is meant to point us back to the One who gave it as a gift of love. When we use water in baptism, we perfect its nature as a means of cleansing. When a man and a woman unite themselves to one another as Christ is united to his Church or as the Persons are united to one another in the Trinity, then they can in that way more perfectly realize their natures as created in the image and likeness of God.

One of the most eloquent witnesses in the contemporary world to this new sort of life to which we are called was the great Orthodox theologian Alexander Schmemann (1921–1983). In his book *For the Life of the World*, Schmemann asked "What is the content of life eternal?"[41]

Among his profound reflections, one finds these beautiful passages—selections which, because of their profound beauty, I will presume to quote at some length.

In the Bible the food that man eats, the world of which he must partake in order to live, is given to him by God, and it is given as communion with God. The world as man's food is not something "material" and limited to material functions, thus different from, and opposed to, the specifically "spiritual" functions by which man is related to God. All that exists is God's gift to man, and it all exists to

---

[41] Schmemann, *For the Life of the World*, 20.

make God known to man, to make man's life communion with God. It is divine love made food, made life for man. God blessed everything He creates, and in biblical language, this means that He makes all creation the sign and means of His presence and wisdom, love and revelation.[42]

The first, the basic definition of man is that he is the priest. He stands in the center of the world and unifies it in his act of blessing God, of both receiving the world from God and offering it to God—and by filling the world with this eucharist, he transforms his life, the one that he receives from the world, into life in God, into communion with Him. The world was created as the "matter," the material of one all-embracing eucharist, and man was created as the priest of this cosmic sacrament.[43] Man has loved the world, but as an end in itself and not as transparent to God. . . . It seems natural for man to experience the world as opaque, and not shot through with the presence of God. It seems natural not to live a life of thanksgiving for God's gift of the world. It seems natural not to be eucharistic.[44]

The natural dependence of man upon the world was intended to be transformed constantly into communion with God in whom is all life. Man was to be the priest of a eucharist, offering the world to God, and in this offering he was to receive the gift of life. But in the fallen world man does not have the priestly power to do this. His dependence on the world becomes a closed circuit,

---

42 Ibid., 21.
43 Ibid., 22.
44 Ibid., 23.

and his love is deviated from its true direction. He still loves, he is hungry. . . . But his love and his dependence refer only to the world in itself. He does not know that breathing can be communion with God. He does not realize that to eat can be to receive life from God in more than its physical sense. He forgets that the world, its air or its food, cannot by themselves bring life, but only as they are received and accepted for God's sake, in God and as bearers of the divine gift of life.[45]

The only real fall of man is his noneucharistic life in a noneucharistic world. The fall is not that he preferred the world to God, distorted the balance between the spiritual and material, but that he made the world material, whereas he was to have transformed it into "life in God," filled with meaning and spirit.[46]

"The world is meaningful," says Schmemann, "only when it is the 'sacrament' of God's presence."[47] Note that the paragraphs I have quoted were in answer to the question, "What is the content of life eternal?" Schmemann believed that the answer to that question was found in the liturgy, which is how we participate now in the heavenly banquet enjoyed by the saints. But that participation is meant to infuse meaning into our entire lives and make our entire lives a preparation for our full enjoyment of that banquet in union with Christ after this life has run its course.

God gives us gifts that are immense, like the universe itself and the order of nature, and gifts that are simple, like the sound of a

---

[45] Ibid., 23–24.
[46] Ibid., 25–26.
[47] Ibid., 24.

beloved song at just the right time to move our hearts or the soft touch of a loved one's hand. If we try to "own" them and "keep" them, we destroy them. If we accept them and value them precisely as gifts of love, they become ours—that is, something shared between God and us, the way the Holy Spirit is shared between the Father and the Son.

So, too, we should understand the human body, and indeed the human person as a whole, sacramentally—as another created thing meant to be an instrument of God's love and grace. It would be odd to call the body an embodiment of God's love and God's grace because the metaphor of embodiment is based on the body. But we want to be clear that although my body is mine, not the government's and not anyone else's, and thus my body should be treated with a certain dignity and respect precisely because it is the body of a person, and persons (body and soul) are due the respect of being "in the image of God," even so, my body is not mine the way my lawnmower or my car is mine. I am a steward of a gift, not the owner of an object.

I am called to render unto others the love that has been given to me. The instrument I have been given to communicate that true, selfless love is my body. It is admittedly, in this life, an imperfect instrument, which will be perfected only in the next life. But to say that the full perfection of the body awaits our resurrected and glorified bodies is not to say that our bodies are worthless dross that we should leave behind. Rather, we see our task as continually offering our bodies up for this transformation from instruments of our own selfish will into instruments of a true, selfless love, made possible in us by the gift of the Holy Spirit, whereby we participate in the eternal communion of selfless, self-giving love shared between the Father and the Son.

Dying at Home

A mistakenly spiritualized understanding of death as separation from the body and from material creation may cause us to misinterpret some very natural, very healthy human reactions as signs of sinfulness. So, for example, many people want to die at home. It is one of the tragedies of our current cultural circumstance that very few actually get to die at home. Why do people want to die at home among the things they have grown accustomed to and with the friends and family they have known and loved? Aren't these "worldly" connections that should be severed to liberate the spirit? If one were a Gnostic, this might seem like good advice. From the Christian perspective, however, free from the ideology of gnostic spiritualism, we would conclude that, unless this connectedness to the material world is calling a person away from God rather than pointing him or her to his love, then denying the dying the comfort of the things and people they know and love during their final days and hours is needlessly cruel.

The dying do not, generally, think they can "take it with them"; they do not generally say, "Bring all my gold so I can stare at it," or "Assemble my family so I can command them." Most people simply want to be in the place they love among the people they love, for this can be a great consolation. On the Christian view, their embodied nature is not foreign to them. Their human connections are not a challenge to God or to their union with him; rather they can be, and often are, a foretaste of that union and deeper communion with God and with their loved ones that they will experience after death.

The Christian faith holds that death does not bring a final separation from all this. Rather, death and the prospect of resurrection promise a deeper connection with the things we love—a connection made by accomplishing the final release from owning and controlling them. They finally become "ours" only when we offer them, and ourselves, up to God as *his*. It is only then that we can receive them back not merely as objects we manipulate but as a pure gift of love. It is only then that we ourselves become the pure selfless gift of love we were meant to be.

On the Christian view, this life is a preparation for heaven not because this life is worthless and all that matters is heaven but because union with God requires a lifetime's effort of preparing oneself to love fully. As the poet T. S. Eliot says, "Humankind cannot bear very much reality." Nor perhaps can they stand the immensity of God's love and his gift of himself all at once, especially since the very grave restriction of our abilities to receive God's love and return it has been our fate since the Fall of mankind. Perhaps the full realization of that love in us can come only when we have been made ready for it. And only God knows when that is.

Grace Does Not Violate Nature but Perfects It

Properly understood, then, Christian teaching about the afterlife involves not an obliteration of the human person or a negation of this life but, rather, its fulfillment and glorification. A common motto in the Church since the time of Thomas Aquinas has been: "Grace does not violate nature but perfects it." Being freed from the slavery of sin and made "perfect" in love does not make us less human or less ourselves. It allows us to become more what we are meant to be—that person who, in our best moments, we have always wanted to be.

Not only do we retain our personal identity, but we also retain those deep connections of love that made life meaningful and that were our "foretaste" of our final union with the eternal Triune love. In that final union with the Triune God, we do not cease being engaged in meaningful activity. Rather, we continue more fully in the activities that Christian tradition understands make life most meaningful: namely, the love of God and neighbor.[48]

Nor does the Christian view of the afterlife cause us to diminish or undermine the importance of this life or any of the elements of true human flourishing. It should not cause us to devalue either the body or the passions of the human soul any more than it should cause us to devalue human reason. Our intellects are finally fully realized by coming into contact with the divine Truth. The Christian view of the afterlife would not cause us to propagate the notion that our being embodied is the source of sin and error. The problem is not in our bodies but in our lack of love or in loving wrongly. The promise of the resurrected life is not that we become less human but finally, at long last, fully human, as the wise, passionate, embodied instruments of love we were always meant to be, living the only kind of existence that could possibly make us truly and lastingly happy. Understood in this way, the Christian message of the afterlife is "good news" indeed.

---

[48] Cardinal Ratzinger, *Introduction to Christianity*, 234, puts it this way: "The Christian message is basically nothing else than the transmission of the testimony that love has managed to break through death here and thus has transformed fundamentally the situation of all of us." And again, in the revised edition of this same work, he says: "Either love is stronger than death, or it is not. If it has become so in him, then it became so precisely as love for others. This also means, it is true, that our own love, left to itself, is not sufficient to overcome death; taken in itself it would have to remain an unanswered cry. It means that only his love, coinciding with God's own power of life and love, can be the foundation of our immortality." *Introduction to Christianity*, rev. ed. (San Francisco: Ignatius Press, 2004), 306.

Whether we live or die, we are the Lord's.

Romans 14:8

Chapter 5

FACING DEATH

We have been attempting to show how the revelation of the risen Christ provides a context of meaningfulness for the next life. By entering the Triune communion of love with the risen Christ in the general resurrection of the body and thus entering into the communion of saints, we do not "lose ourselves" and our loved ones but become more ourselves, more who we were meant to be, more loving, and more able to give ourselves fully to those we love, wherever they may be in time or space.

We have insisted on a connection between the afterlife and this life. We have resisted notions of the afterlife that were at odds with the Christian notion of the human person, human flourishing, and the infinite value of human life. We have said that preparing for death in this life means living a life of selfless love for others; it means dying to self and living in Christ; it means entering into the Trinitarian communion of love as much as we can now because this is our human goal, which, admittedly, will be fully realized only in our final union with God.

But facing death is not merely an intellectual challenge; death is a challenge to one's very existence, and it leaves no part of us, physical, emotional, or spiritual, unaffected. There is a darkness that looms, and if ever there is a time when it becomes necessary to "walk by faith and not by sight," it is in the face of death. Understanding the promise of the resurrection of the body and eternal life can be valuable. It can help calm certain fears and provide needed hope. But we cannot allow the promise of eternal life revealed by Christ's victory over death to become merely a nice story we tell the dying to console them as we tuck them away out of sight. We must live our faith in Christ's victory as an ever-present reality, just as the risen Christ is an ever-present reality. We are called upon to live in the presence of the risen Christ and the communion of saints every day, especially when we are dying or when those we love face death.

How, then, can we live with death in truth and gain the wisdom we need about the limits of this life without being obsessed by death—without becoming morbid? The biblical witness envisions death as an enemy but as an enemy that has ultimately been overcome even though its dark influence still pervades the world. The way to live with it, then, would be not to ignore death but to live with it in union with the Body of Christ. And the most potent way we enter into that union with the risen Christ is in the Mass and in the sacraments of the Church. In the liturgy, we make ourselves one with his death and Resurrection.

Facing Death Liturgically as a Community

How does the Church, as the sacramental presence of the Body of Christ on earth, help its members prepare for death? One way, as we have just said, is to celebrate the Mass reverently and make sure that the crucified and risen Christ is at the center of the Church's life. But a healthy Christian community should also engage in other practices to help prepare people for death—prepare them, that is, without causing them to obsess over death or devalue the importance of life. Some years ago, a friend turned to me during the funeral ceremonies at a church and said: "They do death well here." And indeed, they had. Everything from the viewing of the body, the greeting of the family, and the praying of the Rosary, to the funeral itself, was held in the church. Everything was undertaken in view of the altar, the crucifix, and Christ present in the tabernacle. And there was a deep sense of prayer and respect.

Sadly, many Christian communities in the modern world have forgotten how to bury their dead. When a church does death well, there is a sense of remembrance without having to go through all the details of the person's life. There is a clear sense that the person belonged, that he or she was an important part of the community, that something is missing now, but that we carry on nonetheless because theirs was a life dedicated to this community. So when we carry on their good work (not merely getting on with our day) and dedicate *our* lives to the community he or she served, caring for his or her children and grandchildren, tending the garden, building up the institution in the same spirit with the same vision, then we remain united with them and they with us.

This sense of connection is fostered by (and ultimately must be grounded in) belief in the communion of saints. When those we love die, we do not simply lose them; we gain an even deeper communion with them in and through the union we have with them in Christ. Christ's Resurrection and the doctrine of the general resurrection reveal that our actions, experiences, and relationships are not simply lost or negated with death. They are glorified. Those united with Christ can be present as Christ is present; they are no longer limited by time and space.

But Christians believe in a resurrection of the *body*, not a freeing of a gnostic spirit imprisoned in a body. Orthodox Jews and Muslims share with Christians a belief in the resurrection of the body. This is why Orthodox Jews and Muslims insist on *burying their dead*. They do not burn the bodies and put the ashes in a box on a shelf and then say to visitors, "We haven't quite decided what to do with that yet." We have forgotten how to bury our dead. And it is not a trivial thing not to know how to bury the dead.

To restore its place in the community, the Church should once again take responsibility for burying the dead. All the messy, often distressing "business" that people have to go through to bury their loved ones when they are deep in grief should be handled by their church. What often now takes place in "funeral homes" should happen in the church: the wake, the Rosary, the greeting of the loved ones, probably even the potluck meal.

The church should provide the services and then provide the space for burial near the church. We should restore the practice, lost in the nineteenth century, of burying our dead in the "church-yard" or a nearby graveyard. People shouldn't have to travel miles on special occasions to visit the resting places of their loved ones in some potter's field somewhere; they should be able to pass by the visible symbol of their continued presence on the way to Mass so that the members of the community can be united with their predecessors continually in this way every day. They should find solace in the fact that they, too, one day will rest with those who came before them. Many people, young and old, visit cemeteries regularly, saying they find it spiritually comforting. It puts things into perspective, they say, and reminds them of what is truly important in life.

A healthy Christian community should be attending, accompanying, and supporting the dying as well as attending, accompanying, and supporting fellow members in all the other stages of human development as well: birth, baptism, marriage, and burials. It is not well known now, but there used to be entire liturgical rites and Gregorian chants that communities would use to accompany the dying and ease their passing from this life to the next. The presupposition was that the whole community of friends and family would accompany the dying person on their journey through death and beyond. No one, it was assumed, should have to die alone or die without the support of the community of believers who would care for both their bodily requirements and their emotional and spiritual needs.

Natural death is not the result of a technical failure. Death is a natural end of human life. Christ called upon his followers to understand that "unless a grain of wheat falls into the earth and dies, it remains alone; but if it dies, it bears much fruit" (John 12:24). Later St. Paul would write that "if we have died with Christ, we believe that we will also live with him" (Rom 6:8). This is still the faith of the Church, and the faithful deserve repeated expressions of that faith as they approach their final journey.

Christian churches should recover the liturgies and communal practices the Church used for centuries to comfort the dying and console their families before society decided that dying was primarily a "medical issue." We do violence to the human person when we fail to understand the importance and value of eating and talking with others, of laughter, appropriate touching, music, singing, and the loving presence of friends, family, and community. This is true during our healthy years, and it is no less true with the dying. No one should die alone in a hospital, surrounded by strangers, far from home.

Granted, it could happen that in certain circumstances a person might die alone. In those situations, God's grace alone is sufficient, just as when God says through the prophet Isaiah that even should a mother forget her child, "yet I will not forget you" (Isa 49:15). What about the sufferings and death of the poor, the weak, children, the widows and orphans? Does God not see them? The Scriptures insist repeatedly that he does. Even if and when we cannot be with them, he always is.

God's presence, on the view we have been proposing, is not, however, at odds with our presence. God can (and often does) work in and through the members of the Body of Christ. He does not need them—God works continually in manifold ways we do not perceive or understand—but this does not make our human works of love and care unnecessary. God does not need them, but there are times when we do. As is the case with the sacraments, we as embodied creatures need to feel the cleansing water of baptism and smell the oil of anointing. We need to hear the words of absolution from the priest speaking in the person of Christ. And we need to eat and taste the bread and wine that nourish us in body and soul. These are good things when they direct us to the love and forgiveness they signify. So, too, the presence of loved ones is a good thing when one is in need. They can communicate God in the sense of making present in a concrete way our communion with him. And so we do not say, "I don't know where God is, so I will sit with you." We say, "You know God is here. That is how and why we are here."

We are a communal people whose belief is in a communal heaven: union with the Father, Son, and Spirit in the communion of saints. We live as a "people," and we should be allowed to die among our people. A healthy Christian community would be certain to make present to the dying and to the community-at-large the continuing fellowship we enjoy with the communion of saints. Since "the Church" has always included the communion of saints within the Body of Christ, it makes sense to prepare for a higher participation in that communion by being present to it in an embodied way in a community now. The Christian community would do this, as we have said, liturgically and in the way its members take care of the dying and their family, from final sickness through to burial. The Christian community ought also to surround themselves with signs of the presence of the communion of saints, both with images of the saints and with the presence of the bodies of their forebears in the churchyard. By participating in this way in the death and resurrection of others, we are prepared to enter the communion of saints. By loving God and neighbor now and not making our lives and the lives of others a living hell, we are prepared for a heavenly existence where we will enter perfectly in union with Christ into that perfect communion of love shared between the Father, Son, and Spirit—a love from which "neither death nor life, nor angels, nor principalities, nor things present, nor things to come, nor powers, nor height nor depth, nor anything else in all creation, will be able to separate us" (Rom 8:38–39).

It will be impossible to restore proper respect for the dying until as a community, we once again instill the proper respect for the elderly. In such a community, aging would be seen not as a "disease" but as the natural and healthy course of life, which makes possible new birth and the passage of the generations. So, too, for example, a healthy Christian community would surround itself with symbols and memories of their beloved departed. Even the atheist poet Philip Larkin understood the importance of the presence of the classic churchyard with the graves of the dead. In his poem "Church Going," Larkin says of a church he visits that, although he cannot really understand what goes on inside, he recognizes that a church is a place "proper to grow wise in, / If only that so many dead lie round."[1] Seeing graves in the church-yard reminds those entering the church of the limits to their lives on this earth and of Christ's victory over death. The context also reminds the faithful of their debt to past generations and of what they owe to future generations.

Holistic Medical Care at the End of Life

An incarnational view of the human person, a view guided by the Scriptures that affirms the resurrection of the body, would resist imagining that we are merely preparing a *soul* for its "liberation" from the body and would look, rather, to the story recounted in all four Gospels of the woman who anointed Jesus with expensive oil. When some of those present are critical of this, Christ tells them to let her alone and then, in Matthew's account, says: "In pouring this ointment on my body, she has done it to prepare me for burial" (Matt 26:12; see also Mark 14:8 and John 12:7).[2]

This act of anointing combines in an interesting and import-ant way elements of the physical, emotional, and spiritual. The first and most obvious dimension is physical. Oil is soothing, and the Scripture accounts themselves emphasize the wonderful aroma that filled the room. But to understand the act as purely physical would be a mistake. In Luke's account, for example, the bystanders mistake the act of the woman, who remains unnamed, as something at least potentially sexual. "If this man were a prophet," they complain, "he would have known who and what sort of woman this is who is touching him, for she is a sinner" (Luke 7:39). What makes this woman's act especially significant

---

[1] Philip Larkin, "Church Going," *Blue Ridge Journal*, accessed on Dec. 12, 2021, https://www.blueridgejournal.com/poems/pl-church.htm.

[2] A similar story is recounted in Luke 7:36–50, but it does not contain Jesus's comment about preparing his body for burial.

is the love she shows. She may have been a prostitute before, but she is not now. And her act is in no way lascivious. It is extremely expensive oil, and the woman is not rich. Her act is an expression of her love of and devotion to the Lord.

The third element of this anointing is spiritual. We can see this woman's act as the precursor to the sacrament of the Anointing of the Sick ("Extreme Unction") that remains so invaluable to this day.[3] Anointing bodies for burial was a common tradition in the ancient world. Indeed, what some of the bystanders took to be something potentially sexual ("Jesus is getting a massage from a loose woman"), Christ understood more accurately to be an act of love and a spiritual act of preparation for death. "She has anointed my body beforehand for burying" (Mark 14:8). It is significant that she anoints his body "beforehand" because there would be no chance to anoint it afterward. According to the account in Mark's Gospel, "Mary Magdalene, and Mary the mother of James, and Salome," went to the tomb on the first day of the week, having brought spices, "so that they might go and anoint him" (16:1).[4] When they arrived, however, they found the stone rolled away and the tomb empty. An angel sitting beside the tomb announced to them the good news: "He has risen"—the first proclamation of this good news to anyone in the world.

---

[3] As Jesus says in Matthew's account: "Truly, I say to you, wherever this gospel is preached in the whole world, what she has done will be told in memory of her" (Matt 26:13).

[4] It has become traditional in the West to identify the woman who anointed Jesus's body with the expensive nard as Mary Magdalene. This would create an interesting parallel. Mary Magdalene anoints his body before his death because she will not be able to do so after his death even though she comes to the tomb to do just that. But the truth is, the woman who anoints Jesus is never named in Matthew, Mark, or Luke. And in John, the woman is identified as Mary, the sister of Martha.

There is great wisdom to be gained in this story and in the sacramental tradition of the Church. We ought to see in all the sacraments this invaluable combination of the physical (the bread and wine of the Eucharist; the water of baptism; the oil of anointing), the emotional (the love of parents, friends, God, and the Church), and the spiritual (the work of God's grace in and through the Holy Spirit). Indeed, I would suggest that a proper understanding and appreciation of the sacramental theology of the Church and the holistic, incarnational view of the human person that serves as its foundation—a union of body, emotions, reason, and spirit—can also serve as the best foundation for the proper medical care of the dying. Human persons at the end of life still need the warmth and intimacy of human presence and gentle human touch. It is good for them to hear music and prayer, to smell incense or other pleasing aromas, to converse with others in a fully human way. Affording little more than a short "goodbye" visit to people who are hooked up to machines is fundamentally inhumane to both the dying person and his or her loved ones.

So too, it would be a violation of this holistic view of the human person to allow a false "spiritualist" tendency to cause us to ignore the proper care of the body's needs, including (but not restricted to) the relief of pain. As the body breaks down in the process of dying, the person needs *more* attention to various bodily needs, not less. There will often be more help needed using the bathroom, more frequent washing, more attention to the kinds of food and drink that can either help or hurt.[5]

If human beings were nothing more than physical beings,

---

[5] It is said about Mother Theresa's sisters in Calcutta—and a friend of mine who visited confirms this—that they spend a lot of their time simply cleansing the bodies of the dying. Cleansing and praying seems to make up the bulk of their day.

medical care of the physical body alone would be sufficient. We have bodily needs, certainly, but we also are beings with reason and emotions. The breakdown of the body and the approach of death can bring about a great deal of confusion and a welter of emotions. *What am I to do now? How should I understand my role in life now?* Thus in any serious medical situation, we need to understand, as much as possible, what is happening to us, and we need others to help us deal with the truth intellectually, emotionally, and spiritually.

Palliative care doctors are increasingly finding, for example, that there is an important balance that must be struck when medicating for pain. Pain is one factor that affects the dying, but there are others. Too much pain medication can render patients incapable of understanding their situation or of having the kinds of conversations with their loved ones they need to have. The goal ought to be to preserve the dignity of the person, respecting the integrity of their bodies, and preserving as far as possible their ability to eat, excrete, converse with others, and sleep comfortably and with dignity. But persons at the end of life will also often need emotional and spiritual support as well as clear explanations of what is involved in their medical care.[6]

---

[6] Dr. Cecily Saunders, the founder of Saint Christopher's Hospice in Britain, used the term "total pain" to help correct the notion that pain is merely physical. A consideration of "total pain" will often include psychological, spiritual, and relational elements that affect the degree and character of pain a person has. So, for example, if a person is experiencing emotional turmoil due to interpersonal, psychological, economic, or spiritual reasons, pain medication will not work effectively. For this reason, the hospice movement has long insisted that the unit of care is not the patient but the whole family, especially as the members relate to the patient and the patient's condition. See D. A. E. Shephard, "The Principles and Practice of Palliative Care," *Canadian Medical Association Journal* 116 (5) (March 5, 1977): 522–26. This article was a "Conference Report" of a seminar at which the keynote speakers were

In many instances, emotional support is best tied to the spiritual. One notes, in this regard, psychologist Viktor Frankl's observations, in his book about the German concentration camps, about the importance of preserving some sense of meaning and purpose in one's life.[7] We are beings who live, as Viktor Frankl has said, "*sub specie aeternitatis*": within the context of eternity as a whole. To counter the toxic emotions that can arise at the end of life, it is important for many people that they be assisted in staying connected to what is truly important in life. The Christian view proposes that the meaningfulness and even the purpose of one's life does not end with death. Even if one has only recently been reconciled to friends or family, the promise of the communion of saints is that this reconciliation will continue to bear fruit both eternally and in the years to come. Hence the Christian message of love's victory over death can provide hope at a time when nothing else can. It is the hope that is beyond all merely natural hopes—the hope that only faith in God's love can provide.

Let us emphasize again the importance of the sacraments and the liturgy. People should not die alone. They should be allowed to die embraced by the love of the members of the Body of Christ, embraced, in other words, by the visible signs of love and God's grace that are the special gifts and responsibilities of the Church.

Dr. Elisabeth Kübler-Ross and Dr. Cicely Saunders. Although the article itself is somewhat dated, the notion of "total pain" has remained an important contribution to patient care in the years since.

[7] See Viktor Frankl, *Man's Search for Meaning*, trans. Ilse Lasch, et al. (Boston, MA: Beacon Press, 2006), 73: "Any attempt at fighting the camp's psychopathological influence on the prisoner by psychotherapeutic or psychohygienic methods had to aim at giving him inner strength by pointing out to him a future goal to which he could look forward. Instinctively some of the prisoners attempted to find one on their own. It is a peculiarity of man that he can only live by looking to the future—*sub specie aeternitatis*."

Hospitals can be wonderful for the things they can do and do well. But in a hospital, the likelihood of a person getting music, chant, a communal liturgy, or the simple presence of friends and family around-the-clock, is nearly nonexistent. Many cultures throughout history have developed practices to help "accompany" the dying both physically and spiritually. Only in the modern secularized world have we, it seems, forgotten how to deal with the dying.[8] We have allowed ourselves to be atomized by modern culture into little separate units. And when we do that, we have no power against the institutions that promise to care for us but in fact are increasingly threatening us. The medical community has

---

[8] In the early 1970s, psychologists Robert Kastenbaum and Ruth Aisenberg coined the term *death system* in their popular book *The Psychology of Death* to refer to a society's whole "orientation toward death": "the total range of thought, feeling, and behavior that is directly or indirectly related to death." See Robert Kastenbaum and Ruth Aisenberg, *The Psychology of Death* (New York: Springer, 1972), 191–92. In the latest edition of Kastenbaum's textbook, *Death, Society and Human Experience*, published in 2012, he defined a death system as "the interpersonal, sociophysical, and symbolic network through which an individual's relationship to mortality is mediated by society." See R. Kastenbaum, *Death, Society and Human Experience*, 11th ed. (New York: Routledge, 2012), 102. A society's death system includes ideas about the nature of the human person and how much control we are thought to have over nature; about life, health, sickness, dependence, independence, death, dying, and bereavement. It includes how we view practices in places such as hospitals, hospices, funeral homes, and churches. And finally, it includes the roles played by various persons: the patient, family members, physicians, funeral directors, and clergy. So, for example, a culture that puts emphasis on the uniqueness of the individual will have a different overall orientation and perspective on death and usually different practices than a culture that views individuals has having meaning as parts of the society as a whole. A healthy, integrated death system would enable individuals "to think, feel, and behave with respect to death in ways that they might consider to be effective and appropriate" (*Psychology of Death*, 193). In America, by contrast, argues Kastenbaum, because we as a society ignore the reality of death, many of us do not adequately prepare for it.

an invaluable role to play in treating the dying, but it is only a part, not the whole.

The Culture of Autonomy Gives Rise to Dying Alone

Modern society tends to frame end-of-life questions in terms of individual autonomy alone, not our communal connectedness. This is not entirely wrong since the individual who is dying is the one in need. And yet the Church teaches that, although we are distinctively individual, we are also communal and relational, and thus we ask questions that move beyond mere concern for ourselves. We might ask, for example, "What do I owe others?" and, "What do I owe God?" If my life is a gift entrusted to me by God, and I am called to be a faithful steward of that gift, then I might wish to ask, "What would faithful stewardship entail in these circumstances?" If the fundamental Christian commandments are to love God and love one's neighbor, and if we believe living in accord with these commandments is what makes our lives truly meaningful, then why would we suppose it would be any different in that culminating moment of our life we experience when we face death?

What if we were to think about death as something we undergo in relation to others and to God? Would this cause us, for example, to have conversations with our loved ones not merely about medical and legal directives but also about what is truly meaningful—about those things that have been at the heart of our relationship? We are embodied human persons in relations with others and with God, and in death, we undergo one of the most mysterious and frightening transitions of our lives. It would be a mistake to imagine that we can undergo this major transition without help—without the support of the community that has made possible all the other important moments of growth and transition in our lives. We need the help of God and his Church, and by "his Church," we mean all the members of the Body of Christ: pastors, but also friends, family, and physicians, nurses, and other caretakers who attend to our needs, whether of body, emotions, or spirit. And we mustn't forget the help of the saints and angels who continue to pray for us and who continue to be united to us in our darkest moments. If there is ever a time when the faithful need to hear and feel the sounds of the "divine choir"—all the members of the Body of Christ working together to guide the dying in their time of darkness—it is at the "hour of our death."

And yet, in the end, the only thing that can get us past the darkness is our faith in the victory over death won by Christ in his death, Resurrection, and Ascension to the Father. However beautiful the sound of that divine choir—the care of the medical staff, the prayers of friends, the presence of loved ones—in the end, the blessings of that choir depend upon the One who has in love composed the music they perform.

Dependency and the Dying

If we look upon dependency as a form of weakness, as a lesser mode of being, as being less than fully human, then we might conclude that people who are dying would best be left alone. "I don't want anyone to see me this way—weak and helpless" is a comment one often hears. It is understandable, but is it wise? What if the people you are talking about want to see you, no matter what you think you look like? Perhaps the vanity we all have needs finally to be put aside so we can have those conversations we need to have based on love and not on any attempt to manipulate or control or gain favor with others.

To accept one's life as a human life means accepting it as mortal and as largely dependent on others. To prepare for death, then, would mean precisely not habituating oneself to the illusion of control over life; it would mean accustoming oneself to accepting the gifts provided by others and by God. If we had not realized the value and importance of our dependence on others earlier in our life—if we had been taken in, as so many are, by the illusion of autonomous "control" and the value of individual will-to-power—then perhaps at least the process of aging and death would bring the truth home to us forcefully.

Death, on the Christian account, is not a fatal flaw due to a failure in our technology. It is rather the result of that fatal flaw called sin. Death is a cross we must bear if we are to arise from the slavery into which we have plunged ourselves. Aging is also not a fatal flaw that needs to be fixed or eradicated with modern science and technology. It is the normal, healthy development of the human person within human communities as well as an important stage in the transition to new life. In our fallen condition, aging is a related cross we are called upon to bear as we increasingly empty ourselves of our presumptions to have control over the world. It is a time for giving ourselves fully and finally to God's abundant care, acknowledging with St. Paul that God's grace is sufficient for us and that "power is made perfect in weakness" because it allows the power of Christ to dwell in us (see 2 Cor 12:9). Hence, T. S. Eliot's admonition in "East Coker":

> Do not let me hear
> Of the wisdom of old men, but rather of their folly,
> Their fear of fear and frenzy, their fear of possession,
> Of belonging to another, or to others, or to God.
> The only wisdom we can hope to acquire
> Is the wisdom of humility: humility is endless.[9]

---

[9] T. S. Eliot, "East Coker," section 2 of "Four Quartets: An Accurate Online

The aged and dying reveal to us in a dramatic way the truth of the human condition, a truth we are often uncomfortable admitting, especially to ourselves. Consider this: Why do the disabled and dependent make many of us feel so uncomfortable? Perhaps it is because we see ourselves in them. That is, we see ourselves in them in all the most embarrassing moments in our lives: when we dropped the tray of food in the school cafeteria and everyone laughed and applauded or when we didn't know the answer to the question we were sure everyone else knew. The elderly, the disabled, and the dying are we ourselves when we have been our weakest, our most vulnerable, and our most embarrassed. And no one wants to look or feel that way.

And yet their vulnerability makes them an especially important gift to us all. Remember St. Paul's admonition: "When I am weak, then I am strong" (2 Cor 12:10). So too with us. When we can look upon that weak, vulnerable, socially awkward part of ourselves and say, "Yes, this too, God loves; this too, God sanctifies," then we will finally be on the road to health and human flourishing, both as individuals and as a society.

Recent developments in evolutionary theory have made clear that the old social-Darwinist dictum "survival of the fittest" couldn't be more wrong. What has made *homo sapiens* a dominant species, many biologists are now convinced, has been precisely our ability to cooperate, to act altruistically, and to protect the weakest members of the tribe. A culture that wants to eradicate children with Down syndrome, those with developmental disabilities or brain injuries, and all people who aren't strong and vibrant and productive is to be feared, not fostered—not only because each of us will someday be weak but also because the purveyors of such a

---

Text," accessed Oct. 1, 2021, http://www.davidgorman.com/4quartets/2-coker.htm.

culture are trying to kill what is most human in us. Caring for and living with the weak, those with disabilities, and the dying humanizes us: it teaches us to love selflessly, the way Christ loves us. And it teaches us to love ourselves, even those parts of ourselves we would prefer others not see, those parts that we ourselves would rather not look at.

People who are disabled or dying need our help, but we need them even more. They make us human. God's greatest gift to creatures puffed up with silly self-importance is this gift of humility. T. S. Eliot is right: "The only wisdom we can hope to acquire is the wisdom of humility: humility is endless."

Death and Sorrow

Another question we face is this: If the Christian promise of the afterlife is so wonderful, why are many Christians still filled with fear and sorrow when they face death, either their own or that of a loved one? Does this show a lack of faith? What should be our response at the death of a loved one?

Although profound sorrow and weeping are common reactions to the loss of a loved one, many have concluded that sorrow of this sort is foolish and unbecoming and shows a lack of understanding. In the *Phaedo*, Socrates berates his friends for weeping at the prospect of his coming execution, saying: "What conduct is this, you strange men! I sent the women away chiefly for this very reason, that they might not behave in this absurd way. . . . Keep quiet and be brave." Phaedo says, "Then we were ashamed and controlled our tears."[10]

In a similar vein, the Stoic philosopher Epictetus wrote, "It is

---

[10] *Phaedo* 117d–e; in *Plato in Twelve Volumes*, vol. 1, trans. Harold North Fowler, Loeb Classical Library (Cambridge, MA: Harvard University Press; London, William Heinemann Ltd. 1966), http://www.perseus.tufts.edu/

silly to want your children and your wife and your friends to live forever, for that means that you want what is not in your control to be in your control, and what is not your own to be yours."[11] What you cannot control, you should not be anxious about because to let yourself be anxious or feel deep sorrow at the death of someone you love would be to make yourself weak and dependent on others, which would be ignoble, on the Stoic view. The Stoic concludes from this fact that we should not be too disturbed at their death.

"When anything, from the meanest thing upwards, is attractive or serviceable or an object of affection," says Epictetus, "remember always to say to yourself, 'What is its nature?' If you are fond of a jug, say you are fond of a jug; then you will not be disturbed if it be broken. If you kiss your child or your wife, say to yourself that you are kissing a human being, for then if death strikes it you will not be disturbed."[12]

Elsewhere in the same work, Epictetus says that even in the face of death, one ought to maintain one's poise and equanimity: "When you see a man shedding tears in sorrow for a child abroad or dead, or for loss of property, beware that you are not carried away by the impression that it is outward ills that make him miserable. Keep this thought by you: 'What distresses him is not the event, for that does not distress another, but his judgement on the event.' Therefore do not hesitate to sympathize with him so far as words go, and if it so chance, even to groan with him; but

---

hopper/text?doc=Perseus%3Atext%3A1999.01.0170%3Atext%3DPhaedo%3Asection%3D117d.

[11] Epictetus, *Handbook*, vol. 1, trans. W. A. Oldfather. Loeb Classical Library, vol. 131 (New York: Putnam, 1926), sec. 14. Also available online: http://www.perseus.tufts.edu/hopper/text?doc=Perseus%3Atext%3A1999.01.0236%3Atext%3Denc%3Achapter%3D14.

[12] Ibid., sec. 3.

take heed that you do not also groan in your inner being."[13] When someone you love dies, you can feel *some* sorrow but not too much sorrow—not to the extent that sorrow over their death would overwhelm your ability to reason and manage your affairs.

This sort of advice is not uncommon in hospitals and prisoner-of-war camps. People often say that you cannot allow yourself to get too connected to those who might die because if you do, you will get hurt and not be able to function if and when they die. But "not being able to function" is one thing; "not getting hurt" is another. There may be times when a person dies and those left behind need to keep their wits about them because important decisions remain to be made. But the question is whether stifling one's emotions in the manner the Stoics advise is the necessary precursor to making wise decisions. Sometimes it might be. But it is also not likely to be psychologically healthy in the long run if that person cannot find a way of grieving the loss.[14]

Although the Stoic would see deep grief and inner turmoil over the death of a friend or loved one as "foolish" and a sign of "weakness," a Christian need not. Christians are called upon by their faith to see their embodied existence as meaningful and

---

[13] Ibid., sec. 16.

[14] Jonathan Shay, a psychiatrist who had a great deal of clinical experience with posttraumatic stress disorder in Vietnam veterans, reports in *Achilles in Vietnam: Combat Trauma and the Undoing of Character* (New York: Simon & Schuster, 1995) that one of the biggest causes of trauma among U.S. soldiers in Vietnam was that they were not allowed to grieve the loss of a comrade-in-arms. The body of the dead soldier would often enough be bagged up and shipped off to the States before they even got back to base. He notes that, by contrast, heroes in the *Iliad* were allowed to grieve. Regular truces were called so that the dead could be brought off the battlefield and proper funeral rites could be performed. Soldiers in Vietnam were told to "suck it up," keep their focus, and use their rage to kill more of the enemy. This, suggests Shay, was emotionally and psychologically disastrous.

valuable; it is not something to be shed like a worn-out overcoat, and neither are our relationships.

As we noted above, death is pictured in the Scriptures as the enemy. Christ does not go to his death with calm equanimity. He sweats drops of blood. It is with good reason that Christians call his Crucifixion "the Passion." He is not a model of Stoic *apatheia*. Furthermore, far from being scandalized by Christ's Passion, Christians enter into it weekly or even daily when they celebrate his sacrifice in the Eucharist and in another way when they make "the Way of the Cross." Whenever we reflect deeply on Christ's Passion, we weep at the foot of the Cross with Mary Magdalene and Mary, the Mother of God. The Church's continuing witness to the faith of these women amidst their soul-rending sorrow tells us that even a deep and profound faith in Christ does not keep us from weeping at the foot of the Cross or weeping at the death of a loved one. Jesus himself wept at the tomb of Lazarus (John 11:35) even though he knew he would raise him from the dead.

There is something worth weeping over when we encounter the death of someone we know and love. We weep that, for us now in our fallen world, death of this sort—the blinding rending of the physical body and the soul—precedes our resurrection and final union with God. The Scriptures indicate it was not meant to be this way. It may well have been the case that, before the Fall, Adam and Eve would in due course have been "taken up" into a deeper union and communion with God but without the same decay and struggle that accompanies death now, although this is merely speculation. Without the Fall, perhaps that "assumption" to God's bosom would have been more like Mary's Assumption into heaven or the prophet Elijah's; we don't know. But death as we experience it now was clearly the result of the Fall, and while it prepares us for and makes way for good things—indeed, the very best things—death in and of itself is hard; it is a cross we must bear.

During the course of a meaningful life, a person will feel the full range of emotions. There are ways in which we are called to discipline and direct those emotions, but on the Christian view of human nature and human flourishing, to stifle them when they are a natural reaction to the reality we are experiencing would be like deadening one's sense of touch or stuffing cotton in one's ears. Without emotions, or when the emotional centers in the brain are damaged, people cease to be able to understand the world fully or function in it properly, especially in their relations with other people.

Sorrow is the natural reaction to loss and to evil. Letting sorrow diminish is not a sign that you are "letting go" or that you are letting the person "die" in your heart. On the Christian account of death and resurrection, one can "let go" of constantly thinking about one's deceased loved ones the way that one can let go of constantly thinking about them during life. I don't have to be thinking about my wife to know that I love her and she loves me and that we are bonded together sacramentally. Because we Christians believe that our loved ones are alive in Christ, we know in faith that we need not be constantly thinking about a dead mother or father or son or daughter to know that we are still connected to them in love. We didn't spend every moment thinking about each other when they were alive. We could be active in our own lives because we were confident of each other's love. Precisely because Christians can be confident that death cannot separate them from this love, they can continue to be active even after the death of a loved one.

Thus, a fuller understanding of the Christian teaching about death and the afterlife can help us recognize why sorrow and fear are perfectly Christian responses to death and why their presence need not be taken as showing a lack of faith in Christ's victory over death and the promise of eternal life.

Facing Death While Affirming the Goodness of Life

As we have seen, in the Scriptures, death is not portrayed as a desirable reality; it is dark, frightening, and it at least seems to threaten our very existence. One lesson we might take from the Christian understanding of death and the afterlife we examined above is that death will always, in one sense at least, seem "unnatural." We often perceive it this way, as something not quite right, and we are not entirely wrong in this. Many of us are like Cicero, believing in some sort of immortality of the human person but not quite knowing how or why this might be possible. So, too, on the Christian view, death and decay are in one sense unnatural; they are a result of our fallen state; they are not part of what God in the Genesis creation account called "very good." They are a consequence of sin and made necessary by sin because to eat of the Tree of Life while still mired in sin would be not eternal happiness but everlasting pain, frustration, and suffering.

Biblical revelation and the Church's teaching can help us make sense of why we sometimes think of death as somehow "unnatural"—not the way things were "meant to be." It is in this light that we can understand and appreciate the emotion behind lines like these from Robert Frost's poem "Reluctance."

Ah, when to the heart of man
Was it ever less than a treason
To go with the drift of things,
To yield with a grace to reason,

And bow and accept the end
Of a love or a season?[15]

Or lines like these from the poet Dylan Thomas, who wrote them to his dying father:

Do not go gentle into that good night.
Rage, rage against the dying of the light.[16]

Both poets have captured something authentic in human experience. Christian teaching does not negate these expressions of human attachment to life; rather, it helps us understand this attachment to life more fully and put that desire in its proper context.

The Christian teaching about the afterlife, properly understood, should in no way cause us to diminish the value of this life. Quite the contrary. We should value it as a precious gift of love from God, and as such, it is in an important sense not "ours" to do with as we wish. We did not give ourselves life, so we do not have the authority to take it. To throw it away or risk it needlessly would be unworthy of the gift and the Giver.

Life is a good thing, a "very good" thing, as the Book of Genesis assures us. More life without earthly death is not necessarily a good thing. In fact, it can be a very bad thing, both for the individual and for the community as a whole. We yearn for something that preserves our sense that the spark of spirit and

---

15 Robert Frost, "Reluctance," Poetry Foundation, accessed Oct. 1, 2021, https://www.poetryfoundation.org/poems/53085/reluctance.

16 Dylan Thomas, "Do Not Go Gentle into That Good Night," from The Poems of Dylan Thomas, ed. John Goodby (New York: New Directions Publishing Company, 2017), https://poets.org/poem/do-not-go-gentle-good-night.

life cannot be snuffed out but that also allows openness to the coming of future generations; a view that both connects us meaningfully to the generations that came before us and helps us to look forward lovingly to the generations that will come after us, without somehow making us cease to care about living in the present. The Christian promise of death and resurrection reveals that, in Christ, we can preserve both: the individual spark of life that we sense somehow should not be touched by death and a world that remains continually open to new life.

Christians are called upon to believe that ultimately everything—even the evil we do and the death we have brought upon ourselves—can be reconciled within the divine order of God's loving Providence. There are certainly times in life when we do not see that divine order. It is especially during these times especially when we must "walk by faith, not by sight" (2 Cor 5:7). Why is this necessary? For one thing, we are not God, and we do not have the vastness of intellect to comprehend the Creator's providential plan for his creation—a plan so vast it includes every galaxy and black hole, every atom and quark, every sparrow falling to the ground (Matt 10:29) and every hair on each person's head (Matt 10:30; Luke 12:7). Often, we are simply too close to things to see the overall pattern properly—just as when you are so close to a painting you can see the brushstrokes but not the whole picture. My faith that there is a larger picture even when I cannot see the whole comes from my faith in the Artist. If I have only a torn piece of a painting, I might be able to see only a section that is mostly black. But if I know the painter was Rembrandt and I know how effective Rembrandt was with darkness and light, I trust the painter knew what he was doing, and I search eagerly for the rest of the painting. So too, we trust the Divine Artist rather than merely the look of the colors we happen to see at the moment.

We are far from knowing all the details of that divine Plan, but he has made known to us, in salvation history and in the Scriptures, the basic outline that we need to live our lives. That outline provides for us not a detailed plan for each of our lives but a promise—a covenantal promise like a marriage covenant. God promises to remain faithful in love with a love that is life-giving. We are not forced to say "yes" to that love, but if we do, we can enjoy the life surpassing life, the Trinitarian communion of love into which he is inviting us. Being steward of the gift of my life, I must use it, as I am called upon to use all my gifts, wisely and in loving care for others, according to the divine order, as far as I can discern this order from both reason and revelation.

"Born Again"

Perhaps the only thing to which we can compare this "blind" transition from this life to the next is our birth. If we had been conscious in the womb, as we are now, and if someone had asked us whether we wanted to leave our warm, comfortable fluid "bath" in the womb—to be disconnected from the source of our nourishment and our very blood supply—in order to enter into some "other world" with a kind of life we had never known, I imagine most of us would have said "No, thank you; I prefer to stay right here."

It is one of the great gifts of our lives that, although we remember many things, even some things from our early youth, none of us remembers our birth. If we did, I imagine most of us would have experienced it as a kind of death. And yet, if we had refused to experience this "death" to our earlier life in the womb, we would never have entered this world, with all its expanded possibilities for life—things we could scarcely have imagined in the womb. Even if someone had tried to explain to us in the womb what this wonderful "life" would include after this seeming "death" of our birth, what could they have told us that would have made any sense?

"Will I be able to swim comfortably in fluid as I do now?" we might have asked.

"You will be able to swim, yes, even better than you do now, but you will also be able to walk, run, and even in some cases fly, although flying takes some ingenuity."

"What are walking, running, and flying? I only know swimming," you might then have asked.

What could your parents have replied, other than: "You will have to wait and see. Just have some faith. We love you."

"Will I be fed directly into my stomach the way I am now?"

"You will be fed in even better ways, and you will also able to feed yourself with all sorts of delicious and interesting foods."

"But what else would anyone need other than mother's milk?"

"You need a lot more if you are to keep growing."

"Why do I need to keep growing?"

"You will have to wait and see. Just have some faith. We love you."

"Will I still be warm and loved?"

"You will be warm *and* cold, but both can be wonderful. You will be loved in new and wonderful ways, and you will be able to love others in return in a way you cannot do now. At some point, you will grow enough that you will be able to love in such a way that you can even make another being like you."

"When will that happen? Will it be in a few months—the total length of time I've experienced?"

"I can't tell you that. You don't understand enough about time and free choices to be able to grasp why I cannot give you a definite answer. You will have to wait and see."

"You say that this emptying out of my life right now might seem like death, and it is likely to be painful and frightening. But you say that I have to 'die' to this life to live in this new world. Why are things done this way? Why can't I just spring right out my mother's head, like Athena from the head of Zeus?"

"I don't know why. I only know that it happens this way and that you are called to have faith that the love that created you will give birth to you. Oh, and by the way, those muffled voices you hear? You will be able to understand what they are saying and, in time, even be able to speak back to them. Just have some faith. We love you."

Obviously, we cannot have this conversation with babies in the womb, nor for a good while after their birth, precisely because they cannot understand words. There is no way we can actually communicate to them the reality of what lies ahead for them. Babies simply receive their life in faith and love. They have no other choice, just as in death we have no choice. Perhaps we might see our first birth, then, as a symbol of what our entire lives must be, including that birth we call death.

This analogy between our birth and our death has limitations, of course. Some stories depict death as coming into a white waiting room with lots of bright light, an image that makes sense, given modern operating rooms. But I do not, through my analogy with birth, want to communicate the image that death is like birth *in the operating room*, something that in the modern world can suggest a sterile environment and an impersonal reception. I want with this analogy to emphasize the difference between the comfortable but limited life humans enjoy in the womb and the more wide-open and fruitful life we can enjoy after birth with friends and family.

We recognize the fear that would certainly envelop us if we

were entirely self-aware at birth as we faced the transition from the first state in the womb to the second state outside the womb that would be largely invisible and unknown to us. In both sorts of birth, there would be darkness, fear, and pain. Under the tutelage of the faith, we might come to understand that the pain of both births has a great deal to do with sin and mankind's fallen condition. By this, I do not mean merely that we are beset by the consequences of original sin, although we are. When we attach ourselves to power, wealth, status, and vanity, we tie ourselves to things that cannot last. And if nothing else in our life has stripped us of these illusory goods, death certainly will.

When we sin, we alienate ourselves from God, from others, and finally from our true selves, the self that understands it cannot find its being or goodness apart from God, the Source of all Being and Goodness. If we have alienated ourselves from God and our neighbor during our lives, we have trained ourselves to reject heaven because heaven, on the Christian view, is union with God and the communion of saints. A "no" to God's love and forgiveness is a "no" to union with him. God does not force us to love him; he offers, but we can say no. But saying no to the offer of selfless love is like saying no to the sunshine and healthy food; it is like saying no to the Source of all true Life. One can make that choice, but the person who makes it shouldn't be surprised if he finds himself starving in a lifeless darkness.

Purgatory and Prayers for the Dead

I have said very little thus far about purgatory—or hell. I will have more to say about "final judgment" in the next chapter. But in the meantime, a word is in order about purgatory and the practice of prayers for the dead. Not all Christians believe in purgatory, and I have not thought it necessary to expend the space and effort to defend the doctrine here. Rather, I have attempted to write a book that, although obviously written by a Catholic and from a Catholic perspective, any of our Protestant brethren might still find edifying and helpful. As I hope I have made clear: we all agree that Christ is the center. Our victory over sin and death is won by Christ and by Christ alone. Whatever sacraments, whatever liturgical practices the Church engages in, all are meant to point us toward Christ's death and Resurrection; they help us to enter more fully into union with him—and in him, and "because God's love has been poured into our hearts through the Holy Spirit who has been given to us" (Rom 5:5), we enter more fully into communion with the Father.

During the earthly lives of our loved ones, we frequently ask them to pray for us, and we know they will. And this is important. Their prayers do not *replace* God's grace; they are further expressions of it. God's love does not negate the love of others, nor does the love of our parents and friends negate the love of God. Christians who understand their faith know that God's love is expressed to us in many ways: spiritual graces, the gifts of the Holy Spirit, the beauties of creation, and, often the most wonderful of all, the love of others. We pray for them, and they pray for us. It is one of the ways in which the love we share animates the various members of the Body of Christ. They continue in heaven the activities that established them as members of the Body of Christ on earth: love for God and neighbor and prayer. If we were to pray to the saints the way we pray to Christ—or to put this another way, if we were to pray to the saints as having a power and presence *separate or apart from Christ*—this would be an error on both the Catholic and the Protestant understanding of the faith.[17]

---

[17] There is, of course, at least this one difference between our "beloved dead" and

If, as we said above and as St. Paul tells us, "neither death nor life, nor angels, nor principalities, nor things present, nor things to come, nor powers, nor height, nor depth, nor anything else in all creation, will be able to separate us from the love of God in Christ Jesus our Lord" (Rom 8:38–39), then nothing can really separate us from those to whom we are united in Christ. They continue to pray for us, and we continue to pray for them.

"Why would we need to continue to pray for them?" one of our Protestant brethren might ask, "if they are in heaven." I might suggest that this comment presumes a too-juridical notion of prayer. We pray for our loved ones not only so that they can "pass the bar" of heaven or so that they can get the things they want. Sometimes we give things to our loved ones because they need them, but other times we give them gifts simply as a sign and expression of our love. So, too, sometimes we pray for people because we know they need something, but sometimes we pray for them simply as an expression of love.

And yet, some of those who have died may still be in need of our prayers. All Christians, Protestant and Catholic both, believe that Christ's sacrifice has wiped away the guilt of our sins. But many Protestants have come to accept the fact that many of us still need time for this "justification in Christ" to be made fully present and active in our lives. This is not a question of whether Christ has done something—he has. The question is whether or to what extent I have allowed myself to be possessed by him, to be incorporated into that victory over sin and death. One way of referring

---

the saints. Since we cannot know the full truth about the souls of any other person, we cannot know whether they enjoy the beatific vision or not. Given what we know of those we know and love, we can sometimes make a reasonable guess, but it is still just a guess. When we pray to the saints, however, we pray to those the Church has recognized as enjoying the beatific vision.

to the process of moral and spiritual development whereby we allow ourselves to be changed by the transforming love of Christ is "sanctification." Those who believe in purgatory believe that this process of sanctification may and often does continue after death. Our prayers for the dead would then be an aid to that process, much as we prayed for their continuing sanctification and their deeper incorporation into the Body of Christ during their lives.

So, what shall we say about prayers for the dead? First, it might help to recall that there is a long tradition of this practice going back to the earliest Church. Second, it would be wrong to imagine that, in praying for the dead, we are winning their salvation, just as we err if we imagine that we, in praying for our loved ones who are alive, buy God's favor with our prayers so that he might repay us with things we want. This pagan notion of sacrifice to the gods, Judaism and Christianity did away with. We do not pray in order to earn God's love. God's love comes first. Our prayers are a participation in God's love; they are made possible by God's love.

Finally, we believe that the love and the prayers we have shared with those we have loved during this life do not end with their death. Since those we love remain alive in Christ, we can ask for their prayers, and we can still pray for them.

We pray for them after death as we did during life. If they are in need of the sanctification of purgatory, then we pray that our love will help nourish and strengthen them for that journey. If they still have a need, whatever that need, we pray that God provides it, believing that they will hear this prayer because it is our participation on earth in the glorified Body of Christ. If they are beyond all need, then our prayers are a simple expression of our continuing love. When we pray, we often do not know what those for whom we are praying really need. We just pray, knowing that God will sort it all out. So, too, after death. Is the person for whom we are praying in purgatory? Is he or she beyond all need—or perhaps beyond all hope? We don't know. What we know, because this is what we have been told, is that when it seems as though there is nothing we can do, we should have faith and pray, and let God do the rest.

Being asked by the Pharisees when the kingdom of God was coming, [Jesus] answered them, "The kingdom of God is not coming with signs to be observed; nor will they say, 'Behold, here it is,' or 'There!' for behold, the kingdom of God is in your midst."

Luke 17:21

If it is by the Spirit of God that I cast out demons, then the kingdom of God has come upon you.

Matthew 12:28

But of that day or hour no one knows, not even the angels in heaven, nor the Son, but the Father only. . . . Watch, therefore, for you do not know on what day your Lord is coming.

Matthew 24:36, 42

Again the high priest asked him, "Are you the Christ, the Son of the Blessed?" And Jesus said, "I am; and you will see the Son of man sitting at the right hand of Power, and coming with the clouds of heaven."

Mark 14:61–62

With the Lord a day is as a thousand years, and a thousand years as one day.

2 Peter 3:8

Chapter 6

CHRIST AND THE END OF HISTORY

In November of 1271, on the first Sunday of Advent, Thomas Aquinas delivered a sermon to the masters and students at the University of Paris in which he began with Matthew 21:5; in that verse, Matthew paraphrases a passage from Zechariah 9:9 to refer to Christ's entry into Jerusalem on Palm Sunday: "Behold, your king comes to you, . . . humble and riding on a donkey." Although it is customarily read during the Palm Sunday services, St. Thomas used the verse in this Advent sermon to introduce the topic of Christ's "coming"—his "advent."

Following a long tradition within the Church, St. Thomas distinguishes four different "advents"—four ways in which Christ comes to us. The first is his advent in the flesh in the Incarnation; the second is the advent by which he comes into our souls; the third is the advent in which he comes at the death of the just; and the fourth is the advent in which he comes at the end of time in the final judgment.[1] To this list, we might add his advent to the disciples when he came to them after his Resurrection from the dead and his advent every time the Eucharist is celebrated. Thomas would certainly have been willing to add these to the list—he wrote about the importance of the Eucharist and Christ's Resurrection brilliantly and often—but this sermon was a sermon for Advent, not Easter, and it was a widely accepted rule of preaching at the time that one should keep lists to no more than three or four items. Any more and most people have troubling remembering them. But we should recognize that all of these advents are connected; they are all part of a single providential plan of salvation.

Thus far, we have been focusing our attention on Christ's Resurrection appearances and what they reveal to us about the afterlife since Christ is said to be "the first fruits" of what we, too, will enjoy in the general resurrection. We have also mentioned the importance of Christ's continuing presence in the Eucharist. But these advents are made possible by Christ's Incarnation: his actual coming in the flesh and dwelling with his disciples. I mention here St. Thomas's sermon and its four advents simply to remind us that there was an important advent before Christ's Resurrection, and there is an important advent still to come at the end of time. During the liturgical season of Advent, we can get so caught up thinking about the coming of Christmas that we forget Advent is also meant to direct our attention forward to the Second Coming of Christ at the end of time. It is for this reason that many of the

---

[1] For an English translation, see Sermon 5, "*Ecce Rex Tuus*" in *Thomas Aquinas: The Academic Sermons*, trans. Mark-Robin Hoogland (Washington, DC: The Catholic University of America Press, 2010), 62–78, and my extended discussion of it in Randall Smith, *Reading the Sermons of Aquinas: A Beginner's Guide* (Steubenville, OH: Emmaus Academic, 2016), 4–11, and my analytical outline of it in the Appendix, 240–43.

readings during Advent are taken from the Book of Revelation or involve other readings about "the end times."

Reflections on "the end times" have, at certain times in history, become deranged and dangerous. The fact that Christ himself insisted that "of that day and hour no one knows" (Matt 24:36; see also Mark 13:32; Acts 1:7) has not kept people since then from speculating about when it will come and what it will be like. We need to reflect on the "end times" in the present work, not in order to try to figure out when they will be or what they will be like, but in order to understand the relationship between what St. Thomas Aquinas described in his sermon as "the advent in which Christ comes at the death of the just" and "the advent in which He comes at the end of time in the final judgment." What we will find is that there is one sense in which we are already in "the final times" and yet another sense in which the full realization of what has been promised is still to come.

The End Times and the Old Testament Prophets

Discussions about the "end times" often look back to a famous passage in chapter 12 in the Book of Daniel in which the prophet speaks about "the end of days," when "[m]any of those who sleep in the dust of the earth shall awake, some to everlasting life, and some to shame and everlasting contempt. And those who are wise shall shine like the brightness of the firmament, and those who turn many to righteousness, like the stars for ever and ever" (Dan 12:1–4). At the culmination of the chapter, however, Daniel hears the angel who has delivered this message admonish him, saying: "But go your way till the end; and you shall rest, and shall stand in your allotted place at the end of the days" (v. 13). There is present here, therefore, an interesting combination of urgency (something crucial is coming!) and patience (go your way and rest).

It is also in the Book of Daniel where we find the prophecy about "one like a son of man" coming "with the clouds of heaven" to whom is given "dominion and glory and kingdom, that all peoples, nations, and languages should serve him," and whose "dominion is an everlasting dominion, which shall not pass away, and his kingdom one that shall not be destroyed" (7:13–14). This title, "Son of man," is the one Jesus most commonly uses when referring to himself. And he is clearly referring Daniel's prophecy to himself when, for example, in the Gospel of Matthew, he tells his disciples: "Watch therefore, for you do not know on what day your Lord is coming. . . . Therefore you also must be ready; for the Son of man is coming at an hour you do not expect" (24:42–44). And again, when Jesus is asked by the high priest in the Gospel of Mark, "Are you the Christ, the Son of the Blessed?" He replies: "I am; and you will see the Son of man sitting at the right hand of Power, and coming with the clouds of heaven" (14:61–62).

Many Old Testament prophets speak of "the day of the Lord" that will be "a day of tumult and trampling and confusion" (Isa 22:5), when the nations will be summoned to judgment. Zephaniah prophesies that God has said he "will utterly sweep away everything from the face of the earth" (1:2) and warns his readers: "Be silent before the Lord GOD! For the day of the LORD is at hand" (1:7). So, too, the prophet Malachi warns:

> For behold, the day comes, burning like an oven, when all the arrogant and all evildoers will be stubble; the day that comes shall burn them up, says the LORD of hosts, so that it will leave them neither root nor branch. But for you who fear my name the sun of righteousness shall rise, with

healing in its wings. You shall go forth leaping like calves from the stall. And you shall tread down the wicked, for they will be ashes under the soles of your feet, on the day when I act, says the LORD of hosts. (4:1–3)[2]

Often, the promise of judgment is accompanied by a consoling message that God will save Israel and Judah from the coming destruction. Isaiah warns:

> For the LORD of hosts has a day
>   against all that is proud and lofty,
>   against all that is lifted up and high. (2:12)

But earlier in the same chapter, we find this consoling promise, which is often read during Advent:

> It shall come to pass in the latter days
>   that the mountain of the house of the LORD
>   shall be established as the highest of the mountains,
>   and shall be raised above the hills. (v. 2)

In Jeremiah 30, we find a similar promise about this "day" or the "days" that are coming.

> For behold, days are coming, says the LORD, when I will restore the fortunes of my people, Israel and Judah, says the LORD, and I will bring them back to the land which I gave to their fathers, and they shall take possession

---

2 For other uses of the phrase "the day of the LORD" in the Old Testament, see also Isa 13:6, 9; Ezek 13:5; Joel 1:15, 2:1, 11, 3:14; Amos 5:18, 20; Obad:15; Zeph 1:7, 14; Zech 14:1.

of it. . . . And it shall come to pass in that day, says the
LORD of hosts, that I will break the yoke from off their
neck, and I will burst their bonds, and strangers shall no
more make servants of them. (30:3, 8)

And yet, the prophet warns that the people must also suffer
through tribulation.

Alas! that day is so great
  there is none like it;
it is a time of distress for Jacob;
  yet he shall be saved out of it. (v. 7)

The prophet Amos warns his fellow Jewish countrymen that they
should attend more closely to their own sins and not presume that
judgment is for others only. Since the "day of the Lord" is a day of
judgment against the unjust and idolaters, they should not assume
that they will remain unscathed. "Woe to you who desire the day
of the LORD!" he warns them. "Why would you have the day of
the LORD? It is darkness, and not light" (5:18). Their external sacrifices mean nothing to God, he tells them, without a change of
heart. Rather, "let justice roll down like waters," he tells them, "and
righteousness like an ever-flowing stream" (v. 24), or they, too, will
be consumed by the fires of judgment. So, too, Zephaniah warns
that "the great day of the LORD" will be a "day of wrath," a "day of
distress and anguish, a day of ruin and devastation, a day of darkness and gloom, a day of clouds and thick darkness" (1:14–15).

Many of these prophetic warnings seem to point forward to a
day sometime in the distant future after many troubles and tribulations. Others suggest that the day of the Lord is soon. "Wail, for
the day of the LORD is near!" says Isaiah (Isa 13:6). "For the day is

near, the day of the LORD is near," says Ezekiel (30:3). The day of the LORD "is coming," says Joel; "it is near" (2:1). "Be silent before the Lord GOD!" warns Zephaniah. "For the day of the LORD is at hand" (1:7).

The End Times in the New Testament

The New Testament authors develop this prophetic tradition about the "day of the Lord" in various ways, but all of them associate the "day of the Lord" with Jesus. Paul writes to the Corinthians, for example, that they should discipline a man living with his father's wife, "that his spirit may be saved in the day of the Lord Jesus" (1 Cor 5:5)—a warning that seems quite clearly to refer to the coming judgment at the end of time. So, too, in a subsequent letter to the Corinthians, Paul writes, saying that he hopes "that you can be proud of us as we can be of you, on the day of the Lord Jesus" (2 Cor 1: 14). In Philippians 1:6, Paul assures the Philippians that "he who began a good work in you will bring it to completion at the day of Jesus Christ." And in Philippians 2:16, he says that he has held fast "to the word of life, so that in the day of Christ," he may be proud that he did not labor in vain. In the Gospel of Luke, Jesus uses his preferred title for himself and speaks of "the day when the Son of man is revealed" (Luke 17:30).

In many places, this "day" of the Lord Jesus Christ, "the day when the Son of man is revealed," is associated with the promise of Christ's return. In the Acts of the Apostles, for example, after Christ ascends and disappears from the Apostles' sight, two men in white robes standing nearby say to them: "Men of Galilee, why do you stand looking into heaven? This Jesus, who was taken up from you into heaven, will come in the same way as you saw him go into heaven" (1:11).

There are several Greek terms commonly used to describe this

Second Coming of Christ. One is *parousia* (*adventus* in Latin). So, for example, in 1 Corinthians 15:22–23, Paul says that, "as in Adam all die, so also in Christ shall all be made alive. But each in his own order: Christ the first fruits, then at his coming [*parousiai*] those who belong to Christ." New Testament writers also use the term "epiphany" (*epiphaneia*) to describe his future coming. In 1 Timothy 6:14, Paul writes, "I charge you to keep the commandment unstained and free from reproach until the appearing [*epiphaneias*] of our Lord Jesus Christ." And again, in his Letter to Titus (2:12–13), he exhorts Titus to live a "sober, upright, and godly" life in this world, "awaiting our blessed hope, the appearing [*epiphaneian*] of the glory of our great God and Savior Jesus Christ." In 2 Thessalonians 2:8, Paul pairs the two terms, promising that "the lawless one will be revealed, and the Lord Jesus will slay him . . . and destroy him by his appearing [*epiphaneia*] and his coming [*parousias*]." A third, related term is "apocalypse" or revelation. In 1 Peter 4:13, Peter bids his readers to "rejoice in so far as you share Christ's sufferings, that you may also rejoice and be glad when his glory is revealed [*apokalypsei*]."

The Scriptures indicate that "the day of the Lord" will come quickly, "like a thief in the night" (1 Thess 5:2; 2 Pet 3:10; Rev 16:15), at a time we do not expect, so Christians must be watchful and ready for Christ's return at any moment.

> Watch therefore, for you do not know on what day your Lord is coming. But know this, that if the householder had known in what part of the night the thief was coming, he would have watched and would not have let his house be broken into. Therefore you also must be ready; for the Son of man is coming at an hour you do not expect. (Matt 24:42–44; see also Luke 12:40)

Repeatedly, Christ warns his disciples, "Take heed, watch and pray; for you do not know when the time will come" (Mark 13:33; see also Matt 24:4–5).

And yet Christians are also warned not to be fooled by false reports of his coming. So, for example, St. Paul, who sometimes seems to have expected an imminent return of Christ, writes to the Thessalonians:

> Now concerning the coming of our Lord Jesus Christ and our assembling to meet him, we beg you, brethren, not to be quickly shaken in mind or excited, either by spirit or by word, or by letter purporting to be from us, to the effect that the day of the Lord has come. Let no one deceive you in any way; for that day will not come, unless the rebellion comes first. (2 Thess 2:1–3)

So too, when the disciples ask Jesus, "Tell us . . . what will be the sign of your coming and of the close of the age?" he warns them, "Take heed that no one leads you astray. For many will come in my name, saying, 'I am the Christ,' and they will lead many astray" (Matt 24:3, 4).

Many texts make clear that on "the day of the Lord Jesus Christ," he will return to judge the living and the dead. Indeed, the Apostles gave this doctrine a prominent place in their proclamation about Christ. In Acts 10:42, Peter tells the Gentile crowd in Caesarea that Jesus had commanded him and the other Apostles "to preach to the people, and to testify that he is the one ordained by God to be judge of the living and the dead." Later, Paul, preaching from the Areopagus in Athens, tells the crowd that men everywhere should repent because God "has fixed a day on which he will judge the world in righteousness by a man whom he has appointed, and of this he has given assurance to all men by raising him from the dead" (Acts 17: 31). In his Letter to the Romans, Paul warns that, because of their "hard and impenitent" hearts, they are "storing up wrath" for themselves for "the day of wrath when God's righteous judgment will be revealed" (2:5) "on that day when . . . God judges the secrets of men by Christ Jesus" (v. 16). "For we must all appear before the judgment seat of Christ," he tells the Corinthians, "so that each one may receive good or evil, according to what he has done in the body" (2 Cor 5:10). Paul urges Timothy "in the presence of God and of Christ Jesus who is to judge the living and the dead, and by his appearing and his kingdom" to "preach the word . . . in season and out of season, convince, rebuke, and exhort, be unfailing in patience and in teaching" (2 Tim 4:1–2). The Gospel of Matthew tells us that Christ himself promised, "When the Son of man comes in his glory, and all the angels with him, then he will sit on his glorious throne. Before him will be gathered all the nations, and he will separate them one from another as a shepherd separates the sheep from the goats" (25:31–32).

In addition to the warnings about the coming judgment are the promises of new life: "a new heavens and a new earth," and the resurrection of the dead to new life. And in the Book of Revelation, John says he saw in his vision "a new heaven and a new earth" (21:1). And in the Second Letter of St. Peter, he speaks about waiting for "new heavens and a new earth in which righteousness dwells" (3:13). On that day, the just will be raised from the dead, just as Christ was raised. And so Paul writes to the Thessalonians, assuring them:

> For since we believe that Jesus died and rose again, even so, through Jesus, God will bring with him those who have fallen asleep. . . . For the Lord himself will descend

from heaven with a cry of command, with the archangel's call, and with the sound of the trumpet of God. And the dead in Christ will rise first; then we who are alive, who are left, shall be caught up together with them in the clouds to meet the Lord in the air; and so we shall always be with the Lord." (1 Thess 4:14–17)

And again, he writes to the Corinthians to assure them that "the dead will be raised imperishable, and we shall be changed" (1 Cor 15:52). In John's Gospel, Jesus promises his disciples:

For I have come down from heaven, not to do my own will, but the will of him who sent me; and this is the will of him who sent me, that I should lose nothing of all that he has given me, but raise it up at the last day. For this is the will of my Father, that every one who sees the Son and believes in him should have eternal life; and I will raise him up at the last day." (John 6:38–40)

Is Christ Coming Soon?

Although the New Testament writers are clear that the Old Testament prophecies about "the day of the Lord" are now to be associated with Christ's Second Coming, they do not clear up the question about whether the "day of the Lord" is coming soon or is far in the future. Some texts, such as several in the Book of Revelation, suggest that Christ's coming is soon. Indeed, at the very end of Revelation, we find: "He who testifies to these things says, 'Surely I am coming soon.' Amen. Come, Lord Jesus!" (Rev 22:20; see also Rev 3:11). Paul writes the Corinthians to warn them, "the appointed time has grown very short" (1 Cor 7:29). It is sometimes claimed that Paul thought Christ would return before Paul's death. We will not enter into that debate here. Whatever he may have thought early on, it is clear that, later on, he was convinced he would die before the Second Coming (see 2 Cor 1:8–9, 5:8; Phil 1:21–24, 2:17).

The problem is that some of Paul's earlier comments can be taken either way: as evidence that Christ will return soon or simply that we don't know the day or the hour, so we should stay alert and live lives worthy of Christ. So, for example, in his Letter to the Romans, Paul exhorts his readers to "wake from sleep. For salvation is nearer to us now than when we first believed; the night is far gone, the day is at hand" (13:11–12). And in his Letter to the Philippians, he urges them to "rejoice" and "let all men know your forbearance," for "the Lord is at hand" (4:5). Certainly, every day that passes brings us "nearer" to Christ's coming than the day before. And with Christ's Incarnation, death, and Resurrection, the darkness of night has passed, and a new light has arisen: "the day is at hand." Since we believe that Christ is risen and lives, he is indeed "at hand." Does this mean he will come "soon"? It is impossible to say.

There is an interesting ambivalence, for example, in this exhortation from James 5:7–8: "Be patient, therefore, brethren, until the coming of the Lord. Behold, the farmer waits for the precious fruit of the earth, being patient over it until it receives the early and the late rain. You also be patient. Establish your hearts, for the coming of the Lord is at hand." One might have thought that if the Lord's coming is "at hand," we would not need patience. But instead, we need the patience of a farmer who plants but must wait for "the early and late rain." This image suggests that the Lord's coming is, in one sense, already present—it has been "planted," so to speak— although its full flowering is still to come.

There is also, for example, an interesting application in the

New Testament of an Old Testament prophecy from the Book of Joel, who warned that "the day of the LORD is coming" (2:1). On that day, says Joel, "it shall come to pass," that the LORD will pour out his spirit on all flesh—

> your sons and your daughters shall prophesy,
>   your old men shall dream dreams,
>   and your young men shall see visions.
> Even upon the menservants and maidservants
>   in those days, I will pour out my spirit. (vv. 28–29)

St. Peter quotes this passage when he preaches to the crowd on Pentecost (Acts 2:17–18) when the Eleven were filled with the Holy Spirit. Has the "day of the Lord" arrived, then? In one sense at least, it would seem the answer is yes.

We know, however, that there were also plenty of warnings by writers in the early Church not to lose patience or lose hope. One such prominent warning can be found in the Second Letter of Peter. He exhorts his readers to "remember the predictions of the holy prophets and the commandment of the Lord and Savior through your apostles," but to expect "that scoffers will come in the last days with scoffing . . . and saying, 'Where is the promise of his coming? For ever since the fathers fell asleep, all things have continued as they were from the beginning of creation. . . . But do not ignore this one fact," he tells them, "with the Lord one day is as a thousand years, and a thousand years as one day. The Lord is not slow about his promise as some count slowness, but is forbearing toward you, not wishing that any should perish, but that all should reach repentance" (2 Pet 3:2–9). So they should "count the forbearance of the Lord as salvation" (v. 15), take advantage of the delay, as it were, repent, and live lives of "holiness and godliness, waiting for and hastening the coming of the day of God" (vv. 11–12).

So, too, when Matthew wrote his Gospel, he recalled Jesus's parable of the ten maidens, five of whom were foolish and did not take oil for their lamps, five of whom were wise and took flasks of oil with them. Since the bridegroom "was delayed," all ten fell asleep. When the bridegroom finally arrived, those who had oil for their lamps went in with him to the marriage feast, but the others were left outside. "Watch, therefore," warns Christ, "for you know neither the day nor the hour" (see 25:1–13).

It is worth noting that this parable is about the coming of what Matthew calls "the kingdom of heaven," the term he uses interchangeably with "the kingdom of God." Some of the perplexities we have noted about when the day of the Lord is to come beset considerations about the advent of the kingdom of God. At some points, Christ seems to imply that the kingdom of God is in the future; at other times, he indicates that it is already present: that, in fact, the kingdom has been made present with his coming.

The Kingdom Will Come Sometime in the Future

So, for example, numerous passages in the Scriptures seem to indicate that the kingdom of God is something still to come, sometime in the future. In addition to the parable of the wise and foolish maidens from Matthew's Gospel, we also find in Luke 19 the parable of the talents, which recounts the story of a nobleman who goes into a far country "to receive kingly power and then return" (v. 12). Luke tells the reader that Jesus told this parable "because he was near to Jerusalem, and because they supposed that the kingdom of God was to appear immediately"—the implication being that he wished to correct them on this score (v. 11).

Perhaps the most suggestive scene in this vein, however, occurs at the Last Supper, when Jesus, after breaking the bread and drinking the wine, tells his disciples that he will not eat or drink the Passover again "until the kingdom of God comes" (Luke 22:18), "until it is fulfilled in the kingdom of God (v. 16), "until the day when I drink it new in the kingdom of God" (Mark 14:25).

So, too, in Matthew 8:11, Christ foretells that "many will come from east and west and sit at table with Abraham, Isaac, and Jacob in the kingdom of heaven" (see also Luke 13:28–29, who speaks of sitting at the table in the kingdom of God), implying that the kingdom is an eschatological reality reserved for some future date. In the Gospel of Luke, Christ predicts:

> Nation will rise against nation, and kingdom against kingdom; there will be great earthquakes, and in various places famines and pestilences; and there will be terrors and great signs from heaven. But before all this they will lay their hands on you and persecute you, delivering you up to the synagogues and prisons, and you will be brought before kings and governors for my name's sake....
>
> And there will be signs in sun and moon and stars, and upon the earth distress of nations in perplexity at the roaring of the sea and the waves, men fainting with fear and with foreboding of what is coming on the world; for the powers of the heavens will be shaken. And then they will see the Son of man coming in a cloud with power and great glory. (21:10–27)

All these events clearly seem to be associated with the Old Testament "day of the Lord." Christ finishes his discourse, saying: "When you see these things taking place, you know that the kingdom of God is near" (v. 31).

And finally, in the Gospel of Mark, Jesus tells the crowd that they must deny themselves, take up their cross, and follow him, and whoever is ashamed of him and of his words, "of him will the Son of man also be ashamed, when he comes in the glory of his Father with the holy angels" (8:34–38). And then he promises, "There are some standing here who will not taste death before they see the kingdom of God come with power" (9:1; see also Luke 9:27).

The Kingdom of God Is Present with Christ

Other passages in the Scriptures seem to indicate, however, that the kingdom of God has come with Christ. In the Gospel of Matthew, we are told that Christ's message was "Repent, for the kingdom of heaven is at hand" (Matt 3:2, 4:17, 10:7). And again, in the Gospel of Mark, we read that "after John was arrested, Jesus came into Galilee, preaching the gospel of God, and saying, 'The time is fulfilled, and the kingdom of God is at hand; repent, and believe in the gospel'" (Mark 1:14–15). If we wonder whether his statement "the kingdom of God is at hand" means it is present with him, we need only look a little further, to Matthew 12:28 (and Luke 11:20), where we find Jesus telling the Pharisees, "But if it is by the Spirit of God that I cast out demons, then the kingdom of God has come upon you." And again, in Luke 17:20–21, we are told that, upon being asked by the Pharisees when the kingdom of God was coming, Jesus answered: "The kingdom of God is not coming with signs to be observed . . . for behold, the kingdom of God is in your midst."

Other texts also seem to indicate that the kingdom is present in and with Christ. In several places, Christ associates the call to follow him with the kingdom of God. In the Gospel of Luke, for example, to the man who says, "I will follow you, Lord; but let me first say farewell to those at my home," Christ replies: "No one who puts his hand to the plow and looks back is fit for the kingdom of God" (Luke 9:62). So too, when a rich ruler comes to him to ask, "Good Teacher, what shall I do to inherit eternal life?" Jesus tells him, "Sell all that you have and distribute to the poor, and you will have treasure in heaven; and come, follow me." When the man demurs, Jesus comments, "How hard it is for those who have riches to enter the kingdom of God!" (18:24). And again, when the disciples are keeping some children away from him, Jesus tells them, "Let the children come to me, and do not hinder them; for to such belongs the kingdom of God" (v. 16). And then: "Truly, I say to you, whoever does not receive the kingdom of God like a child shall not enter it" (v. 18:17). And finally, when Peter says to Jesus, "Behold, we have left our homes and followed you," Jesus replies: "Truly, I say to you, there is no man who has left house or wife or brothers or parents or children, for the sake of the kingdom of God, who will not receive manifold more in this time, and in the age to come eternal life" (vv. 28–29).

In all these texts, and others like them, following Christ and entering the kingdom of God are associated with one another. It may be that following Christ is the precursor—the gateway, as it were—for entering the kingdom of God. But it also appears, from the texts we examined above, that the kingdom of God is present *in and with* Christ, as when Christ tells the Pharisees, "behold the kingdom of God is in your midst."

And yet, although the kingdom is made present with Christ, it is not restricted *to* Christ. In the Gospel of Luke, for example, when Christ sends out seventy disciples, two by two, to the surrounding towns, telling them to heal the sick and preach in his name, he instructs them to say: "The kingdom of God has come near to you" (10:9). In Luke's follow-up volume, the Acts of the Apostles, we find the Apostles preaching "good news about the kingdom of God and the name of Jesus Christ" (Acts 8:12). But just a few chapters later, Paul and Barnabas are said to have been "strengthening the souls of the disciples, exhorting them to continue in the faith, and saying that through many tribulations we must enter the kingdom of God" (14:22)—tribulations, clearly, that are still to come. Still later, however, in Acts 28:23, we read that Paul, though imprisoned in Rome, was "testifying to the kingdom of God and trying to convince them about Jesus both from the law of Moses and from the prophets." And in the Gospel of Matthew, although Jesus had come proclaiming that "the kingdom of heaven is at hand," he also says to Peter, "I will give you the keys of the kingdom of heaven, and whatever you bind on earth shall be bound in heaven, and whatever you loose on earth shall be loosed in heaven" (16:19), implying that whatever has been made present with Christ does not end with Christ's departure from this life.

Parables of Growth

Before we comment further on this paradox that we find in statements about "the day of the Lord" and the coming of the kingdom, there is one more set of texts we should consider: namely, the many parables about the kingdom of God that involve organic growth. In the Gospel of Mark, for example, Jesus says:

> The kingdom of God is as if a man should scatter seed upon the ground, and should sleep and rise night and day, and the seed should sprout and grow, he knows not how. The earth produces of itself, first the blade, then the ear, then the full grain in the ear. But when the grain is ripe, at once he puts in the sickle, because the harvest has come. (4:26–28)

Several such parables appear in all three Gospels: the parable of sower some of whose seed fell on rocky ground, some among the weeds, and some in good soil (Matt 13:1–9; see also Mark 4:1–9); the parable of the sower who sowed good seed in his field, but it became mixed with weeds, and the weeds were separated and burned after the harvest (Matt 13:24–30); the parable of the tiny mustard seed that becomes a shrub so large that "the birds of the air come and make nests in its branches" (Matt 13:31–32; see also Mark 4:30–32; Luke 13:18–19); the parable of the yeast ("the leaven") which a woman "hid in three measures of meal," something that would, in time, make the entire loaf rise (Matt 13:33; Luke 13:20–21).

These parables can, I suggest, help us connect the passages in which the kingdom is said to be present now with those that suggest it is still to come. Something can be said to be present and yet not complete. So, for example, we can imagine a farmer saying about a shipment of seed, "Well, next year's crop is here." He might add, humorously, "All we have to do now is plant it, water it, weed it, pray over it for good weather, and harvest it." The "crop" is present in one sense—in seed—but not present in another. There is still much work to be done and much growth that must take place.[3]

Several other considerations are also relevant here. The first

---

[3] In a related vein: My wife once said to me before my birthday, "We have cheesecake for tomorrow." "Where?" I said, going excitedly to the refrigerator to get a slice. "No, no," she replied. "When I was at the store, I bought the ingredients to make cheesecake." Thus cheesecake was "present" in one sense but not in another. Christ crucified and risen is more present to us than that cheesecake was to me when it was present only in its ingredients. And Christ is infinitely more important. But the analogy here is to the desire for something that is present in one sense but whose full realization is yet to come and whose full realization requires some effort on our part.

involves some of the other parables of the kingdom we have not mentioned yet. In Matthew 13, after the parables mentioned above, Christ gives another three that are slightly different. In the first, he says that the kingdom of heaven is "like treasure hidden in a field, which a man found and covered up; then in his joy he goes and sells all that he has and buys that field" (v. 44); in the second, he says that "the kingdom of heaven is like a merchant in search of fine pearls, who, on finding one pearl of great value, went and sold all that he had and bought it" (vv. 45–46). It is sometimes claimed that the treasure in the field and the "pearl of great price" each represent the kingdom, and we are the ones searching. And there is no doubt some truth in this claim. But the reverse is also true: we are the treasure in the field and the pearl of great price, and the kingdom "searches" for us. The text says that the kingdom is like the merchant in search of fine pearls. So, too, in the third parable of the series, Christ says:

> The kingdom of heaven is like a net which was thrown into the sea and gathered fish of every kind; when it was full, men drew it ashore and sat down and sorted the good into vessels but threw away the bad. So it will be at the close of the age. The angels will come out and separate the evil from the righteous, and throw them into the furnace of fire, where there will be weeping and gnashing of teeth. (Matt 13:47–50)

The kingdom is like the net that gathers; we are the fish. The warning is that some caught in the net will be thrown out, just as in the parable of the wheat and the tares or weeds (vv. 24–30), the weeds are harvested with the wheat, then separated and burned.

The sense here is the same as we find in the Gospels of

Matthew and Luke in the parable of the lost sheep, in which a man with a hundred sheep leaves the ninety-nine to go in search of the one who has gone astray. So, too, says Luke in his version of the parable, "there will be more joy in heaven over one sinner who repents than over ninety-nine righteous persons who need no repentance" (15:4–7; also Matt 18:12–14). And again, in Luke's Gospel, we find immediately after this parable another, the parable of the lost coin, in which a woman who has ten silver coins but loses one sweeps her house and seeks diligently until she finds it. "Just so," says Christ, "there is joy before the angels of God over one sinner who repents" (15:8–10). Immediately thereafter in the same chapter, Luke recounts the parable of the prodigal son, who spends his entire inheritance in loose living, but when he returns home repentant, his father forgives him and celebrates his return (vv. 11–32). It is abundantly clear from these texts that the kingdom of God includes a gracious love that is seeking us.

Distinguishing Different "Advents"

So how do we reconcile all these various statements about the kingdom and about the end times? For one answer, perhaps we can look back to the wisdom of Thomas Aquinas. Recall that when St. Thomas was assigned to preach a sermon during Advent—a time when everyone is looking forward to Christ's birth at Christmas but when many of the readings at Mass point us forward to Christ's Second Coming—Thomas's resolution of the problem was to distinguish four advents of Christ: His advent in the flesh in the Incarnation; the advent by which he comes into our souls; the advent in which he comes at the death of the just; and the advent in which he comes at the end of time in the final judgment. Each is distinct, but all four are connected as part of a single providential plan of salvation.

We look forward to Christ's Second Coming, but his Second Coming presupposes the first. And while we await Christ's Second Coming, we do not assume that Christ is simply absent. He is risen and remains present. He reveals that continued presence most fully, and we are able to encounter the risen Christ as intimately as did the Apostles every time we celebrate the Eucharist. When we eat other food, it becomes part of our body. When we receive the Eucharist, we become part of *Christ's* Body. We lift our mortal bodies up to God, as the priest lifts up the bread and wine, and we ask him to transform us into instruments of his grace.

In one sense, the kingdom of God has always existed since all of creation is ruled by God's divine providence. But creation has been subjected to futility, as St. Paul says, and as a result, "the whole creation has been groaning with labor pains," waiting "with eager longing for the revealing of the sons of God," when at last creation "will be set free from its bondage" (Rom 8:19–22). The disorder that was introduced into creation by human sin needs to be rectified, but this is not something man can do by himself because the disorder he introduced into the world is also a disorder in his own soul. Happily, God will not allow man to uncreate what he created. Creation stands in need of renewal, and that renewal must begin with the original source of the infection: mankind. God's divine order must be restored first in us. Hence we have been instructed to pray: "Thy kingdom come, thy will be done, on earth as it is in heaven."

How is God's rule, his divine order, his "kingdom," to be re-established? There are many stages in salvation history, but all of them either lead up to or look back to the central decisive event of history, when the Son of God became man and sacrificed himself to restore communion between God and man and thereby open a path to mankind for the needed transformation from sin and death to a new kind of life, founded on selfless love rather than our selfish will-to-power and domination. And so we say that the kingdom of God was established anew by Christ when the Word became flesh, dwelt among us, and sacrificed himself in love on the Cross. By his death and Resurrection, Christ broke the chains of sin and death. But we, the prisoners whom he has set free, must continue to live in that freedom. God will not work our salvation in us without us. We have our own cooperative role to play, both with regard to the love we ought to show to all God's beloved children and also with regard to putting our own souls in order. We must do our part to re-establish the rule of God and set the world free from its bondage by becoming the sons of God we were created to be.[4]

And yet, this transformation will not happen overnight. Nor was it entirely completed when Christ died and rose from the dead. That key event brought about a new beginning, just as the Jewish people's exodus from Egypt brought about the end of an age of slavery and a new beginning in freedom. Just as the history of the Jewish people did not end at Sinai but rather began anew with new possibilities and a new chance at freedom in obedience to God's law, so too, a new age was established by Christ with a new chance at freedom for those who say yes to God's free gift of grace.

Our time now is something like the time of the wandering in the wilderness of the Jewish people after they made the covenant

---

4   CCC, §1042: "At the end of time, the Kingdom of God will come in its full-ness. After the universal judgment, the righteous will reign for ever with Christ, glorified in body and soul. The universe itself will be renewed: . . . 'At that time, together with the human race, the universe itself, which is so closely related to man and which attains its destiny through him, will be perfectly re-established in Christ' [LG 48; Cf. Acts 3:21; Eph 1:10; Col 1:20; 2 Pet 3:10–13]."

with God at Mt. Sinai. They knew that there would be a happy ending to their story, that they would enter the land promised to them by God, but they did not know *when*. So they had to live each day in faith, trusting that by doing their part in obedience to the law, they would be made ready for that day, sometime in the unknown future, when as a people, they would reach the promised destination.

When we die, Christ incorporates the faithful more fully into his glorified Body—an incorporation that has already begun if we have said yes to him during our lives. But what about those we leave behind? In and with Christ, we do not abandon them; we remain incorporated with them in Christ's Body. The kingdom has been established in one sense, but in another sense, it is still being established, just as after Christ's death, the duty of continuing to establish the kingdom won by Christ was to be carried on by the Apostles. So, in one sense, we have entered "the final times" that the Old Testament prophets foretold. And yet, we are also in the time of tribulation that they foretold as well. When will we reach the end of time—period, full stop? That we do not know. What we know in the meantime is how we should live, that we should love, and that even in death, God will not abandon us. Our situation is like that of the disciples when the risen Christ came to them and told them:

> All authority in heaven and on earth has been given to me. Go therefore and make disciples of all nations, baptizing them in the name of the Father and of the Son and of the Holy Spirit, teaching them to observe all that I have commanded you; and behold, I am with you always, to the close of the age. (Matt 28:18–20)

We are in "the final times" and have been in the final times since the advent of Christ. But the "close of the age" is still to come. Christ's advent has made this new age possible, and he is its foundation. We know that the story has a happy ending, but we do not know when all that was begun in Christ will reach its final culmination. So in the meantime, we must "walk by faith, not by sight" (2 Cor 5:7). And, as Christ warns in the Gospel of Matthew, we must "watch therefore, for you do not know on what day your Lord is coming" (24:42).

So we can, and indeed must, distinguish the different advents of Christ because if we don't, we risk thinking that since Christ will return at the end of time, then he does not come to the faithful at the moment of their death,[5] or since Christ comes to us at the moment of our death, then there is no need for him to come to us in the Eucharist.[6] But this would be to separate rather than

---

[5] Most modern Catholics are not subject to the erroneous belief that we do not achieve our heavenly union with Christ until the Final Judgment. But this doubt has in the past bedeviled some. For this reason, Pope Benedict XII promulgated the following solemn definition in his 1336 bull *Benedictus Deus* (quoted in CCC, §1023): "By virtue of our apostolic authority, we define the following: According to the general disposition of God, the souls of all the saints . . . and other faithful who died after receiving Christ's holy Baptism (provided they were not in need of purification when they died, . . . or, if they then did need or will need some purification, when they have been purified after death, . . .) already before they take up their bodies again and before the general judgment—and this since the Ascension of our Lord and Savior Jesus Christ into heaven—have been, are and will be in heaven, in the heavenly Kingdom and celestial paradise with Christ, joined to the company of the holy angels. Since the Passion and death of our Lord Jesus Christ, these souls have seen and do see the divine essence with an intuitive vision, and even face to face, without the mediation of any creature [DS 1000; cf. LG 49]."

[6] Doubt about Christ's presence in the Eucharist (why do we *need* it if we are going to be with Christ in heaven?) has been historically associated with Protestants, but such doubts have of late become more common among Catholics. To doubt Christ's presence in the Eucharist is to misunderstand the

distinguish the different "advents" of Christ. We would be separating events that are connected rather than distinguishing them as interrelated and connected parts within God's providential plan of salvation. They are distinct events within a unified providential plan. Hence, after the consecration of the Eucharist at Mass, we proclaim one of the formulae called the *mysterium fidei*, the mystery of the faith, each formulation of which has a similar threefold structure: "Christ has died. Christ is risen. Christ will come again"; "We proclaim your Death, O Lord and profess your Resurrection until you come again"; or "When we eat this Bread and drink this Cup, we proclaim your Death, O Lord, until you come again." This faith is the faith of the Church.

We find a nice summary of this faith in *The Catechism of the Catholic Church*. In light of our discussion above, consider the following four statements in the *Catechism*. Notice the places where the text speaks of Christ's "reign" and Christ's "kingdom."

> Though already present in his Church, Christ's reign is nevertheless yet to be fulfilled "with power and great glory" by the King's return to earth [Luke 21:27; cf. Matt 25:31]. (CCC, §671)

> Christ the Lord already reigns through the Church, but all the things of this world are not yet subjected to him. The triumph of Christ's kingdom will not come about without one last assault by the powers of evil. (CCC, §680)

overflowing of the divine gifts and to fail to notice that at Mass we even now participate in the heavenly banquet feast of the Lamb. It is a very real foretaste of heaven, made present to us now visibly and tangibly. This is not a question of "need"; rather, it has to do with the overflowing, gratuitous nature of love.

On Judgment Day at the end of the world, Christ will come in glory to achieve the definitive triumph of good over evil which, like the wheat and the tares, have grown up together in the course of history. (CCC, §681)

When he comes at the end of time to judge the living and the dead, the glorious Christ will reveal the secret disposition of hearts and will render to each man according to his works, and according to his acceptance or refusal of grace. (CCC, §682)

And again, in a later chapter, we read:

The Last Judgment will come when Christ returns in glory. Only the Father knows the day and the hour; only he determines the moment of its coming. Then through his Son Jesus Christ he will pronounce the final word on all history. We shall know the ultimate meaning of the whole work of creation and of the entire economy of salvation and understand the marvellous ways by which his Providence led everything towards its final end. The Last Judgment will reveal that God's justice triumphs over all the injustices committed by his creatures and that God's love is stronger than death [Cf. Song 8:6]. (CCC, §1040)

The message of the Last Judgment calls men to conversion while God is still giving them "the acceptable time, ... the day of salvation" [2 Cor 6:2]. It inspires a holy fear of God and commits them to the justice of the Kingdom of God. It proclaims the "blessed hope" of the Lord's return, when he will come "to be glorified in his saints, and to be marvelled at in all who have believed" [Titus 2:13; 2 Thess 1:10]. (CCC, §1041)

Restoring the Image of God

In Genesis, man is said to be made in the image of God—or more literally, "in our image, after our likeness" (Gen 1:26). With man's first sin, that image became obscured. Some commentators say, rather, that the image was retained but the *likeness* was lost. The point of both interpretations—that the image was obscured or that the likeness was lost—is to make clear that, although we have not lost *everything* imparted to us at creation, our natures are now gravely damaged. The image still bears some resemblance to the original, but it is imperfect and needs to be restored.

Our language is inadequate to capture the fulness of the divine essence, and individual terms often risk communicating the wrong idea, so it is important to understand that, in human persons, being "in the image of God" is not a static condition, like the image in a portrait; it is dynamic and develops. Human beings share in the image of God by reason of their intellect and will. But there are stages of development as the human person grows and matures. We never lose the capacity for knowing and loving God just as we never lose the capacity for knowing and loving others. But we can say no; we can turn away from selfless love to selfish pride and greed. For our fallen natures to be perfected and for that damaged image to be restored, we must conform our lives to God's image as revealed in his Son, Jesus Christ—a transformation made possible by grace when God's love is "poured into our hearts through the Holy Spirit who has been given to us" (Rom 5:5). This is the entire work of the Christian moral life. Furthermore, the work of transformation and the restoration of the image are not completed in this life. The perfect knowledge and love of God is attained only in that union with the Father, Son, and Spirit that is the reward of the faithful in heaven, when we know as we are known and see God face to face in glory, purified of the sinful pride that keeps us from loving fully (see 1 Cor 13:12–13).

The Beginning and End of the End Times

As we have seen, in one sense, "the end times" have already begun with the coming of Christ, and especially with his death, Resurrection, and sending of the Holy Spirit. Now that we live in the light of Christ's death and Resurrection, we have come to realize, under the guidance of the Holy Spirit, that this was the central event of history. Everything in salvation history before it was a precursor to it, and everything since then has been a reflection back on it. We can say (in retrospect), therefore, that it was "the beginning of the end."

We use the expression "the beginning of the end" when the end has become clear but not before. So, too, with the sacrifice of Christ, "the end" has been made clear to us. We now know how the story turns out and that it has a happy ending. We don't know exactly how the happy ending arrives nor exactly when, but that the ending will be happy is no longer in doubt. Humanity will be redeemed, and the futility to which creation has been subjected will be rectified. The faithful will be given victory over sin and death, and the world will be made new.[7] None of this would have

---

[7] See CCC, §1048: "We know neither the moment of the consummation of the earth and of man, nor the way in which the universe will be transformed. The form of this world, distorted by sin, is passing away, and we are taught that God is preparing a new dwelling and a new earth in which righteousness dwells, in which happiness will fill and surpass all the desires of peace arising in the hearts of men [GS 39 §1]." And CCC, §1060: "At the end of time, the Kingdom of God will come in its fullness. Then the just will reign with Christ for ever,

been obvious before Christ; none of it would have been possible without Christ. Knowing it can give us hope.

Knowing the end of the story in this way reveals that history is not merely progress as many modern people think; nor is history an increasing falling away from an ancient "golden age" as many ancient people thought. It is not defined by the conflict between classes or conflict over economic privileges. It is not ruled by human kings and queens and emperors or by large historical-political forces. None of these narratives is completely false, but none captures the central drama of history. What drives history is divine providence and those who respond, either positively or negatively, to the commandments to love God and neighbor. At the end of history, we find Christ, union with whom in the loving embrace of the Father in the Spirit is also the goal of history. Thus, as the poet T. S. Eliot writes, "In my beginning is my end" and "In my end is my beginning."[8]

"Behold," says Christ at the end of the Book of Revelation, "I am coming soon, bringing my recompense, to repay every one for what he has done. I am the Alpha and the Omega, the first and the last, the beginning and the end" (Rev 22:12–13).

But even though it is the beginning of the end, we have not reached the end—full stop. We are still headed in its direction, still drawn by it as our goal. So when will we reach the culmination of this stage of the journey? When will we see what we might call "the end of the end"? That we do not know. Since as 2 Peter 3:8 tells us, "With the Lord one day is as a thousand years, and a thousand years as one day," what we consider "the blink of an eye"

---

glorified in body and soul, and the material universe itself will be transformed. God will then be 'all in all' (1 Cor 15:28) in eternal life."

[8] T. S. Eliot, *East Coker*. "In my beginning is my end" appears in the first line of the poem. "In my end is my beginning" appears in the last line.

could be thirty thousand years. Or it could be the smallest division of a nanosecond. For this reason, we are told, "Watch therefore, for you know neither the day nor the hour" (Matt 25:13).

What some people have thought of as a confusion about the "end times" has, therefore, I would suggest, an important spiritual purpose. Every moment in this life should be lived as if Christ were coming today because, of course, he could. The Second Coming could be in two millennia or in two seconds. It might happen before you finish reading this page. So we'd better be ready now. What would you want Christ to find you doing if he came right now?

And yet, the Second Coming might still be far, far in the future. God alone is the Lord of history, so we need to be ready to dedicate ourselves to our mission for the long haul, not for any immediate reward or an immediate consolation. When Christ will come is not up to us.

Concentrating the Mind Wonderfully on the Things That Are Truly Important

We should think of every moment of life as precious, as irreplaceable, as something to be lived. And yet, this focus on the present moment should not blind us to the passage of time and our connections to the past and obligations to the future. It should help focus our minds in the way death itself can focus our minds. If we are honest with ourselves, we recognize that we could die at any moment. Our lives are tenuous at best. We go on, day by day, as if nothing bad could happen. But then, all at once, perhaps due to the death of someone close to us, death becomes real to us. Not merely "death," but our death—the fact that we will die. It is 100 percent certain. When it will happen is not clear, but that it will happen is.

I once had a student who was working with patients in an end-of-life hospice. "How is it?" I asked him.

"It is really inspiring," he said.

When I asked him why, he replied, "Because the people there aren't worried about the kind of stupid things we worry about. Their minds are focused on what is truly important."

When I asked him to describe the kind of "stupid things" they don't worry about, he replied: "You know, fashion, what's cool, how much money you make, whether you are important."

"What do they focus on instead?" I asked.

"Family, friends, caring for people around them."

What if we could gain sooner the wisdom so many people report receiving in the last few months of their life? What if we could attain that wisdom a good number of years before our death, perhaps simply by considering the prospect of death without being faced with its immediacy? The eighteenth century writer Samuel Johnson is reported to have said, "Depend upon it, sir, when a man knows he is to be hanged in a fortnight, it concentrates his mind wonderfully." The challenge is whether we can have that sort of clarity about what is truly important without the threat of being hanged but simply with the challenge of living as fully as possible each day a life that is finite, always aware of death but refusing to live glumly in its shadow.

Planning for the Future and Living Fully Now

We live with plans for the future, both ours and the future of the community of which we are a part. But we should make those plans with an awareness that we lack control: control of others, control of nature, and control of history. So we set ourselves to our work each day and leave the rest to God. We do not know when Christ will return, so we make the best plans we can, but we get up each day and ask: *What good can I do now? How do I love rightly now, knowing that I am on a journey whose temporal end I do not know? I know I have developing to do and learning to do, so I had better get to it. When the Master returns, I had better be able to show him that I was busy about my work, not beating the other servants* (see Matt 24:49), *and properly developing the talents he entrusted to me, not burying them in the ground* (see Matt 25:14–30).

For these reasons, among others, it is probably best, as C. S. Lewis recommends, for us to leave "futurity in God's hands. We may as well," says Lewis dryly, "for God will certainly retain it whether we leave it to him or not."[9] When World War II began, Lewis gave a lecture at the Church of St. Mary at Oxford explaining why he thought students should continue their education even during the war. As a general principle, he said, it is important to understand that war brings about no uniquely new human situation; it merely reveals the situation we live in every day but without always being aware of the fact. Each day we must face the fact that we might not live out that day. And yet we must make plans and carry out our duties as if we will be alive and active for an indeterminate future.

We can make plans, but we can never trust in those plans. We can trust only in God and in the tasks we have before us now. "Never," says Lewis, "in peace or war, commit your virtue or your happiness to the future. Happy work is best done by the man who takes his long-term plans somewhat lightly and works from moment to moment 'as to the Lord.' It is only our daily bread that we are encouraged to ask for. The present is the only time in

---

[9] C. S. Lewis, "Learning in War-Time," a sermon preached in the Church of St. Mary the Virgin, Oxford, autumn, 1939. This essay is available several places on line, but it appears in print in C. S. Lewis, *The Weight of Glory* (New York: Harper Collins, 1949), 47–63; quote above is on p. 61.

which any duty can be done or any grace received."[10] The ancients, says Lewis,

> thought it good for us to be always aware of our mortality. I am inclined to think they were right. All the animal life in us, all schemes of happiness that centered in this world, were always doomed to a final frustration. In ordinary times only a wise man can realize it. Now the stupidest of us know. We see unmistakably the sort of universe in which we have all along been living, and must come to terms with it. If we had foolish un-Christian hopes about human culture, they are now shattered. If we thought we were building up a heaven on earth, if we looked for something that would turn the present world from a place of pilgrimage into a permanent city satisfying the soul of man, we are disillusioned, and not a moment too soon. But if we thought that for some souls, and at some times, the life of learning, humbly offered to God, was, in its own small way, one of the appointed approaches to the Divine reality and the Divine beauty which we hope to enjoy hereafter, we can think so still.[11]

The Goal of History Is Not in History Itself

There is, however, another important warning in Lewis's words. We should not be putting our hopes in the imminent forces of human history to resolve the problems of history. The salvation of the world is not *from* the world; it is a gift of sanctifying love God makes *to* the world. Since it was his creation, only he can redeem and "re-create" it.

---

[10] Ibid.
[11] Ibid., 62–63.

If one believes that the universe is essentially an empty universe, nothing more than the result of a great cosmic accident of which we humans are an accidental by-product, then it might make sense to believe that there is no afterlife and no purpose to life itself. The most "reasonable" conclusion, given these premises, would be that we came from nothing, by nothing, for no reason. So we should just "make the best of it" while we can. What "make the best of it" might mean would vary from one person to the next. "Making the best of it" might mean "maximizing pleasure and minimizing pain." It might mean living "authentically" in the awareness of one's eventual death, refusing to live in the "illusion" of everlasting life. Or it might involve "making meaning" in whatever way one wills. Any of these conclusions would, given the presupposition of an empty, meaningless universe, "just make sense."

What would not make sense given such a view, however, would be to presume a Christian afterlife without Christ—something akin to "the Church of Christ without Christ" preached by Flannery O'Connor's character Hazel Motes in her novel *Wise Blood*. At least Hazel Motes is honest enough to understand that in this Church without Christ "the blind don't see and the lame don't walk and what's dead stays that way."[12] Without a personal Creator who is willing to forgive sins and redeem and recreate his creation, one is left with the pagan views we examined in the early chapters of this book: Homer's Achilles wandering among the shades of the underworld, or various notions of reincarnation, or a simple obliteration of existence.

What also would not make sense given such a view, moreover, would be selfless acts of love involving personal sacrifice. The

---

[12] Flannery O'Connor, *Wise Blood* (New York: Farrar Straus Giroux, 1949), 50.

presupposition of an empty, meaningless universe simply doesn't provide any foundation for devoting oneself to others in this way. Love does not always involve maximizing pleasure and minimizing pain; quite the contrary, love often involves suffering *with* or *for* others. And the possibility of selfless love is one of those "illusions" in which skeptics who are convinced of the meaninglessness of the universe tell themselves they should not indulge. Furthermore, if the *meaning* you are *making* is your own, it need not include others. Indeed, it is highly unlikely that any two people will "make meaning" in their lives in exactly the same way. Whatever union is built on such tenuous foundations is unlikely to last.

Fortunately, most of us live better lives than our philosophies suggest we might. If people could at some point recognize that the empty view of the world they hold would provide no foundation for the life they know they should be leading—when they recognize that the Way of Love is the Way of Life—then we may find at that moment an opening to the truth of the Christian message. If someone asks, "But don't you think that love is futile? Don't you think that it fails in the end and that hatred and cruelty win out?" what else can we answer other than, "I believe in a Love that transcends all those very real limitations." As Cardinal Ratzinger (Pope emeritus Benedict XVI) has written:

> If it were merely blind chance that threw us into the ocean of nothingness, then there would be sufficient reason for considering ourselves unfortunate. Only when we know that there is Someone who did not make a blind throw of the dice and that we have come from freedom and love

can we then . . . be grateful for this freedom and know with gratitude that it is really a gift to be a human being.[13]

"Only if it is true that the universe comes from freedom, love, and reason," wrote the future pope, "and that these are the real underlying powers, can we trust one another, go forward into the future, and live as human beings. . . . For this means that freedom and love are not ineffectual ideas but rather that they are the sustaining forces of reality."[14]

The Way of Love Is the Way of the Cross

And yet, our limited human loves alone are not sufficient to be the "sustaining forces of reality." As we participate in the *being* imparted to us from the divine Source, so, too, our love, when it is selfless and authentic, is a participation in the divine Love shared by the Father, Son, and Holy Spirit. And in the end, it is the love from this divine Source that cannot die. All that is not love—all that is sin and is contrary to that divine love—will pass away. Wealth will pass away, although the love we showed with that wealth will not. The limited power we possess will be swallowed up into the Source of all power. The pleasures that we enjoy due to wealth, power, status, and fame—the refined enjoyments we get from "having more" and "lording it over others," the satisfaction of being first in line, of being preeminent, of being important in the eyes of those who "matter"—all of these things will decay or be burned away in what T. S. Eliot describes as "frigid purgatorial fires":

---

[13] Joseph Ratzinger, *In the Beginning: A Catholic Understanding of the Story of Creation and the Fall*, trans. Boniface Ramsey (Grand Rapids, MI: Eerdmans, 1995), 53–54.

[14] Ibid., 18.

The whole earth is our hospital
Endowed by the ruined millionaire,
Wherein, if we do well, we shall
Die of the absolute paternal care
That will not leave us, but prevents us everywhere.
  The chill ascends from feet to knees,
  The fever sings in mental wires.
If to be warmed, then I must freeze
And quake in frigid purgatorial fires
Of which the flame is roses, and the smoke is briars.
  The dripping blood our only drink,
  The bloody flesh our only food:
In spite of which we like to think
That we are sound, substantial flesh and blood—
Again, in spite of that, we call this Friday good.[15]

The Love that will have nothing less than all of us, body and soul, will burn away those selfish parts of us that keep us from loving fully in order to prepare us for that further union and deeper communion we are to enjoy in communion with the Father, Son, and Spirit. We cannot share in Christ's Resurrection to the Father if we will not share in his Cross—if we will not die to all selfishness and surrender ourselves to God's gracious care.

The final trial, however, is death. If the other trials of life have not prepared us to receive our lives back as a gift, then perhaps this is what is needed. There is no avoiding the fact that this trial, like many of life's other trials, is not pleasant. It is "bearing a cross." But Christ told his followers that they would have to bear that cross,

---

[15] T. S. Eliot, "East Coker," sec. IV.

both in life and as they faced death. Indeed, not only did Christ tell them, he showed them by bearing his own Cross.

If God's decision to become a limited, finite, vulnerable human person and then allow himself to be tortured and crucified like a criminal on a cross does not convince us that he knows and understands how difficult the journey is—how difficult it is to bear the cross of self-surrender—then could anything ever be sufficient to inspire us to rise to the challenge? At what point do we stop blaming God for not doing enough to inspire us and start taking responsibility for our own refusal to give up our slavish attachments to the "flesh pots of Egypt" and follow Christ, the new Moses, into the wilderness we must cross before we can enter the land he has promised us?

Hasn't Christ been inviting us to this heavenly sort of life our whole lives? Has the witness of his life and death not been inviting us, saying to us, in effect: "I understand that to give up your selfish self-centeredness feels like a kind of death—a death to self. But please understand, you cannot live a real life, the life of love God intends for you, unless you go through that death to self." You cannot get the benefits of commitment without commitment. You cannot get the benefits of a true, honest, selfless relationship if you are unfaithful, dishonest, and selfish. This isn't a question of "punishment"; it is simply a question of reality. "Selfishness" and "love" are contradictory realities. You have to die to the one to live in the other. No one said it would be easy. Again, one would think that by choosing to follow the "way of the cross," Christ would have convinced people that he is very aware (and trying to be completely honest with us) that it is not easy. But does not our experience of love suggest—and does the Resurrection not validate our intuition—that the sacrifice is worth it?

A word of warning on this score is in order, however. In the discussion thus far, I have not said anything about hell. This is a book about the promise of the resurrection not about the dangers of hell. But we should make no mistake: it is a danger. God will not force us to love. God will not work out salvation in us without our cooperation. We can say no. And if we do, God will allow us to say no to that communion of love which is our life, perhaps forever and ever, into eternity. As we saw above, the warnings are clear that on "the day of the Lord," Christ will come to judge the living and the dead.[16]

Those who say no to love of God and neighbor have by this choice removed themselves from the kingdom of God, which is a kingdom of love. If you say, "I do not want to go to heaven if there are Jews and black people there," God will not force you to go there. But if you say that, you are choosing your own hell not only in the next life but now.[17] We all know people, often enough it is we ourselves, who choose to say no to this love. This book has been about the infinite good that God has in store for us, and that should inspire hope. But let us attend to the basic logic that should warn us: to reject an infinite good is to choose an infinite evil. If we need love in the way a young sunflower

---

[16] E.g., Matt 25:31–32: "When the Son of man comes in his glory, and all the angels with him, then he will sit on his glorious throne. Before him will be gathered all the nations, and he will separate them one from another as a shepherd separates the sheep from the goats." Acts 10:42: "He is the one ordained by God to be judge of the living and the dead." Acts 17:30–31: God "has fixed a day on which he will judge the world in righteousness by a man whom he has appointed, and of this he has given assurance to all men by raising him from the dead." Rom 2:5, 16: "the day of wrath when God's righteous judgment will be revealed . . . on that day when . . . God judges the secrets of men by Christ Jesus." 2 Cor 5:10: "For we must all appear before the judgment seat of Christ, so that each one may receive good or evil, according to what he has done in the body."

[17] For a good imaginative account of people making this choice, see C. S. Lewis's *The Great Divorce.*

needs the sun, then turning away from the Source of Love would be like the young sunflower turning away from the sun. The sun does not need to "punish" the sunflower by sending out a solar flare; without the life provided by the sun, the sunflower simply withers and dies. So, too, in a more profound way, when we turn away from God's love, we wither and die. Our message has been, "Choose to live in heaven now—say yes to the gift of divine love shared by the Father, Son, and Spirit each day—and no power on heaven or earth can separate you from that love." But the reverse is also tragically possible. You can say no to the gift of selfless love. You can make your life into a living hell. God will not force you to share the communion of love with him and the saints. And at some point, that decision may become final, and you will have cut yourself off from the Source of all light and life.[18]

This life is not a "mere" preparation for some other one. We have real choices to make, and they are eternally meaningful. We must decide in the here and now how best to love *this* spouse and *these* children, *these* parents and *these* neighbors. That love will be purified, glorified, and expanded in union with God. We experience a foretaste of that "expansion" even now in the growth of children and the ripple effects of one's good deeds. But our love is also always mixed with disappointments. We cannot prevent the

---

[18] We should keep in mind that we may not remain free forever to say yes to God's offer. That is to say, we may corrupt ourselves so severely that, like the addict who is no longer free to choose the love of his family over alcohol or cocaine, we might no longer be free to say yes to God's love, preferring the "fleshpots of Egypt" to the freedom of the sons of God. I will not speculate here on the point at which we might lose that freedom completely. But we should take it seriously as a possibility inherent in our freedom to make choices that end up diminishing our freedom. With every choice for evil, we make ourselves less capable of choosing the good. In some cases, we may even lose the clarity of sense to be able to distinguish the one from the other, with the result that we choose the evil *as* the good. See CCC, §§1056–1060.

effects of sin and our fallen condition from infecting, in one way or another, the fruits of our labors. So what we experience now is merely a foretaste. We see now "in a mirror dimly" (1 Cor 13:12). The pattern of the whole will be revealed to us only later. The significance of our actions will not be clear until that whole pattern is made plain. In the meantime, we love and we obey the commandments of love, for this is our foretaste of the eternal life God has promised us.

APPENDIX:

SHORTER ESSAYS

Reflections on the Passing of a Beloved Neighbor*

One of the problems with having friends in graduate school is that you can't keep them. No one wishes for one's friends to move away, and yet, the longer they stay, the worse it is for them. Graduate school is a transient state one passes through on the way to something else; it's not permanent (thank God).

So when your friends go on job interviews, although you hope they get the job, you know that if they do, they'll be leaving. And if they leave, you won't have them around to shoot the breeze between classes, have cookouts together on the lawn, or play softball in the summers. By the same token, if they stay, there's no future for them: they won't have jobs, a regular salary, a decent place to live, students to teach in classes of their own—all the elements of a full life.

If they stay, the graduate school stipend will end, the institution will no longer keep them on the university's health insurance, and they will be consigned to that hellish limbo called "adjunct faculty," a status one wouldn't wish on one's worst enemies, let alone one's dearest friends.

Now of all the things I was hoping life would not be like, graduate school would certainly top the list. But, as it turns out, there

* A version of this essay was published online at *The Catholic Thing* on Wednesday, November 14, 2012.

is this one noteworthy similarity: friends can't stay—life being as transient a state in the end as graduate school.

Mr. Rowland, my beloved next-door-neighbor, is dying. He is in his eighties, and the cancer that was in his prostate has moved into his spine. The doctors give him six months, give or take.

Good neighbors become part of the comfortable fabric of your life, like the Japanese maple tree in the back yard or the creaky porch in the front. Most days, you don't think about them. But they bring stability and joy because of their presence, and something very crucial would be missing if they weren't there.

You don't have to see them every day to know they're there. You see their trash out, their lights on in the evening, their paper on the steps, and their car in and out of the drive: signs of life, as the saying goes.

They have their customary patterns as you have yours, and you can mark your day by them. "Mr. Rowland was up early this morning," my wife and I say if his car is missing when we go out, or "Boy, Anthony is up late tonight" if we see his lights on later than usual. He cares for his yard in a certain way, keeps his hedges trimmed nicely—so much better than mine—and always diligently sees to the leaves in the fall. Except for this fall. You don't have to see him every day to know something very crucial would be missing if he weren't there.

A neighborhood is a common good, and a common good is not merely an aggregation of private goods. If it were, you could lose a unit, replace it, like a light bulb, and things would go on as before. But that's not the way it is at all. To lose a member of the community is to diminish the whole, to change the essence of the place.

Here's the problem, though: we can't keep Anthony indefinitely any more than we can keep forever that beloved maple tree. Time and God don't work that way. I can't keep Anthony any more than I could hold on to my friends in graduate school. To wish for him to stay indefinitely would be to wish something horrible for him.

Anthony's beloved wife, that miraculous French woman Colette, has been dead now for several years, and he's been wondering, as older men sometimes do after their wives have passed, why he's not yet joined her.

He's a wise Christian man and knows that his life is not his own: that God must still have some work to do—on him or with him. But this doesn't keep him from occasionally entertaining the unavoidable thought: When will I be with my beloved wife again?

It's not clear yet when Anthony will get the call to move on to that full life we enjoy only in union with the glorified Christ, with the only real "tenure" that's not transient or illusory. I know that when the call comes, I will miss him greatly. It would be a cruel friend, though, who would try to keep him a moment longer than his appointed moving day. My concern in the meantime is how to help him pack for the move—and how I'm going to cope when he's gone.

No doubt, when the time comes, I'll need his and Colette's help in the days that follow.

Good Friday, Death, and Christian Life[*]

O, Death
Won't you spare me over til another year
Well what is this that I can't see
With ice cold hands takin' hold of me
Well I am death, none can excel. . . . [1]

These lyrics are from the widely known song "O, Death," a haunting melody that became famous after it was featured in the movie *O Brother, Where Art Thou?* The song, so expertly sung by Ralph Stanley in what is almost a Gregorian chant to the power of death, is haunting precisely because it expresses so well the natural human fear of death.

But is it true that death is something that "none can excel"? Is death really "the final word" over human life? Or is there another word that God has to say on the matter?

In the Second Vatican Council's Pastoral Constitution on the Church in the Modern World (*Gaudium et Spes,* §18), we read: "It is in the face of death that the riddle of human existence grows most acute. Not only is man tormented by pain and by the advancing deterioration of his body, but even more so by a dread of perpetual extinction." Faced with the reality of death, we rightly ask: "What will become of all that I have worked for? What will happen to all those I have loved?" The unavoidable reality of death seems to make human life meaningless. "Why am I here," we ask, "if in the end, it all comes to nothing?"

---

[*] A version of this essay was published online at *Catholic World Report on Good Friday, March 25, 2016.*

[1] "O Death," or "Conversation with Death," is a traditional song, perhaps written by Lloyd Chandler circa 1916, now in the public domain.

In the Scriptures, death is the enemy. It is the companion of sin, and they both must be overcome together. Rather than counseling the faithful simply to accept death as a fact of life, or to welcome death as a gift, *Gaudium et Spes* tells us that the human person "rightly follows the intuition of his heart when he abhors and repudiates the utter ruin and total disappearance of his own person" (GS, §18). It is thus a very human and very understandable reaction to death for the poet Dylan Thomas to beg his dying father, "Do not go gentle into that good night. Rage, rage against the dying of the light." Why? Because God has put in us the seeds of something eternal: a yearning for himself.

"Human beings bear in themselves," *Gaudium et Spes* tells us, "an eternal seed which cannot be reduced to the merely material" (GS, §18). It is precisely because we are not solely material beings that we yearn for something beyond the death of our finite mortal bodies. It is especially when we look at a man or woman in a wheelchair, or an elderly grandmother whose body has withered and failed in so many ways but in whose presence we still feel the power of their indomitable spirit, that we know there is something in the human person not restricted to the current weakness of our material bodies.

Human beings know they must face death, but they also have always yearned for something more—a life that transcends the limitations of this world, including even the boundaries of death. The ancient Roman philosopher Cicero once wrote this about his belief in the immortality of the soul: "If I err in my belief that the souls of men are immortal, I gladly err, nor do I wish this error ... to be wrested from me while I live."[2]

---

[2] Cicero, *De Senectute*, trans. William Armistead Falconer (Cambridge, MA: Harvard University Press, 1923), 85.

Spiritual health involves an acknowledgment of the reality and inevitability of death, but it also involves recognizing in ourselves the desire for a life that transcends the life we see all around us in nature: the kind of life that flowers for a time but then withers and ultimately dies. As humans, we find within ourselves a deep and very meaningful yearning for life in the truest sense, a life free from sin and death: a life we call "eternal life."

Eternal life of the sort Christ promises us is not merely the extension of years—more years to suffer "the slings and arrows of outrageous fortune,"[3] more years to worry anxiously about the ultimate end. This is why, according to *Gaudium et Spes*, "All the endeavors of technology, though useful in the extreme, cannot calm his anxiety; for prolongation of biological life is unable to satisfy the desire for higher life which is inescapably lodged in the human heart" (GS, §18).

When I ask young people whether they want to "live forever," they often will ask me in return, "Do you mean like this? As I am *now*? No," they frequently will reply. Perhaps they sense instinctively that merely extending this life would not yet be enough. Or perhaps they are merely responding to a deep yearning for something *more*: a fuller kind of life, which even the blessings of youth cannot provide.

I also worry that this response might stem from an unfortunate weariness with life. Too many of our beloved young people, as well as our invaluable elderly, consider taking their own lives. We must never allow this sad weariness of life to overcome us. Pope St. John Paul II wrote passionately in his great encyclical *Evangelium Vitae* about the importance of life and of establishing a "culture of life." "The Gospel of life is at the heart of Jesus's

---

[3] From Shakespeare's *Hamlet*, Act III, Scene 1.

message," wrote the pope. "Lovingly received day after day by the Church, it is to be preached with dauntless fidelity as 'good news' to the people of every age and culture" (EV, §1). Indeed, it is precisely when we feel the weariness of life bearing down upon us that we must turn to Christ and unite ourselves more fully with the community of believers in his mystical Body, the Church, in order to be revivified by the Gospel and reassured of the blessings of life.

"Man is called to a fullness of life which far exceeds the dimensions of his earthly existence because it consists in sharing the very life of God," says St. John Paul. And yet this calling to union with God must in no way cause us to devalue human life in this world. Rather, as the saint emphasizes:

> The loftiness of this supernatural vocation reveals the greatness and the inestimable value of human life even in its temporal phase. Life in time, in fact, is the fundamental condition, the initial stage and an integral part of the entire unified process of human existence. It is a process which, unexpectedly and undeservedly, is enlightened by the promise and renewed by the gift of divine life, which will reach its full realization in eternity. (EV, §2; see also 1 John 3:1–2)

Indeed, it is precisely because of this supernatural calling—because the events of our lives now have not merely temporal but eternal ramifications—that, according to St. John Paul II, life "remains a sacred reality entrusted to us, to be preserved with a sense of responsibility and brought to perfection in love and in the gift of ourselves to God and to our brothers and sisters" (EV, §2).

What can give us hope in the face of the utter blackness of death? We cannot see beyond that veil of darkness. Death remains a mystery, and its ceaseless presence can fill us with what is sometimes called existential dread.

> But at my back I always hear
> Time's wingèd chariot hurrying near;
> And yonder all before us lie
> Deserts of vast eternity.[4]

So wrote Andrew Marvell "to his coy mistress." Marvell may have been interested only in a romantic tryst when he wrote those lines, but they're powerful (even if improperly used) precisely because they witness to something authentic in the human condition: an inescapable awareness ("But at my back I always hear"), sometimes dim, sometimes less so, of the inevitable approach of death. Death . . . and then what? "Deserts of vast eternity"? "The grave's a fine and private place," Marvell warns his young paramour, "But none, I think, do there embrace."

Aging and death can make us feel deeply alone in the universe. It seems as though it is a burden we must carry alone. No one can go through this process for us. No one can take our place in death. It is something we ourselves must do.

But are we really alone? Our Christian faith tells us that Christ died for us, and thus we are never truly alone. We read in *Gaudium et Spes*:

> Although the mystery of death utterly beggars the imagination, the Church has been taught by divine revelation and firmly teaches that man has been created by God for

---

[4] Andrew Marvell (1621–1678), "To His Coy Mistress," lines 21–24, Poetry Foundation, accessed Oct. 1, 2021, https://www.poetryfoundation.org/poems/44688/to-his-coy-mistress.

a blissful purpose beyond the reach of earthly misery. In addition, bodily death . . . will be vanquished . . . when man who was ruined by his own doing is restored to wholeness by an almighty and merciful Savior. For God has called man and still calls him so that with his entire being he might be joined to Him in an endless sharing of a divine life beyond all corruption. Christ won this victory when He rose to life, for by His death He freed man from death. Hence to every thoughtful man a solidly established faith provides the answer to his anxiety about what the future holds for him. At the same time faith gives him the power to be united in Christ with his loved ones who have already been snatched away by death; faith arouses the hope that they have found true life with God. (GS, §18)

God made us for himself—to love and serve him and our neighbor in this life and in the next. Perhaps one reason we weep at the death of our loved ones is because we think they are "going away." Too often we think of heaven merely as a place: a place far away, like New York or Paris or the moon. We comfort ourselves by saying: "They've gone to a better place." But we still miss them.

As Catholics we believe in the communion of saints. We are promised that the love we have for God the Father, in communion with the Spirit and the Son, can never die. We do not lose our loved ones, nor they us. Rest assured, our Christian faith tells us, your loved ones are not simply "gone." They abide—with God, and, through God, with you. They continue in their essence as before— loving us, praying for us, being with us. Indeed, in union with the eternal Divine Love, their love for us can be even more intimate. They are no longer merely "beside us" or "across the table" from us.

Now they can be also "above us" and "inside us"—knowing us, as God does, "better than we know ourselves." And we can rejoice in that love and continue to be comforted by it even during the dark times, whether we, or someone we love, faces death.

My own mother died on a cold clear night shortly after the Easter Vigil would have finished. That evening, I was at her bedside instead of at Mass. I was an adult convert, and this was my second Easter as a Catholic. I was filled with deep sorrow at her passing even as I was convinced by my faith that the Lord would be with her. "Yea, though I walk through the valley of the shadow of death," sings the psalmist, "I will fear no evil, for Thou art with me."[5]

And yet, however much we believe in Christ's promise, we weep at the death of a loved one. This is truly human. In this life, we must walk by faith and not by sight. We cannot see what is on the other side of the great darkness. But we know that God is there, and that he—with all his saints in whose lives his love was reflected upon us as light is reflected by a clear mirror—will be there to accompany us, as he has been with us our entire lives, even during those times when he seemed most absent.

There is a lovely little poem written, it is said, by Sir Walter Raleigh in his Bible as he was in prison awaiting execution. It goes like this:

> Even such is time, that takes in trust
> Our youth, our joys, our all we have,
> And pays us but with earth and dust;
> Who, in the dark and silent grave,
> When we have wandered all our ways,

---

5 Ps 23:4, quoted from the more beautiful rendering found in the King James Version.

> Shuts up the story of our days;
> But from this earth, this grave, this dust,
> My God shall raise me up, I trust.[6]

We begin the season of Lent with the ashes of Ash Wednesday, and we hear the priest recite the words: "Remember that you are dust, and to dust you shall return." We end the season with the celebration of Easter, with Christ's victory over death whereby we are raised up with him to that glorious communion of saints who rejoice in the loving presence of the Father, Son, and Holy Spirit, sharing their divine nature and their eternal communion of love. During this season, we reenact the entire journey of human life, "from dust to dust" and then beyond, in the celebration of Christ's Resurrection, beginning at the liturgy of the Easter Vigil as we sing the lines from the great *Exsultet* hymn:

> This is the night
> when Jesus Christ broke the chains of death
> and rose triumphant from the grave.

Yes, we are dust and to dust we shall return. We cannot (as we so often do in our youth-obsessed culture) ignore the reality of aging and death. It is part of the reality of human life. And to live lives that are fully human, we must face the human reality of death. Too often we try to keep it away from us: we hide it away in hospitals and hospices, not keeping it at home. A culture that has not faced up to the reality of death will usually fail to understand the importance and precious nature of life.

Mary weeps at the foot of the Cross, and we weep with her.

---

[6] Sir Walter Raleigh, "Even Such Is Time," at Bartleby.com, accessed October 1, 2021. https://www.bartleby.com/331/487.html.

But we also must not stop there. For beyond the Cross of Good Friday is Christ's Resurrection on Easter morning, his Ascension to God's right hand, and his continual sending of the Holy Spirit to lead us back to him. If we die with him, we will live with him. And the good news is that we can begin that resurrected life with him now but only if we put to death in ourselves all that brings spiritual death—cruelty, hatred, selfishness, and pride—and live in Christ with the new life made possible by the grace of the Holy Spirit, by which "charity is spread abroad in our hearts."[7]

Socrates told his friends who were with him at his execution that all of life is a preparation for death. Socrates was right but not in the way he thought. Life *is* a preparation for death but not merely the death of the body which, as Socrates seems to have thought, liberates the soul. Life should be a constant death-to-self so that we can become, in our own way, like Christ, a selfless gift of self to others. Christ's promise is that this is the sort of life over which even death cannot triumph.

If we spend our lives in the love of God and neighbor then, as St. Paul assures us, "neither death, nor life, nor angels, nor principalities, nor things present, nor things to come, nor powers, nor height, nor depth, nor anything else in all creation, will be able to separate us from the love of God in Christ Jesus our Lord." For "in all these things we are more than conquerors through him who loved us" (Rom 8:37–39).

> Death, be not proud, though some have called thee
> Mighty and dreadful, for thou art not so;
> . . .
> . . . why swell'st thou then?

---

[7] Rom 5:5 from the Wycliff Bible translation.

One short sleep past, we wake eternally
And death shall be no more; Death, thou shalt die.[8]

Such a message is good news indeed, for those willing to accept it—those of us who live, as we all do, "in the valley of the shadow of death."

---

[8] John Donne (1571–1631), "Death, be not proud" (Holy Sonnet 10), lines 1–2, 12–14, Poetry Foundation, accessed Oct. 1, 2021, https://www. poetryfoundation.org/poems/44107/holy-sonnets-death-be-not-proud.

Music for the Dying*

When Elaine Stratton Hild was eighteen, she volunteered to play her viola at a local hospital. On her first day, a nurse asked her to go to the room of a woman who wanted to hear "Amazing Grace." She found the woman alone. Closing her eyes and allowing the music to wash gently over them both, Stratton Hild played the song. When she opened her eyes, she saw that the woman had turned toward the window and stopped breathing. She had died with the sound of "Amazing Grace" in her ears.

More recently, Dr. Stratton Hild (PhD in musicology) has been engaged in a fascinating study of plainsong chants that different communities would sing to dying persons in the Middle Ages. There were entire liturgies to comfort the dying. The presupposition was that the whole community of friends and family would accompany the dying person on his or her journey through death and beyond. No one, it was assumed, should have to die alone. And no one should die without the support of the community of believers who would care for both their bodily requirements and their emotional and spiritual needs.

Medieval people were not alone in this conviction. Many cultures have developed practices to help "accompany" the dying both physically and spiritually. A mother of three children, who had for a time been a novice with a religious community, mentioned that, when a certain bell sounded in that community, everyone would leave whatever she was doing to come to the room of the dying sister. The entire community (spilling out into the hallway) would then sing a chant while the person died.

Most of us in the modern secularized world, it seems, have forgotten how to deal with the dying. Our tendency is to lock the

---

* A version of this essay was published online at *The Catholic Thing* on June 29, 2019.

dying person away in a room so that no one can see this "failure" of our modern technology.

A friend sent a description of Dr. Stratton Hild's work to me several weeks ago after an article of mine appeared in *The Catholic Thing* in which I exhorted Catholic bishops and priests to take more of the burden off bereaved families when parishioners die. The wake, the Rosary, and the funeral should all take place in the Church in full view of the altar and the cross, I suggested, not at an extravagant cost in a creepy funeral "home."

Bodies need not be embalmed—it's a toxic disaster for the environment—and people should then be buried in a simple wooden box in the earth in the churchyard, as has been done for centuries. Spending thousands of dollars to bury a body while leaving Mass as a minor afterthought makes no more sense than spending thousands of dollars on a wedding and leaving Mass as a minor afterthought. (Oh, right; we do that too.)

Listening to Dr. Stratton Hild talk about her work convinced me I had barely scratched the surface of the issue in my previous article. The Church, I am now convinced, should offer its help and the consoling presence of the Body of Christ not only in burial but throughout the entire process of dying. And by "the Church," I don't just mean clerics.

I don't mean to diminish the importance of priests and nuns. I can think of few things more comforting in the hospital than seeing a nurse who is also a religious sister in her habit. Catholics used to see that all the time. We never do anymore. Why we don't is unclear to me. But priests and nuns cannot do everything; they cannot do what only a community can do. And we should not presume to off-load this work on them out of our sight the way we have off-loaded it onto doctors and nurses.

The one thing every dying person I've known has wanted is to die at home. Not one of them did. And in a hospital, the likelihood of a person getting music, chant, a communal liturgy, or the simple presence of friends and family around the clock is almost nil.

We have allowed ourselves to be atomized by modern culture into little separate units. And when we do that, we have no power against the institutions that promise to care for us but which are increasingly threatening us. The medical community has an invaluable role to play in treating the dying, but it is only a part. No one should have to die alone, in the hospital, far from home.

I was privileged recently to participate in a Melkite memorial service for a woman's father who had died. It was sad but beautiful and deeply moving. The only tragedy was that the man couldn't be there to experience it. And I don't mean that as a joke. (He was late for his own funeral?) I mean I can imagine few things more beautiful and consoling to a dying person than to experience this sort of liturgy.

We need to recover the liturgies and communal practices the Church used for centuries to comfort the dying and console their families before society decided dying was a "medical issue." We do violence to the human person when we fail to understand the importance and value of eating and talking with others, of laughter, appropriate touching, music, singing, and the loving presence of friends, family, and community. This is true during our healthy years, but it is no less true with the dying.

Death is not a human failure. It is a natural end of human life. Moreover, Christ called upon his followers to understand that "unless a grain of wheat falls into the earth and dies, it remains alone; but if it dies, it bears much fruit" (John 12:24). Later St. Paul would write that "if we have died with Christ, we believe that we shall also live with him." Is this still our faith? Then we need to surround people with repeated expressions of that faith as they approach their final journey.

WORKS CITED

Becker, Ernest. *The Denial of Death*. New York: Free Press, 1973.

——. *Escape from Evil*. New York: Free Press, 1975.

Benedict XVI. *Jesus of Nazareth: Holy Week*. San Francisco, CA: Ignatius, 2011.

Berdyaev, Nicolas. *The Destiny of Man*. Translated by Natalie Duddington. London: Geoffrey Bles, 1937.

Boswell, James. *The Life of Samuel Johnson*. Edited by David Womersley. London: Penguin Classics, 2008.

Cicero. *De senectute, De amicitia, De divinatione*. Translated by W. A. Falconer. Cambridge, MA: Harvard University Press, 1923.

——. *Somnium Scipionis: The Dream of Scipio Africanus Minor, Being the Epilogue of Cicero's Treatise on Polity*. Translated by W. D. Pearman. Cambridge: Deighton, Bell, 1883.

——. *Tusculan Disputations*. Translated by J. E. King. Cambridge, MA: Harvard University Press, 1927.

Danaylov, Nikola. "The Transhumanist Manifesto." March 11, 2016. https://www.singularityweblog.com/a-transhumanist-manifesto/

Eliot, T. S. "East Coker," section 2 of "Four Quartets: An Accurate Online Text." Accessed October 1, 2021. http://www.davidgorman.com/4quartets/2-coker.htm.

Epictetus. *Handbook*, vol. 1. Translated by W. A. Oldfather. Loeb Classical Library, vol. 131. New York: Putnam, 1926.

Epicurus. "Letter to Menoeceus." Translated by Robert Drew Hicks. Online at http://classics.mit.edu/Epicurus/menoec.html.

Ertz, Susan. *Anger in the Sky*. London: Hodder & Stoughton Limited, 1943.

Ford, Dennis. *The Search for Meaning: A Short History*. Berkeley: University of California Press, 2007.

Frankl, Viktor Emil. *Man's Search for Meaning: An Introduction to Logotherapy*. Translated by Ilse Lasch et al. Boston: Beacon Press, 1962.

Gregory of Nazianzus. *Letter 101 (To Cledonius)*. Translated by Charles Gordon Browne and James Edward Swallow. In *Nicene and Post-Nicene Fathers*, second series, vol. 7. Edited by Philip Schaff and Henry Wace. Buffalo, NY: Christian Literature Publishing Co., 1894.

Heidegger, Martin. *Being and Time*. Translated by Joan Stambaugh. Albany: State University of New York Press, 1996.

Homer. *Iliad*. Translated by Richard Lattimore. "The Chicago Homer." Accessed December 4, 2021. https://homer.library. northwestern.edu.

———. *Odyssey*. Translated by James Huddleston. "The Chicago Homer." Accessed December 4, 2021. https://homer.library. northwestern.edu.

Hughes, Glenn. "The Denial of Death and the Practice of Dying." Ernest Becker Foundation (website). October 1, 2014. https://ernestbecker.org/becker-in-the-press-test-2/.

Ibsen, Henrik. *Peer Gynt*. Translated by William and Charles Archer. New York: Scribner's Sons, 1907.

James, William. *Varieties of Religious Experience*. New York: Longmans, Green, 1901.

John Paul II. "Address of His Holiness John Paul II to Scientists and Representatives of the United Nations University." February 25, 1981. https://www.vatican.va/content/john-paul-ii/en/speeches/1981/february/documents/hf_jp-ii_spe_19810225_giappone-hiroshima-scienziati-univ.html.

———. Faith and Reason *Fides et Ratio*. September 4, 1998. http://www.vatican.va/content/john-paul-ii/en/encyclicals/documents/hf_jp-ii_enc_14091998_fides-et-ratio.html.

———. On Human Work *Laborem Exercens*. September 14, 1981. https://www.vatican.va/content/john-paul-ii/en/encyclicals/documents/hf_jp-ii_enc_14091981_laborem-exercens.html.

———. *Man and Woman He Created Them: A Theology of the Body*. Translated by Michael Waldstein. Boston, MA: Pauline Books, 2006.

Justin Martyr. *On the Resurrection*. Translated by Marcus Dods. In *Ante-Nicene Fathers: Translations of the Writings of the Fathers down to A.D. 325*. Edited by A. Robert, J. Donaldson, A. Cleveland Coxe. New York: Scribner's Sons, 1926.

Kass, Leon. "Triumph or Tragedy? The Moral Meaning of Genetic Technology," *American Journal of Jurisprudence* 45 (2000): 1–16.

Kastenbaum, R. *Death, Society and Human Experience*, 11th ed. New York: Routledge, 2012.

Kereszty, Roch. *Jesus Christ: Fundamentals of Christology*, revised edition. New York: Alba House, 2002.

Lafontaine, Céline. "The Postmortal Condition: From the Biomedical Deconstruction of Death to the Extension of Longevity." *Science as Culture*, 18:3 (2009): 298.

Lewis, C. S. *The Abolition of Man*. New York: Harper Collins, 2001.

———. "Learning in War-Time." In *The Weight of Glory*. New York: Harper Collins, 1949.

Lubac, Henri de. *The Drama of Atheist Humanism*. Translated by Edith M. Riley, Anne E. Nash, and Mark Sebanc. San Francisco, CA: Ignatius Press, 1995.

Macho, Thomas. *Todesmetaphern: Zur Logik Der Grenzerfahrung*. Frankfurt: Suhrkamp, 1987. Translated in Bernard Schumacher, "The Desire for Immortality at the Dawn of the Third Millennium: The Anthropological Stakes." *Nova et Vetera*, vol. 17, no. 4 (Fall 2019): 1221–41.

MacIntyre, Alasdair. *Dependent Rational Animals: Why Human Beings Need the Virtues*. Chicago: Open Court, 2001.

Marx, Karl. "Introduction" to *A Contribution to the Critique of Hegel's Philosophy of Right*, which first appeared in *Deutsch-Französische Jahrbücher*, 7 and 10 (February 1844). For an English translation of the "Introduction," see https://www.marxists.org/archive/marx/works/1843/critique-hpr/intro.htm.

Morgan, John D. "Miguel de Unamuno and Ernest Becker: The Human Person as Mortal." In *Images of the Human: The Philosophy of the Human Person in a Religious Context*, edited by Leonard Kennedy, Hunter Brown, et al. Chicago: Loyola Press, 1995.

Morin, Edgar. *L'Homme et la mort*. Paris: Seuil, 1976.

O'Donovan, Oliver. *Resurrection and Moral Order: An Outline for Evangelical Ethics*. 2nd rev. ed. Grand Rapids, MI: Eerdmans, 1994.

Parkes, Colin Murray, Pittu Laungani, and Bill Young. *Death and Bereavement across Cultures*. New York: Routledge, 1997.

Percy, Walker. *Lost in the Cosmos: The Last Self-Help Book*. New York: Farrar, Straus & Giroux, 1983.

Pew Research Forum. "Living to 120 and Beyond: Americans' Views on Aging, Medical Advances and Radical Life Extension." August 6, 2013. https://www.pewforum.org/2013/08/06/living-to-120-and-beyond-americans-views-on-aging-medical-advances-and-radical-life-extension/.

Plato. *Phaedo.* In *Plato in Twelve Volumes,* vol. 1. Translated by Harold North Fowler. Loeb Classical Library. Cambridge, MA: Harvard University Press; London: William Heinemann Ltd., 1966.

———. *Symposium.* Translated by Alexander Nehamas and Paul Woodruff. Indianapolis, IN: Hackett, 1989.

Rank, Otto. *Beyond Psychology.* New York: Dover Books, 1958.

Ratzinger, Joseph. *Eschatology: Death and Eternal Life.* Translated by Michael Waldstein. Edited by Aidan Nichols, OP. Washington, DC: The Catholic University of America Press, 1988.

———. *In the Beginning: A Catholic Understanding of the Story of Creation and the Fall.* Translated by Boniface Ramsey. Grand Rapids, MI: Eerdmans, 1995.

———. *Introduction to Christianity.* Translated by J. R. Foster. New York: Crossroad, 1985; revised edition, San Francisco: Ignatius Press, 2004.

Rubin, Charles. "Mind Games." *The New Atlantis* 51 (Winter 2017): 109–27.

Saletan, William. "Fear of Immortality." *Slate.* August 6, 2013. https://slate.com/technology/2013/08/aging-polls-and-life-extension-why-dont-americans-want-to-live-longer.html.

Sandel, Michael J. "What's Wrong with Enhancement." Paper presented to the President's Council on Bioethics, December 2002. https://bioethicsarchive.georgetown.edu/pcbe/background/sandelpaper.html.

Sarah, Cardinal Robert. "We Must Rebuild the Cathedral . . . We Do Not Need to Invent a New Church." Address given at Église Saint François-Xavier in Paris, May 25, 2019. *Catholic World Report,* June 21, 2019. https://www.catholicworldreport.com/2019/12/29/cardinal-sarah-we-must-rebuild-the-cathedral-we-do-not-need-to-invent-a-new-church/.

Schmemann, Alexander, *For the Life of the World: Sacraments and Orthodoxy.* Yonkers, NY: St. Vladimir's Seminary Press, 2018.

Schumacher, Bernard N. "The Desire for Immortality at the Dawn of the Third Millennium: The Anthropological Stakes." *Nova et Vetera,* vol. 17, no. 4 (Fall 2019): 1221–41.

Shay, Jonathan. *Achilles in Vietnam: Combat Trauma and the Undoing of Character*. New York: Simon & Schuster, 1995.

Shephard, D. A. E. "The Principles and Practice of Palliative Care." *Canadian Medical Association Journal* 116.5 (March 5, 1977): 522–26.

Smith, Randall. *Reading the Sermons of Aquinas: A Beginner's Guide*. Steubenville, OH: Emmaus Academic, 2016.

Solomon, Sheldon, Jeff Greenberg, and Tom Pyszczynski. *Worm at the Core: On the Role of Death in Life*. New York: Random House, 2015.

Thérèse of Lisieux. *Story of a Soul: The Autobiography of Saint Thérèse of Lisieux*. Translated by John Clarke, OCD. Washington, DC: ICS Publications, 1996.

Thomas Aquinas: The Academic Sermons. Translated by Mark-Robin Hoogland. Washington, DC: The Catholic University of America Press, 2010.

Unamuno, Miguel de. *The Tragic Sense of Life*. Translated by J. E. C. Flitch. London: Macmillan, 1921.

Weigel, George. *Witness to Hope*. New York: Harper, 1999.

Williams, Bernard. *Problems of the Self*. Cambridge: Cambridge University Press, 1973.

Wolff, Catherine. *Beyond: How Humankind Thinks about Heaven*. New York: Riverhead, 2021.